J. COONEY.   July 19 7

dollars and sense

dollars and sense

a guide to **mastering**
your **money**

Art Watkins

 Quadrangle/The New York Times Book Co.

Library of Congress Catalog Card Number: 72-90468

International Standard Book Number: 0-8129-0335-8

Book design by Dorothy Lewis

Production services by Planned Production

To **Molly, Anne, Davy** and **Jo,**
each of whom is very
good in the bread
department

contents

SECTION FOUR
how to cut the monthly cost of *owning* and *operating* your *house,* 95

SECTION FIVE
cutting the high cost of *transportation—your car,* 133

SECTION SIX
how to *stay healthy* and spend less for *medical care,* 161

preface

How to use this book

The basic way to stretch your money and live reasonably well on a given income is to know how to get sound value for your dollar. But sound value in the supermarket is different from sound value in a house you buy or own, or in a car or major appliance or when you buy life insurance. Thus the reason—and purpose—of this book, with more than 30 chapters, is to give you a clear insight into that many different money drains on the typical family budget.

The greatest financial savings—and also the greatest personal triumphs against the high cost of living today—generally can be achieved by directing special attention to those living expenses that account for your greatest family expenditures, which should be obvious but is not so easy to do. For most people these are food and housing (which together drain off 50 percent or more of total family living costs, as shown in Chapter 1), and such things as owning a car, medical expenses and doctor bills (the cost of which in recent years has skyrocketed faster than any other family living expense documented in the government's cost-of-living index).

Though we do not in this book deal with every single such living expense, we have tried to give you a good, clear under-

standing of how to get a sound value from most goods and
services that the typical person commonly needs and buys.
That includes how to buy credit at low cost, whether you're
using it to buy something on the installment plan or simply to
borrow money, how to get low-cost legal counsel, how to save
and invest wisely and, of course, how to save the most on your
annual income taxes, which is actually the very largest annual
expense that many of us are burdened with.

Like most books, this book can be read consecutively and
will pay for itself, we believe, many times over by virtue of the
pithy tips and practical money-saving information that are
sprinkled heavily throughout. It is also designed to be, after
reading, a handy reference book for special information needed
when an important purchase or special financial decision must
be made.

A few qualifications should be stated. Here and there you
will come across facts that have been previously mentioned in
another context. Such repetition is unavoidable in order to
make each chapter self-sufficient. On the other hand, certain
fundamental information applies to various money subjects and
is therefore presented once and elsewhere we refer you to that
basic section on the subject. An example is the art of using
credit and buying on time, which is reported in Chapter 4 and
applies to many different kinds of expenditures discussed elsewhere. And because life goes on, constantly changing from day
to day, certain facts presented in this book are true today but
subject to change tomorrow. Prices change, interest rates go
up—or down—new laws are passed, and as a result, the total
accuracy of all facts and figures in this book as written cannot
necessarily be guaranteed when you may later read it. Much
research and effort, however, has gone into ensuring the basic
accuracy of the material presented.

This book is the result of more than 20 years of research
and writing about many different aspects of consumer money
matters and personal finance for national magazines plus half
a dozen books on related subjects. This book also contains
the fruit—plus lessons from scars—of continual personal en-
counters with family money matters as the result of having a
wife, growing children, and having had several houses, a number of different cars, plus some surprising experiences with

banks, life insurance salesmen, stock market brokers, and income tax men, all of which have contributed to the reservoir from which this book has been drawn.

Above all, perhaps, this book has been viewed as the kind of reasonably complete book on the subject that the author wishes he had available for ready reference and helpful guidance at crucial times in the past for his family and himself. We have also learned much in the process of research and writing this book, and we hope that each reader will also benefit from the result.

ART WATKINS
November, 1972

NEW YORK, NEW YORK

dollars and sense

the art of **spending, saving** and **borrowing money**

Like gold, money by itself is a valuable commodity. Every dollar that passes through your hands has value in addition to the dollar figure on its face. Give it to a banker or lend it to the government or a business corporation (by buying a bond) and you are paid interest for its use by others. Borrow money from the bank or anyone else and you pay a price for renting it from somebody else.

Much money also can be saved—or lost—by the way it is handled day in and day out, and in this first section of the book we present fundamental techniques for handling money efficiently. The typical American middle-income family can expect to handle between half a million and three-quarters of a million dollars over a lifetime of work. That much money will be earned, but how much of it sticks to your fingers and enables you to live well depends on you.

Sharpen your money-handling techniques by being a smart buyer and an intelligent consumer and over a lifetime you can save 10 to 20 percent of the total money that passes through your hands. Simple arithmetic tells us quickly that 10 to 20 percent of a half-million dollars or more of lifetime earnings is by no means peanuts. It could add up to a nice tidy difference in the amount of money you have left over—from as little as $50,000 to as much as $150,000—to afford increased benefits and pleasure from life.

1

basic **money-saving** techniques

Where the greatest savings can be made · Where the money goes · Common money leaks and how to plug them · Seven fundamental tips for cutting buying costs and saving money

It should be obvious that the greatest potential for saving money usually lies in those items that cost you the most money. Anyone can save pennies by intensive shopping from store to store for shoelaces, but the savings will be trivial especially compared with the time and effort expended.

Concentrate your efforts on cutting the cost of your housing and your food, on the other hand, and the savings could mount up considerably. Housing and food together drain off more than 50 percent of the annual after-tax earnings of the typical American family, as shown in the accompanying table of typical living costs. If you are a typical consumer of goods and services, the table also shows that your next largest expenditures each month go for clothing, car and medical care.

But where does *your* money go?

Not all of us, however, are typical consumers and we do not follow the rulebook. For example, a swinging young couple we know spend very little on their housing by renting a couple of rooms in a relative's house, but, boy, do they spend on skiing and surfing and fun and travel—more than 50 percent of their income!

The typical living-cost figures handed down to us by government

3

How most people spend their money

Typical expenses for a four-person American family					What you spend
Item	**Gross annual income**				
	$10,664		**$15,511**		
Food	2,452	28.1%	3,092	25.2%	_____
Housing	2,501	28.6	3,772	30.6	_____
Transportation*	912	10.4	1,183	9.9	_____
Clothing and personal care	1,137	13.1	1,655	14.5	_____
Medical care	564	6.4	588	4.8	_____
Miscellaneous (recreation, travel, tobacco, alcohol, books, records, etc.)	639	7.3	1,056	8.7	_____
Other (life insurance, gifts, contributions, job-related expenses, savings)	539	6.3	903	7.4	_____
Total living expenses and outlays	$ 8,744		$12,249		_____
Income taxes	1,533		2,875		_____
Social security payments	387		387		_____
Total income	$10,664		$15,511		_____

* Chiefly for family-owned cars.
SOURCE: U.S. Department of Labor, Bureau of Labor Statistics, based on living costs in 1969–70; the latest available at the time this book went to press. Budgets for families with higher incomes are not available. The higher the income, generally, the lower the percentage spent for food and housing.

economists also can be thrown out of kilter by special circumstances, such as sending children to college nowadays at a cost of up to $5,000 a year per student. Many a reasonably well-off family putting children through college is reduced to the poverty line when figuring the money left over for all other family expenses.

Not everybody knows where his money goes; yet this *should* be determined and known. Your money may flow out in dribs and drabs or in surprising torrents for expenditures you never realized were as costly as they are. The odds are that you do not really know where your money goes and the proportion of it that is spent for various expenses. Some 8,000 people were interviewed in Michigan and "less than a dozen really knew what they spent and where it went," according to Albert Horner, a Michigan financial expert. An examination of those families' books also showed that in many instances certain supposedly small monthly expenses were substantially greater than ever realized.

Do your living expenses conform fairly closely to those of the average family shown in the table? Are you spending a disproportionately high amount of money for costs that could be sharply reduced? (One such high expense for many families is the high total drained off for interest and credit charges on installment loans, which are curbed only after a family adds up the total cost and in shocked reaction determines to do something about it.)

Go through your checkbooks and bills for the past year. Simply list all the checks and money paid out under the appropriate headings and add up the totals. This is a quicker and easier chore than you may think, and it can be fascinating as well as revealing once you get into it. A hazy gray area will be what happened to all that pocket cash and daily money spent, the nickels and dimes, quarters and dollars paid out here and there with no record of them. Such daily expenses can be estimated and don't have to be tracked down to the last penny. They should, however, be scrutinized because sometimes they add up to a major leak.

Before starting a family accounting of money spent vow that there will be no bloodletting and no reprisals. There will be surprises, we assure you, but that's par for the course. Before accusations are thrown around, between husband and wife, or parents and children, establish a clear understanding that no one will be executed for treasonable family spending regardless of the findings. The purpose is to determine first where the lion's share of your family expenditures go and thus where the greatest possible savings may be made, and second where unknown money leaks exist so that you can do something about them.

The most common money leaks

Women tend to go overboard for "vanities" such as cosmetics and contact lenses (seldom worn after purchase), for home furnishings and expensive clothes impulsively bought. "There isn't a woman in America who doesn't have a clothing skeleton buried in her closet and recognized as a great mistake soon after being purchased," says Luise Addis, a leading home economist. (But spending extravagantly for an expensive dress or another personal item is not necessarily all that bad, says Dr. Morton

S. Eisenberg, a New York psychoanalyst. It's an instinctive method of relieving tension or depression, he says, citing the woman who will say, "I felt so blue I went out and bought a dress and felt much better afterward!" Allowing oneself an occasional fling can be excusable.)

Typical money leaks for men tend to be the purchase of a bigger and newer car than necessary, or spending a lot of money on hobbies like boats, bowling, golf, snowmobiles, hunting and fishing, and model trains or racing cars. No man—or woman—who is dedicated to a sport or hobby need cease at once or face dire consequences in order to preserve the family's resources. The point is, do your thing but also recognize its true, actual cost and whether or not you and your family can afford the pleasure—or extravagance—or whether you're willing to curb other expenditures to pay for your special interest in life.

Other common family money leaks are going overboard on sweets and cakes at the supermarket, which take a surprisingly big bite out of many food budgets; frequent eating out in fancy restaurants; spending extravagantly and unnecessarily for children; spending money freely on gifts galore for friends and relatives, especially at Christmastime; keeping up with the Joneses (which returns a questionable dividend in status and prestige); and one of the newest and most insidious, going hog-wild on tempting credit card purchases that give little lasting pleasure.

A survey of some 500 young couples by *Redbook* magazine spotlights another major leak and a special trap to avoid: the "foolish expenditure" for household items and home improvements. Door-to-door salesmen walk off with a large amount of this wasted money. Couple after couple ruefully reported being taken by such slick operators, who had eased their way into the living room to sell expensive fire-alarm systems, built-in house vacuum systems, water softeners, storm windows and particularly encyclopedias for children. One woman says, "How stupid can you get? We let this man talk us into a $400 encyclopedia when our son was only ten months old!"

This and other buying traps can be avoided by developing a basic technique for buying almost anything anytime. It consists of seven fundamental principles that not only can save you money for the rest of your life, but can also help you obtain better value and greater pleasure for your money. Some of them may not be new to every reader, but they are summed up here for other readers who may be unaware of them.

1. *Shop and compare prices.* This is, of course, the standard advice continually given to consumers, yet it is amazing how many people do not shop and compare prices before buying. That includes buying an expensive car from the first dealer visited, signing up for years of life-

insurance premiums from the first salesman who calls without checking on insurance sold by others, as well as buying an expensive encyclopedia or home-vacuum cleaner system from a glib salesman without checking its cost and value with other sellers.

Make a rule never to spend more than $10—all right, $25 or $50, if you will—for anything anywhere without pricing and evaluating the same merchandise elsewhere. Some salesman will press you hard, saying here's the chance of a lifetime to buy their Little-Giant Earthshaker at an absolutely rockbottom bargain price, but if you wait till tomorrow it will be too late. Nonsense. Others will claim that it's a fixed-price item available nowhere else at a lower price. That's seldom true. Identical merchandise is often sold by different people at different prices. That goes for the same new cars sold by different dealers, to TV sets and children's shoes.

There's a limit, of course, to the amount of shopping that justifies the money saved, the extreme limit being ridiculous all-day shopping to buy low-cost shoelaces. As a rule, the higher the price, the greater the potential savings possible by shopping around. Time sometimes can be saved by telephone shopping, and a quick check on the price of many different items can be obtained from a mail-order catalogue kept at home, such as the Sears Roebuck or Montgomery Ward catalogue. But remember that mail order prices should be adjusted upward to allow for delivery and installation charges when necessary.

2. *Strive for quality.* Don't be a low-price sucker. That's a person who shops all over and never buys anything unless its the absolutely cheapest available, but then often ends up with shoddy goods that are the most expensive because they must soon be replaced. Pay a little more for high quality when necessary and you almost always will save money. A good suit may cost 50 percent more than a cheap suit, but it could last twice as long and then be 25 percent cheaper in price than the cost of *two* cheap suits. The same value principle applies to shirts, underwear, household appliances and many other products or merchandise you can cite (other than the latest high-fashion gown from Paris where exclusive style determines its price).

It does not necessarily follow, however, that the higher the price, the higher the quality. No general rule can be given on price versus quality for everything you may buy because of many variables that intrude. And sometimes, different versions of the same product will be on sale at different prices according to quality. The Sears Roebuck catalogue, for example, lists two to three versions of many individual products as "Good," "Better" and "Best." "Good" is really ordinary quality, "Better" is in between, and "Best" is their highest quality.

John Ruskin said it:

> *It is unwise to pay too much, but it's worse to pay too little.*
> *When you pay too much, you lose a little money—that is all.*
> *When you pay too little, you sometimes lose everything*
> *because the thing you bought was incapable of doing the thing*
> *it was bought to do. The common law of business balance*
> *prohibits paying a little and getting a lot—it can't be done.*
> *If you deal with the lowest bidder, it is well to add something*
> *for the risk you ran, and if you do that you will have enough*
> *to pay for something better.*

3. *Patronize good stores and reputable dealers.* Confine your shopping to people who take pride in their business and don't dispense shoddy goods. A good store will back up its merchandise, provide service when necessary and quickly replace defective products with no backtalk or delay. All your shopping need not, however, be limited to a few places. Not at all. Off and on, other stores and dealers will be worth a visit or two. But in the main it can pay to be known and recognized by people whose products and services you buy regularly, and often there will be a special additional bonus. The proprietor will tell you when a special, desirable item is available at a low price—and also when not to buy something.

4. *Consult the Better Business Bureau (BBB).* There are BBB offices throughout the U.S. and Canada, and though not all are as helpful or consumer-protective as they might be, many can indeed be helpful. Call the nearest one to you—listed in the telephone book—to check on any store, contractor, serviceman or other firm you may deal with for the first time but know nothing about. Is the man reliable?

The BBB people do not answer that question directly, however. You must understand their reports and read between the lines. A BBB staff person will tell you if a particular firm has a record of uncorrected complaints against it. Beware of any firm that has a record of one or more complaints against it which it has not corrected. Go elsewhere. On the other hand, a firm with no BBB record is not necessarily dependable. That could mean only that no one has complained about it to the BBB. Check further on it.

The Better Business Bureaus also publish some good pamphlets and booklets on many different products and services. Write for the latest list of available ones, including a stamped, return-addressed envelope, to the Council of Better Business Bureaus, 1101 17th Street, N.W., Washington, D.C. 20036.

5. *Check on product ratings.* The quality, price and other facts about products vary from year to year, as well as from brand to brand. Reports on them are available in the annual buying guides published by *Consumer Reports* and *Consumer Bulletin,* both available on newsstands and in many libraries. Also see their monthly magazines; see back issues reporting on a particular product you're interested in at your library.

6. *Know when and how to bargain and negotiate for good terms and the best price.* As in an Arabian bazaar, prices in America are frequently subject to a negotiated reduction. The initial price asked for many for-sale products are, in fact, often set high deliberately to allow the seller a cushion for bargaining. That goes for appliances, home furnishings and home improvements, virtually every used item you may buy, for legal and other professional work you hire, and especially for buying or selling a car or a house where often hundreds if not thousands of dollars can be saved merely by asking for a lower price. That doesn't mean you must haggle and aggressively chop away to gain a price advantage. It means knowing how to play it cool and among other things, pause and hesitate at the right moment. Always assume that a price is subject to reduction or that better terms can be had merely by asking.

A prime prerequisite for successful bargaining is to know the value of the item sought. This may take a little research to determine but it's invaluable information. It permits you to make the proper initial bid price and leave a cushion to raise the ante and still not overpay. You'll be surprised, however, how often a low initial bid will be accepted.

Expert negotiators in business and those who negotiate labor contracts have found that as a rule the lower the initial bid made during bargaining, the better the final terms for you at the end. Successful horse traders know this instinctively and therefore make an extremely low first bid or offer—and are ready to come right back with a higher one, if necessary. That's unless their first offer is naively accepted, which sometimes happens. Conversely, when you are selling something, the higher your initial asking price, the higher the final price likely to be obtained. There are exceptions, to be sure, the danger being that an extremely high initial asking price will frighten off potential buyers, as in selling a house, as reported in Chapter 7.

Sometimes, of course, a price is absolutely firm. You can't expect a price deduction on toothpaste at the drugstore, a tankful of gasoline or the electric bill from your local utility where the rates are fixed. Also, of course, aggressive bargaining can be carried too far and a rude buyer will be flatly turned away. So keep your cool, be friendly and polite and learn to sense when you have obtained the best possible price and terms.

Bargaining is an art and takes confidence and practice. To sharpen your technique, try it when little is at stake. The typical person's chief enemy is his own fear and embarrassment at bargaining, and especially at making an initially low bid or high offer, depending on whether he's buying or selling something. This fear often can be overcome by knowing values.

7. *Know your money strengths and weaknesses.* Everyone has both. Review your past and how and why you have done well and not well with money. Do you commonly commit certain mistakes that cost you money? How can you avoid repeating them? What kind of purchases generally turn out well for you, and what kind do not? Probe a little deeper and you'll probably discover a pattern of similar causes and conditions that underlie your successes on the one hand and your failures on the other. Right then and there you will have made a big step forward in saving a lot of money in the future. The chances are that past mistakes you have made will boil down to violating one of the basic money-handling principles we have just presented.

MONEY-SAVING TIP: In nearly every family it is either the husband or the wife who is the better money manager. That spouse should handle the family finances.

Annual income twenty pounds, annual expenditures nineteen-six, result happiness. Annual income twenty pounds, annual expeditures twenty pounds ought and six, result misery.
—CHARLES DICKENS

2

how to get the most **interest** on your **savings**

Banks that pay the highest interest on savings · Credit unions · How compound interest should be figured · How safe is your money? · U.S. savings bonds · Up to 8 percent a year from bonds

The interest rate paid on money depends on the kind of bank and the type of savings account you choose. Not everyone gets high interest on his money simply because many people don't realize one bank often will pay a greater interest rate than another, and in addition a bank often will offer special kinds of savings accounts that pay higher interest than their regular savings accounts.

There are three main kinds of banks: savings banks (also called mutual savings banks), savings and loan associations (also called building and loan associations, cooperative banks and homestead societies) and commercial banks. Of the three a savings bank or a savings and loan association generally pays the highest interest and one or the other is usually the best place for keeping serious long-term savings.

A savings bank is any bank with the word "savings" in its name, such as The Thrifty Man's Savings Bank. There are a few exceptions in the Midwest where some commercial banks have "savings" in their names.

There are some 500 savings banks (plus 1,300 branches) in the U.S. located in the following 17 states:

Alaska	New Jersey
Connecticut	New York
Delaware	Oregon
Indiana	Pennsylvania
Maine	Rhode Island
Maryland	Vermont
Massachusetts	Washington
Minnesota	Wisconsin
New Hampshire	

If you do not live in one of these states, no law can prevent you from banking by mail with a savings bank in one of the above states. But, if money is kept in a bank in another state, complications can arise to tie up the money in case of the depositor's death. So, before banking in another state, take steps to avoid such difficulties. Check with the bank or an estate tax lawyer. This advice also applies to checking accounts and other money and property you may possess outside of your own state. In recent years savings banks have paid interest up to 5 percent per year on regular savings accounts, more on special accounts described below.

The maximum interest rate a bank is permitted to pay is set by the government, and in addition, it is raised or lowered from time to time, but not all banks pay the top allowable rate. Those in competitive large cities and metropolitan areas generally pay the highest rates while outlying banks, in some suburbs and many small towns, generally pay the lowest. Here again, banking by mail, from a small town to the nearest big-city bank, for example, could earn you extra money.*

The highest interest rate is generally also allowed to the 6,100 savings and loan associations in various parts of the country, though not all will necessarily pay the highest interest allowable by law. And in some areas savings and loan associations are sometimes allowed to pay a slightly higher maximum interest rate than all other banks.

Third are the commercial banks, the most numerous with one on Main Street in nearly every city, and in all about 14,000 nationwide. If a bank

---

* Interest rates not only vary from bank to bank but historically they have also fluctuated up and down from time to time. In the early 1950's, for example, maximum bank interest rates ranged as low as 1 to 2 percent, and did not reach 5 percent on regular savings accounts till 1970. No one can predict future interest rates. To protect against a possible decline in interest rates, you could put your money in a time-deposit account or in certificates of deposit, described later in this chapter.

offers checking accounts, it almost always is a commercial bank and offers savings accounts, too (plus a variety of other commercial banking services, like safe deposit boxes). Many also call themselves "full-service" banks. They have paid interest rates on regular savings ranging recently up to about 4½ percent, but quite a few, particularly in suburbs and small towns, have paid no more than 3½ to 4 percent.

Credit unions

Besides a bank, you can save money with a credit union savings account. Credit unions are nonprofit associations sponsored by fraternal organizations and labor unions (for their members), by commercial firms (for employees) and other groups of people with a common bond. Everybody saves together and interest rates paid on savings accounts often range higher than those paid by a bank; in recent years they have gone up to 7 percent and occasionally higher. There are some 20,000 credit unions in the U.S.

How the interest on your savings is figured

It is figured in different ways, mainly according to the kind of savings account you have. By and large, the best kind is a Day-of-Deposit to Day-of-Withdrawal account, or DD-DW one. Regardless of when money is deposited or withdrawn, interest is paid on the money for every day it's in the bank.

That's not so with the usual "regular" savings account, which pays you interest only on money on deposit for the full interest-paying period, which is usually three months. Sometimes you are offered a few days "grace" on money deposited or withdrawn. The grace-period account is often played up big by some banks because it sounds great in advertisements, but the benefits you get may not be great.

It works like this: You may deposit money on any day up to the tenth of the month with the money earning interest retroactively from the first of the month. That's fine, except that if your money is deposited a day or more after the grace period, it doesn't begin earning interest until the first of the next month, sometimes not until the first of the next quarter. Moreover, if you withdraw money before the end of an interest-crediting period, you usually lose all the interest on the sum withdrawn for the whole interest-crediting period.

In addition, with a grace-days account, some banks pay interest only on the lowest sum of money in your account during each interest period.

Others pay on the average balance, and still others pay according to complicated rules such as first-in, first-out, or FIFO; this means, in effect, that no interest is paid on money withdrawn before the end of a particular interest period.

A regular savings account with a grace feature is useful only if you regularly deposit money as late as the tenth of the month and do not make any withdrawals except planned ones at the end of interest-crediting periods. As a general rule, a DD-DW account is better for most people, especially those with active savings accounts.

Such facts are important to know, especially before depositing or withdrawing a large sum of money. Before doing it, ask the bank exactly how much interest you may gain or lose. Move it in or out of a bank at the wrong time and more than a few dollars can be lost.

Compound interest

Compound interest is interest paid on interest. The frequency of compounding, like interest rates, also varies from bank to bank, though this is also played up by some banks far out of proportion to its value.

Not long ago in New York City, for example, the Dime Savings Bank spent a lot of money ballyhooing to the public that all money on deposit with it was "compounded daily!" This actually meant practically nothing, as the interest paid on $1,000 in a savings account for one year and compounded daily would earn you a mere 25 cents more, or just over two cents more per month, compared with the same money compounded quarterly at the same annual interest rate. The accompanying table shows how compound interest works.

Growth of $1,000 in a compound interest savings account

	Effective annual interest rate	Total annual interest	Total money at end of year
Compounded Daily	5.12%	$51.20	$1,051.20
″ Quarterly	5.095%	$50.95	1,050.95
″ Semiquarterly	5.06%	$50.60	1,050.60
″ Annually	5.00%	$50.00	1,050.00

You can see that compounding starts at a snail's pace and the frequency of compounding (daily, quarterly, and so on) doesn't make much difference on small sums over a few years. With a large sum over a period of years, compounding can indeed make a difference. Not all banks, however, always compound your interest. Be sure, then, that your money is compounded and that your large savings are compounded at least quarter or semiannually.

Time-deposit accounts

This is how to earn extra interest on long-term savings. You sacrifice liquidity by tying up your money for a specific period of one to two years or more but you gain extra interest. A bank willingly pays higher interest for money it knows will not be withdrawn shortly, for this is money that the bank can put to work for a longer time.

You open a long-term savings account with a fancy name, like "Golden Passbook," "Bonus" or "Super Pacemaker" account, which pays from ¼ to 1 percent higher annual interest rate than is paid on regular savings accounts. When maximum interest rates recently paid by savings banks were 5 percent on regular savings, interest rates on time-deposit accounts went up to 6 percent. In return, you agree not to withdraw your money for a certain period of time, usually a year or two. You generally must start off with a minimum deposit of $500 to $1,000, and after the specified minimum time period is up you may have to give notice—30 to 50 days, as a rule—before withdrawing your money. Suppose you need to withdraw money before the minimum time is up because of an emergency? Many banks will let you do this, but then, naturally, you will lose some of the bonus interest, since federal law requires that a premature withdrawal be penalized with loss of up to three months interest.

CD's (Certificates of Deposit)

A CD is, in effect, the same as a time-deposit savings account with a higher-than-normal interest paid for money kept in a bank for a stipulated period of time. It may be as little as 30 to 60 days, but it's usually for at least one to two years. In return you're paid from ½ to 1 percent or so higher interest than is being offered at the time by regular savings accounts.

Like regular savings accounts and time-deposit accounts, the top interest rates paid for CD's also vary from bank to bank. Not all banks pay compound interest on CD's (as with time-deposit accounts). So before tying up money in a CD, or in a time-deposit account, shop around. Ask hard questions about possible small-print catches, as well as the compound interest being paid or not paid.

How safe is your money?

More than 95 percent of all bank accounts are insured to the tune of $20,000 per person per account. Be sure that your savings are insured or they could be wiped out if a bank goes broke (and some go broke off and on). A commercial bank or a savings bank should display the seal of the Federal Deposit Insurance Corporation (FDIC) or be insured by a state insurance program. A savings and loan association should be insured by the Federal Savings and Loan Corporation (FSLC) or by state insurance. Since not as many credit unions carry such insurance (because it is new with credit unions as of 1971), checking on insurance for a credit union account is particularly important.

Suppose you have more than $20,000 in a bank account or spread among several accounts including a checking account? It may or may not be insured in full since the total sum of money deposited under one name is usually insured only up to $20,000. Say, for example, you have a total of $22,000 in two savings accounts, $18,000 in one and $4,000 in another in the same bank. If the bank goes bust, you would be covered for only $20,000 of that total and you'd lose $2,000. On the other hand, a joint account in the names of husband and wife is insured up to $40,000, or $20,000 per name; and a three-name account (father, mother and child) would be insured up to $60,000 (the same $20,000 per person). The rule is, therefore, don't keep more than $20,000 per person in any one savings account, regardless of how many different accounts you may have. Turn such accounts into joint or trust accounts, or put the additional money over $20,000 in another insured bank. If in doubt about this, check with a knowledgeable banker.

Earn up to 13½ percent interest?

This was a widely publicized claim and the subject of a book, but it's largely a snare and a delusion. It's theoretically possible if you wish to go into the full-time business of switching your money from bank to bank and exploiting grace days and special savings features offered by some banks some of the time. In addition, one of the banks must let you borrow against your savings with no interest charged on the loan for a few weeks after the loan is made. You switch your money from bank to bank, take advantage of interest-free loans for short periods and milk each account for its maximum interest, keeping the money on deposit for the fewest allowable days each month. If you do it right and the banks involved don't catch on fast and throw you out, you can achieve the satisfaction of 13½ percent interest on your money, at least according to the crafty author of the book on the subject. A man in Chicago with $100,000 tried to exact that much interest from his money, transferring it back and forth between two savings and loan associations and taking advantage of different grace days offered by each. He was soon discovered by officials at each of the savings and loans, who knew each other, and he was thrown out of both places.

U.S. savings bonds

The government Series E savings bond is a good way to get good interest on a small sum of money, but you must keep each bond to maturity (five years and ten months) to get the full 5.5-percent-a-year interest. If you cash one in earlier, the interest is less, going down in steps according to how long you held it.

Government savings bonds may not pay you the highest possible interest, but they can be bought painlessly with an automatic payroll savings plan, they are exempt from state and local income taxes and from personal property taxes and an investment in U.S. savings bonds is a patriotic gesture.

Up to 8 percent a year from bonds

Buying high-quality bonds can earn a greater return on your money—up to 8 percent, sometimes more—than is obtainable in a savings account. A point to remember is that a bond is a loan of money to the government or to a corporation for which you are paid interest till the loan is paid off and you get your money back.

There are three main kinds of bonds: those issued by the U.S. government, including U.S. Treasury "bills" and "notes," the safest of all bonds, since they're backed by the U.S. government; municipal bonds issued by states, cities and towns, which pay a relatively low interest rate but the interest is tax free, which gives them special appeal to a person in a high-income tax bracket; and corporate bonds, which generally pay the highest interest rate but which run the gamut from high safety to high risk.

The best way to buy bonds is through a good stock broker who knows the business or via a mutual fund that specializes in buying bonds and bonds only for its shareholders. (See Chapter 28.) You can also buy through a local bank and government bonds direct from the U.S. Treasury. But before buying from a bank or a broker, determine what the brokerage commission will be. Good bonds can earn you excellent return, but the buying and selling of bonds can be tricky at times because of cross currents in the market, which are constantly changing and which are difficult if not impossible to describe in a book. So it's important to investigate carefully before buying and deal with a good bond broker.

How fast do your savings grow?

If you save $10 a month at compound interest of	You will have this much money after			
	10 yrs.	15 yrs.	20 yrs.	25 yrs.
4%	$1,467	$2,450	$3,650	$5,114
5%	1,545	2,657	4,084	5,912
6%	1,628	2,886	4,581	6,667

$50 a month saved at				
4%	7,334	12,251	18,251	25,572
5%	7,725	13,285	20,420	29,560
6%	8,140	14,420	22,905	33,835

$100 a month saved at				
4%	14,667	24,501	36,501	51,144
5%	15,447	26,571	40,836	59,121
6%	16,281	28,863	45,813	66,669

NOTE: The sum of money you will accumulate for any other amount saved regularly can be easily figured from above. For example, $20 a month saved will give you twice as much as $10 saved at the same interest rate, above. Similarly, $40 a month saved will give four times as much as $10 saved; $75 a month, half again as much as for $50; and so on.

CHECKLIST: GETTING THE MOST INTEREST ON YOUR MONEY

1. Put your serious savings in a bank or credit union that offers the highest interest rate, usually a mutual savings bank or a savings and loan association.
2. Don't lose interest by depositing or withdrawing money at the wrong time. Choose a day-of-deposit-to-day-of-withdrawal account that pays interest every day your money is in the bank.
3. Obtain the highest interest on long-term savings with a time-deposit account or a certificate of deposit.
4. Be sure you're getting compound interest.
5. Be sure your savings are insured, especially if you have more than $20,000 in any one bank.
6. Consider the purchase of bonds to earn as much as 50 percent more interest than generally earned in banks. But buy bonds carefully, stick to high-grade issues and deal with a good bond broker or with a bond mutual fund.

MONEY-SAVING TIP: Interest for nearly three to six months can be lost when money is withdrawn from a savings account before the end of an interest-paying period. Wait till the end of the period, or take out a short-term passbook loan to be repaid at the end of the interest period. The interest preserved should more than cover the loan cost and save total loss of your interest.

3

getting the most from
a **checking account**

*Getting the most checks at low cost · No-charge checking
accounts · Avoiding common mistakes that cost you
money · Special facts to know about checks*

In recent years there has been a decided thaw in the attitude of many
banks toward personal checking accounts. Now most banks not only
welcome your checking account, but many will virtually beg for it just to
get your money business. That could save you money on check costs and
also save time and money in other ways, too.

More than 50 million Americans now have personal checking accounts,
but not all get the full advantage from them. Quite a few additional
Americans don't have them but should. Bankers shake their heads with
puzzlement at the people streaming into banks and post offices every day
for money orders at 25 to 50 cents apiece, while checks for the same
purpose cost no more than 10 to 15 cents and sometimes nothing. Moreover, checks are just as safe, simpler to use and can save the time and
expense of buying a money order each time one is needed.

Two main kinds of checking accounts

They are the "special" and the "regular" checking accounts. They're
offered by nearly all commercial banks (many also called "full service"

banks), by savings banks in a few states (Delaware, Indiana, Maryland, Massachusetts, New Jersey, and possibly Connecticut and other states in the future), and by savings and loan associations in Rhode Island (possibly other states in the future).

A special checking account usually costs 10 cents to 15 cents per check plus a possible maintenance charge of 50 cents to $1.00 a month and that's it. The exact charge varies from bank to bank. Write 15 to 20 checks a month and a special checking account will cost you about $1.50 to $3 a month.

The cost of a regular checking account depends on your account activity and the amount of money kept on account from month to month. Generally, you're charged a fixed fee for every check written and every deposit made, such as 7 cents per deposit and 5 cents for each check written. There also may or may not be a monthly maintenance charge of 50 cents to perhaps $1.50 a month, the charge varying according to the bank.

On the other hand, you get a credit of from 10 to 20 cents for every $100 in your account during the month, your average monthly balance. Some banks charge you nothing if you keep a few hundred dollars in the account at all times; you get free checking, in other words. The required minimum balance for free checking varies from bank to bank as does the charge made for checks written and deposits made. No bank, by the way, pays interest on checking account money because that's prohibited by law.

Which checking account for you?

A special checking account is generally better only if you write a relatively small number of checks each month and you keep no more money in your account than required to cover the checks you write.

A regular checking account is generally better if you write a relatively large number of checks and particularly if you maintain a few hundred dollars or more average balance in your account all the time. Because checking account charges vary from place to place, you should compare the cost to you of each type of account in your area according to the number of checks you write and the average deposits made each month from your past checking account statements. Also figure in, of course, the credit earned on your average monthly balance. Call a few different banks to get checking account costs.

A regular checking account also may speak better of you than a special checking. Some people consider that a regular checking account is for the sophisticated person who is likely to be more financially stable than one with a special checking account. This isn't always true but it's what some people think.

With a regular checking account, it could pay you to transfer a few hundred dollars from a savings account to the checking account and let that be your continuous balance cushion from month to month. What you save on monthly checking account charges could be greater than the interest otherwise earned each month on the same money in a savings account. This doesn't always pay, however. Because it depends on interest rates versus checking account costs in your area, you must figure it both ways to see which would save you money.

Some banks offer you free checking if you open a savings account with them. You generally must put about $500 to $1,000 in the savings account and agree to leave it on deposit for a year or more. You are paid the prevailing interest rate on your savings, in addition to writing all the checks you want each month at no charge. This can mean an effective return of over 8 percent a year on $1,000 worth of savings put into such a savings account. For example, Joe Willison and his wife have an active checking account which formerly cost them about $3 a month or $36 a year in service charges. The $1,000 in his new savings account saves him that $36 a year, via free checking, and also earns him $45 a year as a result of $4\frac{1}{2}$ percent interest; thus a total return of $81, or over 8 percent a year on his savings. Actually, he saves more because he writes more checks nowadays, makes as many deposits as he wishes at no charge, and he doesn't have to maintain a steady balance in his checking account other than required to cover his checks.

A no-charge checking account is the cheapest of all to have. It's usually a regular checking account that requires no minimum balance and you write all the checks you want at no charge. Its availability depends on where you live and the competitive banking situation in your area. Banks offer no-charge checking as a loss-leader to attract new business. It's on the basis that if you open a checking account with them, you'll also open a savings account and do other business with them, such as getting a car loan and opening a safe deposit box.

Remember, however, that convenience and special services offered by a particular bank also makes a difference. It doesn't necessarily pay, for example, to open a checking account with a bank on the other side of town just for a free checking account, as Elaine, a young career woman, found out. Naturally she wanted to take advantage of no-charge checking, but she soon found that she was taking taxis to rush to the bank before it closed and that cost far exceeded her savings.

A convenient neighborhood bank can by itself be a money-saving consideration. On the other hand, many banks let you bank by mail and you hardly ever need go to the bank personally (provided you can cash checks, as necessary, at other places). By all means choose a bank offering low-cost checking, but also weigh in its suitability and charges for your other needs. For that matter, use two banks, if desired, though by and large, it's not good to open a lot of accounts in different banks.

Avoiding common mistakes

Don't make checkbook errors. This is the most common mistake of all, committed by seven out of ten people with checkbooks. It can lead to embarrassing overdrafts, a banker's euphemism for a bounced check (at a cost of $3 to $4 per bounce), and possible "Mayday" calls from creditors. The most common are failure to record checks written (especially those written away from home); failure to allow for checks that haven't cleared the bank at check-balancing time each month; and failure to deduct service fees, maintenance and other charges levied against your account each month.

Don't cash checks that you intend to cover with a deposit in a day or two. The computers nowadays operate with lightning speed, with checks cashed in the morning reaching their home bank in another part of town and chalked up against your account before the day is over. If you lose, it can cost you a $3 to $4 "Ins." charge (for insufficient funds, another bounced check).

Don't postdate checks. That, of course, is putting a future date on a check so that it won't be cashed beforehand. Often it is and the check zips through the bank's clearing department because clerks look mainly at the sums involved and often miss the date.

Don't write a lot of little checks. Pay bills monthly rather than weekly. Don't cash checks frequently just to keep yourself in pocket money; cash fewer large checks (unless, of course, pocket cash is too easily spent).

Don't spend money for checks printed with your name, address and phone number, especially those expensive personalized checks with your picture or a fancy scenic background. That's all right if you don't mind paying extra. Though banks don't broadcast it, simple checks with your name or two names on them generally are printed for you at no cost. Your address on your checks plus a special color or other design (and sometimes your telephone number, too) costs you from one to two dollars for every 100 checks.

Consolidate your checking accounts. This generally means a joint husband-wife checking account, which can save you money, compared with the cost of separate accounts. The combined monthly balance for two or more accounts shoveled into one account can reduce if not eliminate the total service charge.

Other tips

You may stop payment on a check when you decide you don't want a check you've already given out cashed. A check may go astray in the mail, or you may have overpaid a bill by mistake. Call the bank and tell them to stop the check, giving them details. Ordinarily, you must follow this up with a letter confirming the stop in writing.

A certified check can be useful, since it allows you to pay by check a person who doesn't know you or who wants assurance of your solvency. Your bank marks the check "Certified," and sets aside money from your account to cover it. If you don't use the check, you must return it to the bank before the money can be restored to your balance. The certification charge is nominal.

Once you write a check, it's valid for six years, though most banks will question any check more than six months old. And, despite a common misconception, checks can be both drawn and cashed on Sundays and holidays.

Like money kept in a savings account, money in a checking account should be in a bank that's covered with insurance. Remember that you're insured only up to $20,000 per person and that limit applies to the total money in one name in all accounts within one bank. If you and your family have a greater amount in one bank, spread it among different names or joint accounts for insurance on the total amount.

If someone alters or forges one of your checks, the forger or the bank that cashes it is normally responsible, not you. Sometimes, though, things can get sticky and the bank or person who cashed a forged check can try to make you pay. Because of this and because forgeries are on the increase, avoid the possibility. To play safe, forgery insurance can be obtained fairly inexpensively by adding it to your homeowners' insurance policy. Write checks clearly and properly, use ink, not pencil (seemingly obvious advice but you'd be surprised how many pencils are applied to checks). Leave no space for anyone to add to your written numbers or spelled-out figures. And don't write checks payable to "Cash" or to the "Bearer." If one is lost, anyone can cash it. If a check is lost or stolen, notify your bank at once.

How to balance a checkbook quickly without errors

1. When your monthly statement comes, mark off each item on the statement corresponding with the cancelled checks and the deposits in your checkbook record. Do this first, because cancelled checks are usually returned in the same order as listed on the statement.

2. Rearrange the checks in sequence of date or number, thus in the same order as your checkbook record. If, by the way, you still are a slave to the old-fashioned stub method, you can save time and trouble by switching to the modern method of recording checks with a "check-register," rather than stubs. Ask your bank for one.

3. See that each cancelled check matches its entry on your checkbook record. Set aside cancelled checks that are not recorded.

4. Enter any cancelled checks that were not recorded. Enter any service charges and other deductions made on your statement but not yet entered in your checkbook record.

5. Is your deposit record accurate? Any deposit on the statement but not in your record should now be entered in your checkbook.

6. Strike a new checkbook balance, including all cancelled checks, deposits and other sums noted on your statement.

7. Add up your "outstandings," the checks and deposits you made which are noted in your checkbook but not on the statement (because they did not clear the bank in time). *Add* the sum of outstanding checks to your checkbook balance. *Subtract* the sum of outstanding deposits from your checkbook balance at the end of the month. The final balance figure you now have should agree with the end-of-the-month balance on your statement from the bank.

If the two figures do not agree, how much of a difference is there? If the difference is a figure that is divisible by nine (such as $18 or $81), you've probably made a transposition error somewhere. That means writing $18 for $81, or $137 for $173, or vice versa. That's a common mistake in which the difference between the two figures is always divisible by nine (the way bank auditors catch this error). A glance down your monthly figures should catch the transposed number quickly.

If the difference is only a dollar or two and doesn't bother you, forget it. Adjust your balance up or down by this small difference and let it go at that. Many people do this simply because tracking down a gremlinlike mistake of small size isn't worth the trouble. If, however, you are a person who is compelled to balance your checkbook to the last penny, you'll probably have to go over all your figures from start to finish, and also

check each of the computations noted above. If you still haven't found
the error, check the bank statement. It's conceivable that the bank erred.
Then call the bank.

> **TIP:** Save time and trouble when you balance your checkbook
> (or do your income-tax and other accounting) by adding up
> the dollars and not the cents in a column of figures. Add to the
> bottom total $1.00 for each sum of 50 cents or more; ignore
> each sum of 49 cents or less. That's how auditors and accountants
> speed up their work. Invariably your sums will fall within a
> dollar or two of the exact total and average out accurately.

4

how to cut **credit costs** and **borrow money** at the best terms

The five best ways to buy now and pay later · How to avoid high interest and credit costs · How lenders size you up for a loan · How your credit rating is determined · Saving money when you pay cash · Using credit cards · Avoiding common credit traps.

Never forget that when you buy now and pay later it costs you extra. The price goes up by an interest charge of from 10 to 24 percent and some times as high as 48 percent, depending on the item purchased, the kind of credit obtained and your state's legal ceiling on credit costs.

Looking at it another way, you can save that much by paying cash. But not everyone can pay cash, and besides, credit is often handy if not indispensible for letting us buy and enjoy things we otherwise could not afford, and we pay while using them. About 90 percent of all home buyers must borrow (via a mortgage loan) to buy a house, about 60 percent of all cars are bought on time, and the next most common consumer purchases bought heavily with installment loans are home appliances and furnishings. Without credit to buy such things, many of us would indeed be deprived. There are also credit cards, which afford us the ultimate in buying convenience but while some cost you nothing to use, others can cost you a piggyback interest charge added to the price of each purchase.

Knowing a little about credit can save you a lot of money almost every day you venture forth to buy almost anything, as well as save you money on most of the specific needs and wants in life that are the subject of the rest of this book. Probably the most money can be saved by remembering that it's almost always cheaper and better to shop and arrange for your own credit and for your own time installment loan, compared with financing a purchase directly through the store or dealer from whom you're buying.

The five best and cheapest ways to borrow and buy

Borrowing from yourself is the cheapest of all. You do it with a bank passbook loan or a life-insurance loan.

A bank passbook loan requires that you have money in the bank. You get a passbook loan and your savings are held by the bank as collateral. You pay about 5 to 7 percent interest but because your savings continue to pay interest the loan runs about 2 to 3 percent net cost to you, the difference between the loan interest paid out and the savings interest continuing to be paid in. The money borrowed is used to pay for whatever you're buying, and you then repay yourself later as you can.

Why not just withdraw your own money from the bank? That costs nothing, of course. The answer is that a passbook loan gives you incentive to repay yourself and build up your savings again when otherwise you might not, which is the main reason for a passbook loan. The only other purpose of a passbook loan is to preserve interest on savings when you must withdraw money from a savings account at a time that would cost you lost interest, as we mentioned in Chapter 1.

A life-insurance loan involves borrowing against the cash value built up in a life-insurance policy you own. Up to 95 percent of that money ordinarily can be borrowed at a cost of 4 to 6 percent annual interest. The cash value of a policy is given in a table in the policy. You repay the loan whenever you wish or not at all. That's the catch. If you don't repay it, your interest cost mounts up every year and, in case of death, the insurance sum paid to a beneficiary is the policy face value less the money out on loan. Many people don't repay life-insurance loans and end up paying a lot of interest on them over the years. Thus it is a loan recommended only if you have the self-discipline to repay it.

Third best is a personal bank loan given on your signature alone if you have good credit but more often it requires the posting of collateral to back up the loan if you don't repay it. Interest charges generally run about 6 to 8 percent, more or less, and the typical collateral used are stocks or bonds deposited with the lender until the loan is repaid.

Borrowing from a credit union is generally the next best and cheapest loan. The charges run from about 6 to 12 percent a year, and you're given cash which you repay the credit union in monthly installments. At the end of the year, some credit unions will give you a rebate on the interest if they've had a good year and there's a surplus.

Last is a bank loan, the most common and widespread type of consumer loan. It is obtained directly from a local bank and, like a credit union loan, the money obtained is used to make a cash purchase. But you should shop from bank to bank since the interest rates range from about 10 to 15 percent a year and some banks charge less—or more—than others. Of course, shopping from bank to bank all over town everytime you need a loan can be a bore and a waste of time and the money sometimes saved doesn't justify intensive shopping. Many local banks offer competitive rates and it generally makes sense to do most of your bank business with one or two of them. Before getting a large loan, however, make a few calls to other banks to be sure that the terms offered by your favorite local bank are not out of line.

Most banks offer special "car loans" and "home-improvement loans," but by and large these are the same kind of loans at about the same interest rate as loans made for other purposes. One exception is an FHA-Home Improvement Loan, made to you through a local bank and not directly by the government. It can save you interest on money borrowed to fix up a house.

Incidentally, no one should be afraid to walk into a bank, any bank, for a loan. Some people are reluctant to do so because they don't wear fashionable clothes or are just plain afraid of banks. As a result they pay more for a higher-interest loan—one of those described below—when they could save money with a bank loan—more on this in a moment.

Dealer financing

This is the kind of loan we mentioned earlier with which a seller pulls out papers to finance what he's selling you. The cost ranges anywhere from about 15 percent up to 48 percent, depending on the store and state credit laws. Department stores and mail-order houses generally charge 1½ to 2 percent a month, which means 18 to 24 percent a year interest. Except for certain large stores and national store chains, which provide their own financing, most stores and other sellers serve as middlemen for local banks or finance companies, which really finance the purchases. The dealer serves as the financing agent so that he can make the sale, and often he also earns a commission on the financing (as well as a profit on the merchandise sold). Arrange for the financing yourself and that same commission could end up in your own pocket (via reduced financing charges) and you also save with a lower interest rate.

You can also borrow money quickly and easily from a consumer finance company but the cost can run up to 48 percent interest; or from a pawnshop or a loan shark where the sky's the limit. A high-interest consumer finance company is recommended only if you have been turned down by a bank or two and are in urgent need of the money. A pawnshop is a last resort and a loan shark can be as vicious as a tiger shark.

How much are you paying for credit?

The main cost is the interest rate, and sometimes other charges are added in. By law, the interest must be stated clearly on the loan papers you sign in terms of true annual interest. Thus, all you need do is look for this, right?

Wrong. Many lenders omit the true interest rate from their forms or put it in other ways. Some lenders will, for example, tell you that it's "a 6 percent rate," or a "7 percent add-on rate." That's a common method of figuring credit charges with what are called "discount" and "add-on" loans. The true annual interest is roughly twice the stated rate.

A $1,000 add-on loan for one year at 6 percent means that you get $1,000 but you repay $1,060, which is 6 percent added on to the sum borrowed. You repay it in twelve monthly installments, and the actual interest rate over a year on the balance due works out to almost 12 percent. A 6 percent discount loan for $1,000 has the lender deduct $60, giving you $940, but you repay $1,000 in monthly installments. The true annual interest on the balance (which recedes monthly following each payment) works out to a little over 12 percent.

As mentioned above, there are stores which charge interest at a monthly rate, such as 1½ or 2 percent a month, which results in a true annual interest of 18 or 24 percent a year.

You also may be charged for credit life insurance, which is a short-term policy to insure that the lender will be repaid in case something happens to the borrower. Some lenders also add a few other charges to a loan for "servicing cost," a credit check or "maintenance fee." There are no standard costs, which means that you, the borrower, must check the total cost you must pay for a loan and not just the annual interest rate.

The total cost can be figured easily by adding up the total sum of all installments to be repaid and subtracting the money being borrowed. Simply multiply the monthly installments times the number of repayments. Consider, for example, a loan or purchase of $1,000 that calls for repayments of $60.21 a month for 20 months. That adds up to $1,204.20, the total money you pay for the $1,000 borrowed. Your total loan charges come to $204.20 ($1,204.20 minus $1,000). It's as simple as that.

A special trap to avoid is the "balloon" note, a tricky kind of financing that may sound cheap but isn't. Your monthly installments are kept down to make them seem low, but the very last installment is a high, one-time, final repayment to pick up slack and erase the loan at a ballooned sum. Take that $1,000 loan just noted which calls for 20 payments of $60.21 apiece. A balloon note for that same $1,000 loan might call for regular monthly payments of, say, $50 a month for 19 months, then a final, 20th payment of $254.20 to clean up the loan. Thus the same $1,204.20 to be repaid. Such loans are actually not identified "Balloon Note" at the top of the page, and you won't see that word anywhere. You have to read the contract, and be sure that it calls for all the same repayments, and not for a ballooned payment that would hit you hard at the end.

Credit cards

A credit card can be not only a great convenience but also indispensible. On a business trip Bob Cachit, a friend of ours, was refused a car he needed though he had plenty of cash with him, which he offered as security. He had no credit card, however, and was refused a car by three different car rental firms. Too many cars are rented and never returned, he was told, so that cars were limited to people with good credit ratings, as evidenced by their credit cards.

But, since the price you pay for a credit card depends on the kind of card, you should know the differences among the three main kinds. First is the T&E card (which means Travel & Entertainment) offered by American Express, Carte Blanche and Diners' Club. They are accepted by many if not most large hotels, restaurants, airlines, car rental companies, many gas stations, and a variety of stores and other businesses throughout the world. One of them is all you generally need to get by nearly anywhere. With one you also can cash checks and obtain travelers checks in most cities. That's usually done, for example, with an American Express card at American Express offices located in many large cities of the world.

The T&E card costs you a membership fee of about $15 a year. You're expected to pay your bills on time and no interest is charged unless you

do not pay within 60 days. Then you pay 1½ percent a month (18 percent a year) for up to $500 owed, 1 percent (12 percent a year) on more
than $500 owed. The same interest is also charged when you buy some-
thing like airline tickets on a monthly installment plan.

The second kind of credit card is the bank card like BankAmericard
and Master Charge. Like a T&E card, it allows you to charge almost anything in many places, but unlike a T&E card it also gives you the added
privilege of borrowing money quickly and easily (though that's a booby-
trap as much as a privilege). A bank credit card costs you nothing to
obtain, which makes it sound cheap. However, you must pay your bills
for purchases made with the card on time—usually within 25 days of the
billing date—or you are charged interest. Sometimes there is also a
monthly service charge or maintenance fee, depending on the bank. In
addition, a charge is always made on money borrowed from the bank
with a bank credit card. The interest starts up on the day the money is
borrowed, and not 25 days later as some people mistakenly believe.

The total annual cost of a bank credit card therefore can run higher
and much higher than the cost of a T&E charge. (This writer has regularly
used a T&E credit card for more than ten years and never once had to
pay an interest charge.) A bank credit card is therefore recommended
only if it will really be cheaper for you, which means paying the bank on
time each month and avoiding those mounting credit charges. It is also
recommended only if you require a credit card to do a lot of local travel
and business with small local firms and restaurants which accept a local
bank credit card but not necessarily a T&E card.

Banks love credit cards because they know how human nature works.
Anne Fuzzleheit gets a bank credit card because it costs nothing to obtain,
and she vows to pay her bills promptly to avoid late-payment interest
charges. The bank knows, however, that like most people Anne will
gradually drift into paying those bills late and, besides, the credit card
will probably tempt her into spending more money than she ever did
before. That's just fine with the bank, because the greater the credit card
volume Anne builds up, the more money the bank may earn on her
account. According to an official of the Bank of America, the country's
largest bank and the Big Daddy of the bank credit card, such business
is ". . . still the area where we obtain the highest rate of return in the use
of funds anywhere in the bank."

We have deliberately played down the bank credit card because it is
so disarmingly easy to get and sounds cheap. But it's also disarmingly
easy to use and could cost you a lot of money. If you can handle one
economically, fine; if not, avoid the bank credit card.

If you do get one, it may not be good to get it from your regular bank where you have a checking or savings account. If you don't pay your credit card balance because, for example, you're mistakenly billed for a sum you don't owe (and a bank's computer can make exasperating mistakes like any other computer), your bank could take the money from one of your accounts. You're out of luck till the problem is resolved. Your responsibility for money owed on a credit card is spelled out in the agreement made for accepting a credit card. You automatically subscribe to the agreement when you begin using the card without necessarily signing any paper. Obtain the credit card from another bank to forestall such complications.

The third kind of popular credit card is the *single-use* card which is offered to credit-worthy patrons by department stores, oil companies, hotel and motel chains and car rental firms, among others. It generally costs nothing to obtain, and its chief purpose is to encourage you to do business with the people who issued the card. No interest or other carrying charge is usually made if you pay your bills on time. Depending on the issuer, however, you may be charged 1½ to 2 percent a month on bills not repaid within 25 to 30 days of the billing date.

Credit cards summed up

Don't go overboard on credit cards. Most people need no more than one or two regular credit cards at most (not necessarily counting store charge-account cards). We mentioned that a single well-known T&E card can get you by nearly anywhere in the U.S. and the rest of the world. The only other regular credit card generally required is a single-use oil company card for buying gas. Another card or two may be handy if you travel a lot or your business requires being able to flash the right credit card at any time.

A person with a wallet of different credit cards not only pays extra for many of them but he's often asking for trouble. Every card that is lost or stolen can cost the owner up to $50 in forged charges; by law that's the limit of your responsibility for a lost or stolen personal credit card (not applicable to business credit cards taken out for you by the company you work for). You're liable for nothing if you notify each credit card issuer promptly about cards lost or stolen. But reporting a stolen credit card promptly is not necessarily simple and easy. Try to telephone a bank or other credit card issuer any evening or on a weekend and see what happens.*

One other money-saving fact about credit cards is to know its total

---

* No one answers.

price to you when you add up all purchases made that would not be made without a credit card. That means, of course, everything from spur-of-the-moment eating out to a trip to Europe which sounds so nice when you may pay for it later. That depends on you and, if the cost is too high or you want to save a lot of money, there's an easy solution: destroy your credit cards.

How a bank or other lender sizes you up for credit

Bob Quackenbush never has trouble getting credit (to buy a new car, for instance) and always gets credit at a low cost. His cousin Ray does have trouble and pays higher interest and financing charges. The difference is that Bob meets certain qualifications as a good credit risk, while his cousin does not. Here is what they are when a bank or any other lender, including a store-owner you're buying from, sizes you up for credit.

We've mentioned that you should not be reluctant to apply for a bank loan. You don't have to wear a tie or be fashionably dressed to be welcome at the bank loan desk. The color of your skin and the length of your name also count less than many people think. Bankers are hard-nosed people who lend money to make money. To them, the heart of the matter is whether you will repay a loan and repay it on time. Meet that basic criterion and a ring-tailed monkey straight out of a tree would be given a loan as quickly as any human being. So long as you're reasonably neat and presentable, in farmer's jeans or workingman's overalls, that man at the bank desk may be smiling and friendly but he's viewing you with a cold eye focused virtually entirely on the kind of credit risk you represent. He also knows that some of the fanciest-dressed applicants are the world's worst spendthrifts.

He judges you primarily according to the three C's of consumer credit: Capacity to repay, Capital worth and Credit experience.

Capacity to repay is estimated by your monthly income less your total monthly living expenses including other debts. Is there enough left over to afford a loan?

Capital worth has to do with ownership of a house (a plus sign but not essential), and how much savings, life insurance, stocks and other assets you have. If you can't repay the loan, will the other assets cover it?

Credit experience is your past promptness record of paying other loans and regular bills (telephone, electric, etc.). One banker puts it this way: "Banks view seriously *payment on due date.*" Money on loan costs banks extra for each day overdue so banks put great emphasis on a "good pay" record. A "slow pay" record is not good but not necessarily by itself a disqualification. For example, you may have had a major fiscal setback in the past, after losing a job or because of a medical emergency, which put a black mark on your credit history. But if you resumed paying your bills later, that black mark ordinarily is erased.

Some people mistakenly believe that they will be automatically refused credit because they've never borrowed money before and therefore have to establish a credit record. This is a popular myth but untrue. Don't deliberately take out a loan that's unneeded just to repay it and establish a good record. That's usually a waste of time and money. Nearly everyone applying for credit the first time is judged in other ways, such as type of job, income, assets, how he or she has handled a checking account and his record for paying routine family bills.

On the other hand, involvement in lawsuits, tax liens and legal judgments can hurt you even though you've come out of court triumphantly every time. Court actions are noted on credit reports and frighten lenders. They fear that such a person can cause more fuss and bother than his loan business is worth. People who move around a lot (transients) are also viewed dimly by lenders, for an obvious reason. The lender wants to know that you'll be around to repay and a long list of different addresses on your record casts doubt on this. Conversely, if you have lived in one area for a long time and have deep roots in your community, you are viewed as a desirable borrower.

A "secured" loan is also easier and cheaper to obtain than an "unsecured" one. It's secured when it's for a house, car or appliance which can be repossessed, if necessary, so that the lender's risk is relatively small. It's unsecured when no such collateral is there to back up the loan. The lender's risk is greater and generally the financing charges are higher.

The final decision about whether or not you will be given credit is based on the lender's feel and judgment, the known facts about you mixed with intangibles about the kind of person you are. "We're never 100 percent sure that a person will repay and we make mistakes," one banker told us. He added, "But we have to be right in the great majority of loans or go broke fast in this business."

What is your credit rating?

The chances are that credit and other information about you and nearly every reader of this book are on file in a special cabinet not far from where you live. There are such records for more than 110 million Americans, and what's in your file not only can affect you when you buy something on time, but also when you apply for a job, for life insurance or if you need government security clearance. But now you, too, may know what's in your file, as noted below.

Actually, the typical credit file or report does not grade you with a credit rating per se; it contains facts about your job and income, whether you own a house or rent, about your charge accounts and credit cards and your record of paying bills and loans. Facts about your "character" and living habits legally may not be included (though personal information may be contained in an investigative report compiled for other reasons by a private company or government agency like the F.B.I.).

Credit records are compiled and kept up-to-date by some 2,500 local credit bureaus and credit reporting agencies in the country. Information in them comes mainly from sources you've given on credit applications you've filled out. It's confidential information, however, and available only to stores and others with a legitimate business interest in knowing about you. It is otherwise made available only when requested by a court of law, government agency or a firm that requires security clearance on you for national defense reasons. The Fair Credit Reporting Act of 1971 makes it illegal for anyone to disclose your credit file for any other reason or to any other person, such as a nosy neighbor or business competitor or prying newspaper reporter. It's also illegal for anyone to obtain a credit report on you under false pretenses, under penalty of up to a year in jail, a $5,000 fine or both.

Anyone is, however, entitled to know what's on file about himself. You simply call or write the local credit agency and ask. They're usually listed in the classified telephone pages under "Credit Bureaus" or "Credit Reporting Agencies." There may be a small charge to pull your file and tell you. There's no charge, however, if you're turned down for credit and want to know why. Then you must request a look at your file within 30 days. The bank, finance company or other firm that refused you must, by law, tell you which credit bureau its information came from.

If you're refused credit by a bank, store or other firm with its own internal credit bureau report, the nature of the report must be disclosed to you, but you must request this in writing within 60 days of the turn-down. Firms that do have their own in-house credit departments also may label you with a credit rating—such as A, B, C, or "Good pay," or "Poor Pay." That's about the only instance when you're given a credit rating and it's for use only within the particular firm. (Credit ratings are also given for businessmen for commercial credit.)

A good time to check your credit file is after you have had a financial reversal caused by loss of a job which has resulted in your being unable to pay your bills. Though you are now back on your feet financially, that past black mark may still blot your credit record. See the local credit bureau and often the black mark can be removed, or at least explained so that it will no longer hurt you. Other adverse data included in credit reports have to do with a law suit, a tax lien, a legal judgment, bankruptcy or an arrest or conviction for a crime. Such information, however, must be removed after seven years or after the statute of limitation that applies expires, except for a personal bankruptcy which may remain on record for fourteen years. These time limitations do not apply, however, when you apply for certain jobs ($20,000 a year and up) and if you're being checked out for a life insurance policy of $50,000 or more.

Other facts about your credit

Many people buy on time simply because they think the dealer will give better service if the item hasn't been paid for but that's a fallacy. Most dealers pass your loan papers on to a bank or finance company, and you generally must repay the lender even if the item bought is not satisfactory. Buying on time is no guarantee that you'll get better repairs or better service. Those factors depend on how you choose your dealer and product.

Save money by paying cash rather than charging with a credit card. Many store owners and others who accept credit cards will give you a break on the price if you pay cash, but you must ask about this. Charging with your credit card can cost the seller up to $7\frac{1}{2}$ percent of the price for processing the credit card order. Taking cash costs him nothing and saves him processing time and trouble, and as a result he may cut the price accordingly.

Remember that interest charges for credit are tax deductible on income tax returns but credit charges listed as "service fees" or "maintenance costs" are not necessarily tax deductible as described in Chapter 31.

Don't take on loans to be repaid that add up to more than 15 to 20 percent of your net take-home pay. With $15,000 net income, for example, that means no more than $2,250 to $3,000 of total installment loans and debts to be repaid. Stay on the low side if you're conservative or financially hard-pressed; on the high side only if you have good control over your finances and are not pressing to make ends meet every month.

How to beat the computer

Joe Doublo was being dunned repeatedly for a bill he had paid, and each time he fired back a letter saying he had paid. But, since computers can't read, the bills kept coming. Sound familiar? Because computer billing is particularly common when you buy on credit, we should add a few words

Four ways to buy a $450 color TV set

Buying method	Time annual interest	Monthly payments over two years	Total finance charge	Total cost
Cash	—	—	—	$450.*
Bank or credit union installment loan	12%	$21.17	$58.28	$508.28
Store loan or revolving credit charge	18%	$22.45	$88.80	$538.80
Finance company loan	24%	$23.81	$121.44	$571.44

* Possibly less if you request a discount. But don't say, "How much off if I pay cash?" Say instead, "How much off do you give people who pay cash?"

about it here. They also apply in most other instances of computer billing.

It's not the computer, of course, that can't read, it's the person who mans it, the computer jockey. To put an end to computer billing mistakes, tear the billing card or statement in half and return it together with a letter to a specific person at the company that's billing you. If necessary, telephone the firm to get the president's name or the name of the credit department head. Write a cool, factual letter giving the facts—and hope for the best.

The trick is to deal with a specific person, not the computer or its nameless jockey. If a letter doesn't work, try to get the man on the phone. If it's long distance, call collect. Send copies of your letter to the Better Business Bureau, the President's Commission on Consumer Affairs, or the appropriate consumer-help office where you live, such as your state attorney general.

CREDIT CHECKLIST

1. Save money by borrowing from yourself with a passbook or life insurance loan.
2. The next best and cheapest loans are usually a low-interest personal bank loan, a credit union loan and a regular bank loan.

3. Arrange for your own time-installment loan rather than accepting the usual financing offered by a car dealer, store or other seller.
4. Shop for the best terms.
5. Read the contract before signing anything. Determine the total credit cost, including interest and other possible charges. Request an explanation of anything you do not understand, and don't sign until it's clear.
6. Don't sign a loan contract with blank spaces to be filled in later by the seller. If it can't be filled in now, sign later and only after all blanks are filled in.
7. Put everything in writing. A verbal promise is worthless. You may be told, for example, that there's no service charge on a loan if you repay in 60 days, but, if this is not in writing, it could cost you money.
8. Borrow from a consumer loan company only as a last resort, but try several first for the best terms.
9. Don't go to loan sharks and debt poolers.
10. Don't stock up on credit cards; one or two well-known ones are all you'll generally need.
11. Use a bank credit card only if you will pay bills promptly and avoid interest charges.

your **food** and **supermarket** bills

When you enter the supermarket be prepared to spend from 25 to 30 percent of your after-tax income. It's a little less for some families, more for others. In every case, though, it adds up to a hefty chunk of money month after month. You can save pennies, nickels and dimes by weighing every item, comparing and choosing economically before purchase. You can save considerably more—many dollars—by imaginative planning, shopping and cooking.

5

the intelligent shopper's guide
for **cutting food bills**

by Jo Watkins

Everyone is aware of rising food prices and nearly every consumer is worried about the family's food budget. You may feel low when you see those depressing tables in the newspapers purporting to show how little an average family spends for food when your food budget seems unmanageably higher. But those "food budget" figures can be misleading—almost everyone buys paper products, cleaning supplies, many five-and-dime-store and department store items when shopping for food. In real life the money spent by an average family for all those nonfood items can increase the total supermarket checkout bill by one third more than what's spent for food only. All those government figures on family food costs pertain only to the food items on that checkout tape.

In fact, your "food" bill may not be as swollen as you think. If you're typical, your food bill accounts for only about 75 percent or so of your total supermarket bills. Perhaps a better term for the total would be "marketing budget." You can determine it by subtracting your nonfood items from your sales slip when you get home. (An easy way to do this is to set aside all nonfood items when you unpack after a marketing trip and add them up separately.) That should tell you if you really are or are not extravagent in your buying, cooking and eating habits (or perhaps you have teenage boys!). In the one case you can probably use help and in the other you will feel better with the assurance that you're doing fairly well already. Actually, nearly every shopper can do better on her marketing budget if only because the rules are continually changing and new ways to cut that bill are being developed all the time.

Planning, shopping, cooking

How good are you at each of these? The answers will be reflected in several places, but the one we'll mainly deal with here is your pocketbook.

Planning comes first, of course. Naturally, you know that making a list is supposed to save you money, almost by magic, when you shop for food. But planning really starts way back when you choose your home or apartment.

1. *Get the best kitchen you can.* You know that an efficient kitchen can save you time and energy. Do you realize that it can also save you money? Adequate and well-arranged storage space—shelves, cupboards, refrigerator, possibly freezer—makes it easier for you to store your food purchases in a logical way so that a half-used can of peanuts won't turn up six months later behind the macaroni, rancid, and the little jar of pimientos won't come to light, moldy, behind a gallon of milk. A good refrigerator will keep your food in better condition, longer, than will an old relic.

A good stove will maintain even heat—your biscuits won't burn in the oven and your stew won't scorch on the back burner. Thoughtful use of your minor appliances can result in serious savings—you can make baby food in a blender for far less money than you'd pay for those cute little jars. (But if you do buy little jars, *don't* throw them out—make them pay for themselves by recycling them as nail and screw holders, picnic sugar bowls, spice jars, jam and jelly jars—paint their lids for these last.) A food mill can ready leftover vegetables for soup or leftover roasts for hash, a soufflé or a mousse. Your waffle iron will produce much better waffles than your supermarket's freezer will, and for much less money. If you make a double batch, you can freeze half and, presto, a convenience food! In addition, if you have a good kitchen, you'll be happier about the time you spend there and more willing to cook from scratch, which is usually cheaper, because your good equipment almost guarantees successful cooking. You have to bear in mind that if your oven is so undependable that three out of four cakes fall, it's not only your morale that suffers, it's your food budget, too. In such a case, a store cake would be a bargain.

2. *Educate yourself.* Read cookbooks, learn about nutrition, find out how to use the less expensive cuts of meat and learn what *your* markets call them. Experiment, on a small scale, with the unfamiliar. Try lentils as a supplementary source of protein, for example, but don't make five gallons of lentil soup if you've never tasted it. Learn about the cooking of countries which have very little meat—China, for example, and

India. Collect recipes which use those fish that are still inexpensive. Use tuna, but try the other canned fish, too. And don't forget cheese and eggs—nourishing, delicious and infinitely adaptable. There are whole cookbooks devoted to egg and cheese cookery.

3. *When you sit down to make a shopping list:*

Think about the way *your* family, not a hypothetical statistical family, eats and acts about food. In *our* family "ice cream and cookies" for dessert is translated as "nothing for dessert" while "pudding" *is* "dessert" and if dessert is a homemade pie, supper itself can be eggs and chili (or buttons and grass, for that matter). If you buy unsuitable things just because they're cheap, or glamorous or your friends think you ought to, they'll probably go to waste—and you'll be wasting your food money.

Think about your abilities and available time, what's in season and good and cheap, what's in the newspaper food ads, what you have in the refrigerator and on the shelves, special needs for a special occasion coming up, and what you're hungry for.

Check any special diet needs. Special diets can either increase or decrease food costs. One family we know decided to remove a few dozen excess pounds and found their food costs went down remarkably during that period—they had eliminated desserts and most starches and baked goods. In another family a too-plump teenager went on an all-meat diet— their costs skyrocketed.

Check your staples, not only because it's annoying to run out, but because a special trip to the store for a pound of sugar costs money and time—and you're likely to fall prey to that old bugaboo, impulse buying, and bring home half a dozen things you don't really need.

Check your emergency shelf. It doesn't, of course, have to be a separate area, but you should have enough canned goods, convenience foods, etc., on hand so that you can deal with very bad weather, unexpected guests or the flu with some degree of equanimity.

Check your garden, if you have one. The author's wife felt a little silly one day lately when she came home with some supermarket radishes only to find that the author's daughters' first radishes were ready.

If you like to make detailed menus, do so, with the help of newspaper ads for specials (especially on meats), your cookbooks and your imagination, but don't make up complete menus if knowing what you're going to cook and eat for the next week bores you silly. If that's your case, make your list more general: Write down "meat for four main courses," "salad greens," "vegetables and fruits," and so on, and then fit them together as you cook through the week. But of course if the birthday kid has requested butterfly leg of lamb and you know perfectly well everyone will want baby new potatoes and creamed peas with it, then, in that kind of situation, you'd do better to write it all down.

Make your list with the layout of the market where you mean to shop in mind. You'll save time and avoid back-tracking—an impulse buying trap. Start out with the areas where you mean to be flexible. For example, if that chuck on the fantastic sale turns out to be a fantastic piece of bone and fat, you won't want it—so go look at the chicken, and then buy the vegetables to accompany it.

Consider comparison shopping. It's sometimes a good idea, to be sure, but don't spend more money on gas driving around town bargain hunting than you save in the markets, and remember that your time may have value, both economic and personal. If you make the cookies at home from scratch with the eight-year-old incipient cook, they will be at least as cheap as the ones on the big sale at a distant market and you will have spent your time *and* money in a more "valuable" way.

Now you're ready to go shopping. Take your mind and your memory as well as your list and your money. If you can leave your baby behind you'll save time and distraction; if you can leave your bigger kids behind, you may spend less—kids are notorious impulse shoppers. So, allegedly, are men. But of course if your husband markets with you regularly he can become as impervious to the hard sell as we hope you are.

Dishing out the money

So here you are in the supermarket, ready to spend that 25 to 30 percent of your after-tax income. How can you keep the outlay as low as possible while still providing meals for your family that are satisfying both nutritionally and, if you will, esthetically?

Well, don't come too often! Statistics indicate that if you market only once or twice a week you will probably spend less—you will of necessity have planned more carefully. And your cart will be so full of necessities that there won't be room for items you don't really need!

Don't stay too long! Supermarket surveys show that you spend an extra 50 cents for every minute over 30 that you are in the store.

Stick to your list, within reason, but be willing to be flexible. If something you've planned on is much more expensive than you thought it would be, switch to something less expensive but similar.

Try to develop blind spots for sensational displays of the latest junk products, but remember to keep aware of genuinely helpful new products.

Buy the right size. Often, but not always, the largest size will be the most economical, but this won't be so for you if it will spoil before it's used up, or if you lack sufficient storage space. Gallon bottles of milk *are* cheaper, but, when little kids are pouring, buying quart containers can prevent lots of crying over spilt milk and broken glass. And don't buy six months' supply of paper goods, no matter how super the sale, if the only storage space available is a damp basement—moldy tissues won't make your next cold any more cheerful.

Buy house brands if they are cheaper. Usually they are, but once in a while house brand prices do creep up to and even pass name brand prices for food of similar quality, so check.

Read the labels. Chicken-and-noodles and noodles-and-chicken are not the same thing. The first item mentioned must be the largest component, and so on down the list of ingredients.

Don't buy a higher quality than is necessary for the use you have in mind. You don't need whole tomatoes for a stew or pineapple rings for a fruit cup—the chunks and pieces are generally cheaper.

Do buy convenience foods when the convenience, for you, outweighs the cost. Use them for emergency shelf items, when a baby sitter is tending the children (wouldn't you rather have her give her attention to the kids than to the stove?); when you or another family member is sick; for days when your time is worth more than money; or if you really are a terrible cook and don't care, or you're a very nervous new cook but have to give a dinner party. Of course some of these leaks can be plugged by advance planning—you can fill your freezer with your own convenience foods when you're on a cooking binge. Remember, too, that some convenience foods are true bargains. It costs much more to produce orange juice from scratch than it does to use it in its convenience forms— canned, frozen, in containers or in bottles.

If your store uses unit pricing, accustom yourself to using it. It's a handy tool and will make comparison between brands and sizes easy. Markets which do have it say surprisingly few people use it. We think that, like zip codes, it may be slow to catch on, but once people become aware of its potential for helping them, they'll use it. If your store doesn't have it, you can suggest that they get it. Meanwhile, do it for yourself. Do a few items every time you shop, save your notes and soon you'll have a list that's comprehensive enough for your own needs. Do remember, however, that prices change.

Consider buying some of your food in small shops. If you're lucky enough to have a neighborhood butcher (a real neighborhood butcher, not a glamorous meat market for the rich), try him out. You may be surprised to find that you can buy meat for little or no more money per actual serving than you'd pay in a supermarket. Often it will be better quality meat and more carefully trimmed, which means more usable meat for your money. The butcher may be able to help you save money by telling you how to use unfamiliar meats or less expensive ones than a recipe calls for. Some supermarkets have meat departments which will give the same service, but most have neither the time nor the desire to.

When you are out in the country check roadside stands for produce in season, eggs, and so on, but know what current prices are in town and check quality closely. If there is a buyers' cooperative near you, you might want to join it. You'll probably have to do some of the work, but some coops do a very good job of paring costs for their members and it might be worthwhile for you.

You may be tempted by aggressive salesmen or ads to buy a food-freezer plan, or to buy frozen meat in bulk. These plans *can* be true bargains for you, sometimes, but before you buy, or sign a contract to buy, be very sure that you know very definitely what you are getting and not getting and the actual costs; be very sure you are dealing with a company with an established reputation for quality and integrity. If you don't, you may find yourself with 100 pounds of $2.00 stew meat, or a tiny freezer, a freezer load of frozen turnips and a bill for $700!

Another way of saving money on food is raising some of it yourself. But don't do this unless you enjoy it—the out-of-pocket costs can be very small, but it does take time, energy and diligence. You don't have to have an acre of land. A very small patch (6 feet by 10 feet) will keep a family in lettuce for a summer. In three times that space you can have not only the lettuce but also some broccoli, cucumbers, radishes and tomatoes. To make this an economically sound proposition, start most things from seed and don't spend a fortune on expensive fertilizers and tools—keep it simple and small. If you're planning to stay in your present house for a number of years, you might want to consider planting some long-term items—asparagus plants, raspberry bushes, fruit trees. They all add glamour to your garden as well as to your table, and you'll save money on these luxury foods almost as soon as they begin to yield. And if you do move away, they may enhance the value of your property.

Now you're back home with all those brown paper bags of food. Unpack them quickly but carefully and store them properly immediately so that there will be no diminution of quality due to mishandling. Now comes the moment of truth.

There can be no overemphasizing the importance of good cooking. You can buy the most beautiful food, but if you haven't chosen what your family likes, if you don't cook it well and serve it attractively, you will contribute more to the garbage disposal problem than to your family's economic and physical well-being. So learn to be a good cook! Every meal, no matter how simple, should have something to make it special, even if it's just croutons in the salad, basil in the spaghetti or cucumbers in the liverwurst sandwiches. Plan on having leftovers (and look on the inevitable unplanned ones as bounty, not burden). Your own inspired creation, made from the day before yesterday's lamb, plus zucchini and tomatoes from your garden or your pantry shelf is likely to be much better, much much cheaper than a dab of meat, specially bought, mixed with a packaged "extender."

And don't forget that an occasional wild extravagance—the very first blueberries, if that's what makes *you* happy—is not an inexpiable sin. You can let blueberries substitute for the cherry tree in A. E. Housman's poem:

> *And since to look at things in bloom*
> *Fifty springs are little room,*
> *About the woodlands I will go*
> *To see the cherry hung with snow.*

After all, there are just so many blueberry seasons in a lifetime.

6

the 10 best ways to save
in the **supermarket**

Some of the following tips may be familiar to you but are included here for the sake of completeness and also because many a young wife or bachelor may not be so knowledgeable and experienced. They also include certain points mentioned in the previous chapter which deserve elaboration.

1. *Know nutritional values.* You can spend a lot of money for glamour foods and other tempting items that are bloated in price (and often calories, too) but skinny in real food value, and in just the opposite way buy lower-priced foods abundant in nutritional value. This is old advice handed out by home economists but nevertheless still one of the most important ways to eat well economically. The heart of the matter is to develop a pattern of buying food for balanced meals. Send for *Price List 11, Home Economics, Food and Cooking*, free, from the Superintendent of Documents, Washington, D.C. 20402.

2. *Buy meat with the highest protein per dollar.* Meat is the largest single portion of most people's food bills. According to whose figures are used, it accounts for 25 to 40 percent of a family's total food bill. The best buys are the lowest in cost for protein content. Chicken and lean hamburger are usually two of the best in this respect, as shown in the following table. Conversely, veal cutlets, pork and lamb chops are highest in price for the little protein they contain. The table also shows how to save money by sprinkling your menus with meat substitutes, with dry beans leading the list; not everybody may like dry beans, of course, but

50

an imaginative cook can make them appetizing (baked, in bean soup or cold bean salad, for example).

Choose meats and meat substitutes, by and large, from high up in the table, and don't go overboard for items at the bottom though their price per pound may make them seem cheap. The prices in the table are from a supermarket survey made not long ago in the Northeast. They obviously will vary somewhat from one part of the country to another and also from time to time as meat prices fluctuate.

Obviously, as the price of any food item above goes up or down, its price for protein received will be higher or lower and your values should be adjusted accordingly. Some items will cost more and others less in

Cost of protein from cooked lean meats and meat alternates

Food	Recent retail price	Grams protein per pound	Cost of 20 grams protein*
1. Dry beans	$0.19	95	2 cents
2. Peanut butter	.62	124	5
3. Eggs, large	.51 (dozen)	85	6
4. Chicken, fryer	.42	65	7
5. American cheese	.89	100	9
6. Beef liver	.75	85	9
7. Turkey, ready-to-cook	.56	66	9
8. Tuna fish	.38 (6½ oz. can)	45	9
9. Hamburger, regular	.79	82	10
10. Ham, whole	1.00	58	17
11. Frankfurters	.89	54	17
12. Pork roast, bone in	.85	49	17
13. Sirloin steak	1.32	70	19
14. Chuck roast	1.10	56	20
15. Round steak	1.79	86	21
16. Haddock, filet	1.39	61	23
17. Bologna	.63 (8 oz.)	27	23
18. Bacon, sliced	.98	42	23
19. Rib roast of beef	1.29	53	24
20. Pork chops	1.55	48	32
21. Lamb chops	1.85	51	36
22. Veal	2.15	56	39

* One-third of amount recommended for a 20-year-old man by the National Research Council, 1968.

relation to the others, but by and large the order of the foods in the table should not change too much. You'll generally receive the most protein per dollar from those at the top of the table and the least from those at the bottom.

Figuring your protein cost based on a new and different price takes a little arithmetic: Divide the new price of any item by its protein content from the table. For example, round steak could rise to $2.10 a pound. It always contains some 86 grams of protein per pound (from above). Its latest protein cost to you is therefore 2.4 cents per gram of protein ($2.10 divided by 86), or 24 cents per 10 grams. The main point is that certain meats and meat alternates give you more nourishment and nutritional value per dollar than others, and the table shows you which indeed give you more for your money.

3. *Don't spend extra for the very top grades.* The highest-grade meats and produce are the best looking and the most uniform in size. "Choice," generally the top-grade beef available, may be juicier and more tender than lower grades but the next two grades, "Good" and "Standard," usually have less fat and more protein. Some stores also label these latter grades as "Budget Beef" but don't be put off by this label. It can be your best buy.

Produce that is labeled U.S. Grade B or U.S. Standard can also be a better buy than Grade A, which may be better-looking. In other words, buy Grade A for the table, Grade B for the pot. Similar savings can be made with other foods, such as nonfat dry milk (with the same calcium content at half the price of fresh milk); margarine for butter; and Grade B eggs, which are just as wholesome as Grade A but not as good-looking. When a recipe calls for milk, you can use dry milk plus water; when it calls for butter, margarine can be used, and so on.

4. *Beware of fake specials.* Not every "special" costs you less. You must know prices and values. Be sure you're getting a legitimate special, which can indeed save you 20 to 30 percent, sometimes more. Most specials go on sale from Wednesday to Saturday, but shop for them before 4 P.M., the earlier, the better. You'll get the freshest food and not risk losing out when all the specials are bought up by the early birds.

5. *Don't go hog-wild at sales.* A top government home economist says, "Some people buy as if there's never again going to be another sale." The solution: Buy only what you need now. Leave everything else.

6. *Choose convenience foods carefully.* Some are unbeatable, others cost you dearly compared with the price of buying the same food in its natural form and preparing it at home. Frozen orange juice and canned peas are two convenience foods often cited which cost less than

the raw product. On the other hand, premixed pancakes cost about 25 percent more than the homemade kind, frozen pies up to 100 percent more, and frozen dinners as much as 200 percent more than the same dinner made in your kitchen.

Of course, spending a little extra now and then to save time and effort with a convenience food can be worth the expense, if only because having frozen or other almost-ready-to-serve food on hand in an emergency could save the expense of a last-minute jaunt to the store. On the whole, however, if you tend to buy a lot of convenience foods, analyze the real cost of each and eliminate the expensive and unnecessary ones.

7. *Buy in bulk, but not always.* The giant economy size is not always cheaper by the dozen. Unit pricing can save you money here. Know which of your foods and supplies are cheaper in bulk and which are not, then of course get the best buys in each. For example, sugar and flour are usually cheaper in large bags than in boxes, and milk by the half-gallon or gallon is cheaper than two separate quarts.

8. *Buy in season.* Beef, pork and veal tend to be least expensive in the spring (the time to stock a freezer), and fresh tomatoes are generally cheapest in July. Like the swallows in summer, nearly every food has its season, the time when the greatest supply is available at the lowest cost. Buy out of season and you pay extra.

9. *Leave husband and children at home when you shop.* More than one of those food studies always being taken show that a husband trailing his wife in the supermarket causes the average check-out bill to go up by $2 or more. Men and children are often suckers for eye-catching tidbits and other items which a hardened woman shopper knows the family doesn't need. There are exceptions, of course, like the economy-conscious man who checks every item with a slide rule to determine the best buy.

10. *And don't buy on impulse.* This oft-mentioned trap cannot be overemphasized. Use a shopping list and stick close to it, but don't hold rigidly to it when, for example, you encounter an unexpected special that can mean tidy savings.

section three

how to **buy a house** in the 1970's

More than 60 percent of all American families own their own houses. Although housing costs have risen much faster than general inflation, literally skyrocketing in recent years, those who own their houses have enjoyed lower housing costs* than those who rent. We know families today who must pay terrifically high rents for not very large apartments, whereas others nearby who own houses pay considerably less money for more living space. Buying almost always has been cheaper than renting in recent decades, though there are exceptions and things may change in the future.

The key to buying a house, and living economically in it afterwards, is knowing how to judge house values and buy well. Big money can be saved by knowing how to get a good house at the right price, by choosing a house that will retain its resale value (if not increase in value) and by buying a soundly built house that will be economical to maintain—with low fuel bills, for example— as well as one that will not require expensive repairs. Each of these vital aspects of buying a house is dealt with in the following section. Even if you live in an

---

* Except for some people who live where property taxes have gone through the roof, though most still pay less than renting comparable housing.

apartment or are a confirmed renter, knowing about them can direct your attention to important facts about your present housing.

But first, should you buy or rent—which is cheaper or better for you? How much house can you afford? And perhaps most important today are major changes going on in housing that could, in fact, be adding up to a housing revolution in the U.S.

7

before you **buy** or **rent**

*The changing house market · Should you buy or
rent? · How much house can you afford?*

When people decide to buy a house, they usually dive into the classified
pages of the newspaper and pore over the ads for houses, and then spend
weekend after weekend chasing down the most likely contenders for their
money.

Hold on. Before plunging into the house-shopping game, stand back
and get a perspective on the ocean you're diving into. What kind of house
do you really want? Where should you live?

The answers to those questions can be sharply different from what
they were just five to ten years ago because of significant changes that
have been going on in housing. These changes not only can affect every
home buyer, but they also can affect you if you now own or rent and are
not even considering a change in your present housing; before you may
realize it, what's going on could well cause an abrupt change in your
future housing plans.

The changing housing market

One of the most significant changes in American housing is that the
traditional single-family house on the traditional private lot is becoming

57

more and more expensive and less and less available, and as a result, the
era of the private one-family house could well be vanishing in the U.S.
Back in the boom housing years of the 1950's, the private one-family
house accounted for 85 to 90 percent of all new housing built and sold
in the U.S. As many as 1.5 million a year were built.

Today, however, and particularly since the middle 1960's, diminishing
numbers of private houses have been built. In recent years, the single-
family house has accounted for less than 40 percent of all new housing.
Fewer than 500,000 private, single-family houses were built in 1971. The
traditional single-family house has become too expensive for all but well-
heeled home buyers (except in small towns and outlying areas). Prices
today for the smallest minimal-size one-family house with three bedrooms
and a modicum of land in most suburban areas of the country *start* at
$30,000 to $35,000. For a better house, with more space and, say, a
second or third bathroom, and located in a nice suburb within convenient
commuting distance to a downtown job, you generally will have to spend
at least $40,000 to $50,000.

Prices for single-family houses have climbed sharply chiefly because
of soaring land prices in desirable residential areas within commuting
radius of large metropolitan centers where many people must live.

Average prices for a private lot for a single-family house now run
about $8,000 to $10,000, more or less, in typical American suburbs; in
many places they run higher. For example, the average price for residential land in northern New Jersey, just west of New York City, had by
1970 climbed to over $16,000 per house lot, and was still climbing.
Naturally, the price of the land is included in the price you must pay for
a house. Land now accounts for an average of 20 to 25 percent of the
sales price of a typical new house. Thus, a house selling for $40,000 is
by itself actually worth no more than about $30,000 to $32,000; the other
$8,000 to $10,000 goes for the land it's built on. Construction labor and
materials for houses have also been climbing steadily in prices. And as
new house prices rise, so do old house prices, since each has a leveling
effect on the other.

However, other compensating changes in the housing market have occurred, since business, like nature, abhors a vacuum. More and more
apartments, particularly garden apartments, have been built. In the mid-
1950's, apartments accounted for only 10 to 12 percent of all new housing
built. By 1971, apartment construction was booming as never before, and
it accounted for close to 50 percent of all new housing being built, giving
us, in all, a record 750,000 new apartments in one year.

Growing numbers of other kinds of housing were also being built to make up for reduced new single-family-house construction. These included the single-family "townhouse," an up-to-date version of the old colonial townhouse. In the early 1970's, townhouses were accounting for about 20 percent of all new housing being built. Most are two- and three-story single-family houses with two to four bedrooms. Townhouses, apartments and other forms of multifamily housing require less expensive land than single-family houses. In a desirable suburb, for example, residential land may cost about $45,000 an acre, not an uncommon figure. But no more than two to three single-family houses generally can be built on each acre; hence a land cost of up to $15,000 per each home buyer. Put townhouses or apartments on the same acreage and housing can be built for 10 to 30 families per acre, thus a land cost down to $1,500 to $3,000 per family. Thus, much cheaper housing per family and more housing for more families.

Another notable change in housing is the growing number of complete houses being produced in large part or virtually in full on factory assembly lines and then shipped for speedy erection on home-building sites in cities, suburbs and elsewhere. This includes what is called "modular housing," and it is giving us new kinds of housing for sale. By the early 1970's, more than 50,000 such assembly-line housing units were being produced each year. The growing trend toward the factory mass production of houses holds out the promise (finally) of arresting the upward spiral of construction costs and ultimately giving us lower-cost houses (though it may do little or nothing to reduce the cost of land for housing).

There is also the mobile home, to date the most complete kind of factory-made, whole house. It is the fastest-growing segment of the housing industry, though many people refuse to recognize it. By the beginning of 1973, mobile homes provided permanent, year-round housing for more than 7,000,000 Americans, and new ones were being built and sold at a rate of over 600,000 a year. Once delivered, most mobile homes are seldom if ever moved again. Roughly half of all mobile home inhabitants and about half of all new buyers were young married couples 19 to 34 years old; the second largest group of owners and buyers are at the other end of the social cycle, couples 55 or older.

The typical mobile home contains two to three compact bedrooms, a surprisingly modern kitchen and living area, comes with built-in furniture and furnishings and sells for a mere $7,000 to $8,000 (plus land). Larger mobiles with three bedrooms and air conditioning sell for $10,000 to $18,000; some of these custom models are equivalent in looks and space to one-story ranch houses selling for $25,000 or more in price.

In short, a mobile home provides more square feet of living space by far than any other kind of housing today. Admittedly, some mobile-home parks are unattractive and some are shabby trailer camps and shanty-towns, but an increasing number of new ones are surprisingly attractive (though often these are set behind fences or trees and not noticed when you drive by on the highway).

What does it mean to you, the home buyer? The changing shape of the housing market means that if your heart is set on buying a roomy one-family house, especially on a big lot, you may be in for dis-appointment—and tears. That's unless you're fairly well off, or are willing to move to a distant suburb or country area, where house prices are lower, or if you are willing to buckle down and shop long and hard to find a rare traditional house at a price you can afford.

Be prepared, in other words, to pay a high price for the luxury of a traditional single-family house. An exception is one of those lower-priced houses in a small city or town which are becoming the few remaining places where such houses still can be found at an economical price.

All is not necessarily lost, however. If you have children, and desire a house of your own, consider a full-fledged townhouse with three to four bedrooms or another kind of attached, single-family house. Such housing often offers as much interior living space as a traditional one-family house but at less cost. You pay less because there's less outdoor land of your own (which is no loss considering the outdoor maintenance that is also eliminated). For a couple with one or no children, a smaller townhouse could be ideal. And if you're pinched hard for money, don't pass up the possibility of a mobile home without looking into its availability where you live.

You may lean strongly toward apartment living yet at the same time be strongly attracted by the income-tax savings (with property taxes and your mortgage interest payments each year being deductible on federal and state income-tax returns) and the immunity from future rent hikes. Then consider a cooperative apartment or a condominium which offer much the same financial benefits as ownership of a private house.

Should you buy or rent—which is cheaper?

In general, owning a house will cost less than renting if you live in it for at least three to four years before selling. It takes that long for the equity built up in a house to offset the initial buying costs. After that time a house can mean additional money in the bank for you for each addi-tional year you keep it. A study by the editors of *Better Homes & Gardens* showed that a person buying a $20,000 house with a 10 percent cash down payment and a 7½ percent 20-year mortgage was $3,500 ahead of renting after five years, $12,000 ahead after ten years and $40,000 ahead after 20 years!

That's compared with paying an annual rent equal to 12 percent of house cost, or 1 percent of comparable house cost a month ($200 a month in this case), a good rental figure for comparison purposes. Rental costs also included another 1 percent a year for insurance and maintenance. If you rent, the study also takes into account getting 8½ percent a year return on all the excess money, over rent, not spent, but invested instead, such as that 10 percent down payment needed to buy and own a house.

For buying the house, the study takes into account $300 for initial closing costs (to obtain a mortgage), $1,000 for moving in (for refrigerator, furnishings, etc.), 3 percent of house price a year for property taxes, plus that 1 percent a year for insurance and maintenance. It also figures appreciation in house value of 2 percent a year because of inflation, approximately average for houses in recent decades, plus income-tax savings of 20 percent of the annual property taxes and mortgage interest charges.

Your income-tax savings will vary, of course, according to your income-tax bracket. The other percentages cited can be used to compare the cost of buying a house of any price with the cost of renting.

The case for buying well, however, hinges on two basic assumptions: that you buy a reasonably good house and one that is located in a desirable area so that its resale value is not suddenly shot out from under you. We mentioned earlier that most people who have bought houses in recent decades have ended up financially well ahead of the game compared with renting. That's particularly true for those who later sold at a fat profit, with inflation having pushed up the price of their houses well over what they initially paid to buy.

Still others, however, have houses which are not very good or more frequently they had the ill fortune to buy a house in a poor location or a poor neighborhood that has gone downhill, carrying down with it the resale value of their houses. Despite inflation, their houses are worth less and sometimes considerably less than what they paid for them. That puts special emphasis on buying a good house and also buying one in a good location. These two vital factors are dealt with in following chapters.

The case for renting. It can be a shaky case because renting works in your favor only if you save or invest all the money in excess of rent that would otherwise be spent for a house. Another study, for example, compared two brothers, one of whom, Dan, bought a $24,000 house with a $3,500 down payment and a 30-year mortgage. His brother

Sam rented for $300 a month and invested his $3,500 in "good growth stocks."

Thirty years later Dan's house was worth $45,000, the study assumed, based on an average increase of just over 2 percent a year, while brother Sam's nest egg in stocks had increased in value to $46,437. That's 9.3 percent a year compounded, "a modest long-term average increase." After 30 years of renting, that supposedly put Dan $13,000 ahead of his brother who bought a house, and it takes into account a variety of annual costs and savings for each brother as a result of buying or renting and not just what each ends up with after 30 years.

There are, however, two very shaky assumptions in this study. One, it assumes that Sam rented his apartment for a flat $300 a month all that time, which blithely ignores the tendency of rents to increase. The other is that people who rent don't always follow through on a long-term savings or investment program with money saved each month by not owning a house. In addition, few people have the skill and talent to average 9.3 percent a year in the stock market, which is actually a whopping good return seldom achieved by nonprofessionals in the stock market, as noted in Section 9 of this book.

What about future housing inflation, a definite consideration whether you buy or rent (as it will affect the cost and rentals for apartments, as well as the future resale value of a house you buy)? Will it continue to boost housing costs, pushing up house values and apartment rents? No one can say for sure. A moderate, continual inflation is likely since it has been a way of life for centuries. But in the immediate future the price of housing, which is affected so much by supply versus demand, will depend largely on how fast new-house construction can fill the great existing need for new houses. Economists say that in the U.S. it will take at least through the 1970's and possibly until 1980 before our nationwide housing shortages are overcome and there is enough housing for all. Consequently, excess of demand over the supply for houses is likely to be working for you if you buy or own a house in the next decade. There will be exceptions, to be sure, with pockets of overbuilt housing here and there in many areas where house prices and values will come down, as will apartment rents. If little or no future housing inflation occurs and a house you buy falls off in value by about 2 percent a year, the BH&G study says that buying and owning a $20,000 house will still put you ahead of renting after some 7 years, and after 20 years you would be ahead by $6,400.

The future supply and demand for housing also depend on the future growth of our population, in other words, the U.S. birth rate, which has been climbing for decades. One of the biggest influences on new housing has always been the number of "new family formations," the economists' phrase for young couples who get married and need a new house or apartment. But, of all things, the U.S. birth rate has taken a surprising turn downward in the early 1970's (because of the pill or any other explanation you may apply). If, as a result, our population growth slows down in the future, as some experts believe, then the future demand for housing will ultimately diminish. That could change the whole picture of buying versus renting. That prospect, however, is something to consider chiefly for its effects on us 20 to 30 years from now, or in the 1990's (which is really looking forward). That's when today's baby crop will grow up, get married and enter the market for housing, just as the World War II babies of the 1940's were beginning to get married and exert large pressure on the demand for housing in the late 1960's and early 1970's.

Which should you do? There is no pat answer. Don't kid yourself about the financial pros and cons of buying versus renting today just because you happen to lean one way or the other. Strictly on economic considerations, buying a good house is likely to be cheaper than renting in the next 10 to 20 years, particularly since it's also a method of forced saving with an investment that is likely to keep its value, if not increase in value. True, your property taxes may continue to climb (as will rents). But buying a house stabilizes your basic long-term housing at the price paid to buy it today and your mortgage is paid off in cheaper dollars tomorrow because of inflation.

The income-tax benefits of buying could save you much money on both state and federal income taxes. You may abhor the responsibilities and upkeep burden required for traditional house ownership, but this can be largely avoided by buying a townhouse, cooperative or condominium apartment, each of which offers the same financial benefits and income-tax breaks of regular home ownership without all the same upkeep responsibilities. Renting, on the other hand, could be cheaper if you can find a good rental place at a reasonable price, and if you are sufficiently disciplined and knowledgeable to invest the difference in cost profitably. (How you might achieve up to 10 percent a year from investing is given in Chapter 29.)

Personal considerations may be more important to you than the cold dollar figures involved. A house of your own could be a great source of pleasure and joy and particularly advantageous with children. You may like puttering around the garden and the do-it-yourself opportunities to improve your house. Such things can make a powerful case for owning a house even if it costs more money.

Or you may be inclined the other way, detesting all those chores and fix-up requirements with a house, desiring only a good janitor to remove them from your back. Renting an apartment offers more freedom of movement from one location to another, which could have strong appeal for you. These and other personal leanings, for or against renting or owning, are obviously important. So don't necessarily weigh the case for buying or renting strictly on a dollars-and-cents scale. Don't be a cynic who, Oscar Wilde said, is a person who knows the price of everything and the value of nothing.

How much house can you afford?

If you buy a house, according to the conventional wisdom, it should cost no more than 25 percent of your net income. With a net income of $10,000 a year, your take-home pay, you may spend up to $2,500, or $208 a month for mortgage payments, property taxes, insurance, heating bills, maintenance and upkeep.

Another rule-of-thumb says that your monthly expenses for basic housing costs (taxes, mortgage payments and insurance) should not exceed your net annual income divided by 60. With $10,000 a year net income, you therefore can spend up to $167 a month for those expenses ($10,000 divided by 60). Earnings of $15,000 a year will allow up to $250 a month for them. Turned around, this rule allows up to 20 percent of your annual income for basic housing costs, and allows another 5 percent for heating, upkeep and repairs. (We noted earlier that the average annual total housing expenses for typical families approaches 30 percent of annual living expenses. This higher figure includes the cost of household furnishings, appliances, utility bills and other such accessory costs.)

There is also the old moss-covered rule, now obsolete, that you may buy a house priced up to two-and-a-half times your annual income. Thus a $10,000-a-year income should permit the purchase of a $25,000 house; a $15,000-a-year income, a house of up to $37,500. That's obsolete now because it was a rule formulated way back when mortgage interest rates were no more than 5 percent or so (and interest rates have since climbed 50 percent or more) and back when property taxes were comparatively low. Most important, the sales price of a house is not indicative of its ownership costs. For example, the annual property taxes on a $30,000 house may run no more than $600 to $700 a year in one area but up to two to three times as much in another area. Don't go by the two-

and-a-half times income rule. The important thing is to determine what the *actual* total price of buying and owning a particular house will cost you.

Try to stay within the 25 percent of annual income rule, not counting accessory costs for furnishings, appliances and utility bills. You may stretch the rule and pay more if your income is on the rise, or if you have a tidy nest egg that permits buying a house with a large down payment and a comparatively small mortgage, thus reducing monthly mortgage payments. On the other hand, if you have reached an income plateau and your earnings are not likely to increase in the future, it's prudent to stay below the 25 percent rule. This also may hinge on other family expenses. For example, a family with growing children and possibly more children coming would do well to be conservative on housing. Ironically, of course, it is the young family with children and a limited income that often has the most urgent need of the most house.

How much you can spend for a house, your absolute limit, can be determined only by you. It's your monthly income minus all other essential monthly expenditures. You can determine what you now spend for housing with the table given in Chapter 1. This figure is your starting point, though many people begin stretching it as they find that the house they really want will cost more, and that in turn will require tightening your belt on other nonhousing expenses.

HOW MUCH DOES A HOUSE COST TO BUY AND OWN?

1. *Cash needed to buy and move in*

    Cash down payment: 5 to 35 percent; on the lower
        side for a new house, high side for used house $_____

    Closing costs: for title insurance, mortgage, other
        fees: about 1 to 2 percent of house price, more
        or less, depending on house   _____

    Lawyer's fee: ½ to 1 percent of house price   _____

    Annual property taxes: up to 100 percent of the
        annual property taxes payable in advance   _____

    Insurance: roughly ½ percent of house price,
        usually payable in advance   _____

    Moving and settling-in expenses: $500 to $1,000 or
        up, depending on house, improvements, furniture
        and equipment required   _____

    Contingency: ½ to 1 percent of house price   _____

    Total cash required to buy and move into house   _____

2. *Monthly ownership expenses*
   Mortgage payment: Principal _____ _____
                     Interest   _____ _____
                                                  Total   _____
   Property taxes: 1/12 of annual taxes   _____
   Insurance: 1/12 of annual premium   _____
   Structural upkeep and maintenance: 2 to 3 percent
       of house price divided by 12   _____
   Central heat   _____
   Air conditioning   _____
   Other   _____

   Total gross monthly cost of home ownership   _____

3. *Annual income-tax break* (as result of property
   taxes and mortgage interest payments being tax
   deductible)
   a. Total annual property taxes and mortgage interest
      payments from above   _____
   b. Annual federal income tax savings, 10 to 50
      percent of total on above line, depending on
      your income-tax bracket   _____
   c. Annual savings on state income taxes   _____

   Annual income tax savings, 3b plus 3c   _____

4. *Total net annual house ownership cost*
   a. Total monthly home ownership costs from 2
      above multiplied by 12 $_____
   b. Subtract annual income-tax savings from 3 above   _____

   Your net annual home ownership cost $_____

8

shopping for a house

Choosing where to live—the all-important location · Should
you buy a new or an old house? · Using a real-estate broker

Where you decide to live, the location of your house, is obviously of great
importance. It will shape the lives of everyone in your family. The location in relation to one's job is of primary concern, and this should not
exceed 40 minutes commuting time to work, according to the U.S. Savings & Loan League, a veteran group with much housing research under
its belt. You may have to settle for a longer commute, but then you should
look for easy travel or be prepared to tolerate exhausting daily trips.
Draw the appropriate circle on a road map centered around your employer and that will show you your primary shopping area for a house.

When you're looking at houses, devote time to judging the neighborhood and nearby areas as well as the house itself. Obviously, you will
want to live in a neighborhood that you will enjoy and not only one that
is likely to remain stable and pleasant, but also one with people you will
like and find congenial, especially if you have children. That means,
literally, shopping for an area to live in that has people already there
whom you will want as friends, people not too sharply divergent from
you in social and intellectual ways and by and large with similar affluence,
again especially if you have children. A prominent sociologist says that
this last is of great importance—though not everyone may agree with

him—because families with sharply divergent incomes follow different child-rearing practices which can lead to poisonous rows among neighbors.

Some home buyers shop for a place to live, a particular area or neighborhood, even before they start looking at houses. Naturally, they size up the local schools, stores, shopping center, church and other features they want nearby; these are the obvious check points to make when you are considering a house anywhere.

To find out accurately about them, don't necessarily take the word of a real estate broker or house salesman. Dig a little deeper, as Joe Fostermacher and his wife did before buying their present house. They browsed on Main Street, visited the local Town Hall, had dinner at local restaurants and got to know a few bartenders well. They picked up invaluable information about the local builders but, most of all, they got an inside tip from a local storekeeper about a great house going on the market, which enabled them to buy it before anyone else got wind of it.

Another couple, Bill and Judith Gaddis, explored a Hudson River village they liked, eating and drinking in a local restaurant and pub. Later, when they read an advertisement in a metropolitan paper describing a house for sale there, they saw the house at once. Because they already knew the village, they could buy the house immediately, making a bid for it just ahead of another buyer who wanted it. Where to live, the location, can be more important than the house you choose, as a flaw in a house generally can be remedied more easily and cheaply than a flaw in the surrounding community.

New versus old house—which is better?

One of the biggest advantages of a new house is that it usually requires a smaller cash down payment than a used house, any age. Limited cash resources could therefore restrict your choice to a new house, which often can be bought with as little as 5 to 10 percent of the sales price in cash. A used house usually (but not always) requires from 20 to 35 percent of the house price, and the older the house the higher the down payment.

A new house starts you off with a clean slate. There should be no major repairs and headaches as a result of age and deterioration. There will be inevitable settling-in adjustments, however. Doors and windows will stick, baby shrubbery and grass must be coaxed along to grow and, like a ship on a shakedown cruise, there will be snags to be eliminated. Because most new houses are located in outlying areas, growth pains are also experienced settling down with new roads, services and distant shopping.

With a used house, any age, you can usually move at once into a house ready to live in, and it's generally located in an established neighborhood. It may take more cash to buy, but it will generally offer shorter and faster commuting to work since more used houses are located close to cities and built-up areas where people work.

But, like a pig in a poke, a used house can have unseen faults, minor or major, even structural boobytraps which entail a hefty expenditure for repairs. It depends on the house, of course, which calls for a thorough check of its condition, before buying.

Should you use a real estate broker?

Why not? A good broker can save you money, as well as help you obtain a good house. Most brokers, however, deal mainly with used houses. One will cost you no money since his sales fee, usually 6 or 7 percent of the house price, is paid by the house seller. Occasionally, you might save money by dealing direct for a used house, as a seller will sometimes come down in price by an amount equal to part or all of the sales fee he otherwise would have to pay a broker involved. Use one or more brokers and also look for a house on your own. Some used houses, however, are sold only through brokers, so getting one might require a broker.

A good broker will show you around an area, answer questions, help you bargain and negotiate for a house, arrange a myriad of details and also help you obtain a mortgage. But there are brokers and there are brokers. By and large, the best real estate brokers are "realtors," a label that may be used only by a licensed real estate broker who is also a member of the local board of real estate brokers. These generally are more established brokers who make real estate their full-time occupation.

9

judging the **design** of a **house**

What good design is · How a house should fit your family · Key elements of design · 22 common design traps to avoid

Divide your inspection of a house into two stages. First is its architectural design, which includes, of course, its style, appearance, over-all looks, how well it is set on its site and oriented in relation to the overhead sun, the best view, and its privacy from neighbors and traffic. Good design also means sensible design for living, the difference between a house that is deceptively easy and pleasant to live in and one that is a nightmare for its occupants.

Is the floor plan well-designed, the rooms arranged sensibly in relation to each other and also in relation to the front and back entrances to the house? Imagine yourself living, circulating and working within the house. Will it be efficient and easy?

Are the rooms large enough and well planned, with good window placement, ample storage and laid out for convenient furniture location? Certain rooms, like kitchen and bathrooms, rate top priority inspection, since people spend so much time in each. Many, however, may look attractive at first glance but are deceptively ill-designed. Run-down and inadequate kitchens and bathrooms are two of the biggest drawbacks found in used houses, and they are expensive to redo.

70

The design of a house also should be suitable for your family's special needs. If you entertain frequently, for example, a house should be suitable for entertaining, with roomy and pleasant dining and living rooms and a pleasant outdoor patio or terrace. The children's rooms and TV play area should be isolated from the entertaining center, or civil war could result. If personal family activities are especially important—music, handcrafts, a hobby or an avocation—obviously you will want appropriate design. For that matter, you may like nothing more than quiet repose, not a house with a sun porch or patio flush next to the neighborhood basketball court. How do you and your family live? Think this through and judge the design of a house accordingly.

Was the house designed by an architect? Only a minority of houses are, and most development houses lack full or even partial architectural grace and aplomb. A custom-built house by a good architect for that alone could call for a premium price, and premium attention from you. But there is no such thing as the perfect house. Even the best Frank Lloyd Wright house was not perfect. But be flexible and tolerant. Don't set your standards too high but, on the other hand, don't accept flaws that you'll be unable to cope with.

TWENTY-TWO COMMON LITTLE TRAPS

Here are common design flaws to watch out for in houses.
1. No separate entranceway or foyer to receive visitors.
2. No opening in the front door, or no window or glass outlook to let you see who's at the door.
3. No roof overhang or similar protection over the front door for shelter from rainy weather while you are fumbling for your key, or to protect guests waiting to enter.
4. No direct access route from the driveway to the kitchen.
5. No direct route from outdoors to bathroom so that children can come in and out with minimum bother and mud-tracking.
6. Gas, electric and water meters inside the house or in the garage or basement, rather than outside. Outside meters obviate the need to let meter men in every month.
7. Fishbowl picture window in front of the house, exposing you to every passerby.
8. The nightmare driveway that opens out on a blind curve so that you cannot see oncoming traffic when backing out. A driveway that slopes up to the street is almost as bad, especi-

ally for trapping you on an icy morning when the car won't start.

9. Isolated garage or carport with no direct or protected access from car to house.

10. Accident-inviting doors that open toward the basement stairs.

11. Cut-up rooms with windows haphazardly located. Sometimes too many doors make it impossible to arrange furniture.

12. Windows in children's rooms that are too low for safety, too high to see out of, too small or difficult to get out of in case of fire.

13. A hard-to-open window over the kitchen sink, usually a double-hung type. An easily cranked casement window is usually best here, a sliding window second best.

14. A window over the bathroom tub. This can cause cold drafts, as well as rotted window sills as a result of condensation.

15. Stage-front bathrooms placed squarely in view of a space like the living room, or smack in view at the top of the stairway. Ideally, one should be able to go from any bedroom to the bathroom without being seen from another part of the house.

16. Only one bathroom, especially tough on you in a two-story or split-level house.

17. No light switches at each room entrance and exit.

18. No light or electrical outlet on a porch, patio or terrace.

19. No outside lamp to light up the front path to and from the house.

20. Noisy light switches that go on and off like a pistol shot. Silent switches cost only a little more, and no new house can be called modern without them today.

21. Child-trap closets that can't be opened from inside.

22. Midget closets that are hardly big enough for half your wardrobe. Also watch out for narrow closet doors that keep half of the closet out of reach without a fishing pole, basketball-player shelves too high for a person of normal height and clothes poles so low that dresses and trousers hit the floor.

10

judging the **construction** quality of a **house**

How to tell if a new house is soundly built · The vanishing builder · Who can check a house for you · How to tell if a used house is in good condition

The builder is the key to the construction quality of a house and especially with a new house you buy. If he's good and reputable, you hardly need go further. If anything's not right, a good builder will return and make amends. If he's not reputable and couldn't care less, the house you buy may look pretty sound but it's likely to be rife with cheap construction and poor quality in ways the untutored eye (which means anyone who is not a home-building professional) cannot detect regardless of how much time you may spend probing the house on tiptoes and knees. And then later when something goes wrong and you chose the wrong builder, you will get long practice in Whistling Dixie while you're waiting for *him* to return and correct things.

Check the builder first and above all. Is he experienced, with a track record of plenty of other good houses built locally that have stood up well for their buyers and owners?

By and large, a good builder lives nearby, has been in business for a number of years and operates under his own name, like "Jonathan Aley, Builder," Westport, Connecticut, rather than a generic name like "Heavenly Acres, Inc.," or "Splendiferous Homes, Inc." An impersonal corporate name could mask the quick-buck builder who puts up a group of houses to make a killing, takes his profit, folds his corporation and vanishes.

The vanishing builder

There is no surer way to get stuck with a new house than to buy it from a "vanishing" builder. The builder may seem completely trustworthy, and the house may be spanking new and look as solidly constructed as any other. It may even have been approved by the Federal Housing Administration or the Veterans Administration.

But if something goes wrong with it, the builder is no longer around. It may be a small thing—a warped door, sticky windows or a busted faucet; or it may be something really serious, such as chronic flooding of the basement, a defective furnace or a bad septic tank. Your calls for help go unanswered. Or you may find, to your surprise and distress, there's no phone listing for him. He may have gone out of business or left town quietly. Whatever has happened, he has vanished as far as you are concerned, and you are left high and dry.

Take the case of the Johnsons and ten other families who bought $30,000 to $35,000 houses in a new development called Paradise Knolls. After they had moved in, the Johnsons' house developed a series of troubles due to poor drainage. The septic tank system constantly overflowed. "The sewage smell is awful," Mrs. Johnson reported. "Water has seriously damaged our floor tiling, and the wallboard is mildewing. We brought in 32 truckloads of earth to divert the water. It only comes in slower. The State Supreme Court granted us a $3,000 judgment against the builder, but we can't collect."

Other families in Paradise Knolls must cope with similar problems. They have tried for months to get the builder who had built and sold the houses to remedy the situation—but to no avail. He is from another part of the state and won't make the repairs. In effect, he has "vanished." It is said, however, that he is building elsewhere under a different company name.

How do such builders get away with it? One widespread method used by such builders (who often don't know much about house construction) is to form a corporation to build the houses and then dissolve it as soon as the houses are sold. This way, the company cannot be prosecuted when the houses start to collapse. Another scheme is to drain the corporation of all its assets, so that when the homeowners try to collect, the builder can plead that the corporation is bankrupt and unable to pay for damages. In most cases, there is little law enforcement agencies can do for the defrauded homeowners.

Before buying a new house, then, be sure to find out how long the builder has been established in business locally, in addition to noting the type of company name he uses. Check with his bank—get its name by asking the builder or one of his salesmen, a routine question no one should shy away from. Visit the bank and ask about the builder. You're a potential new customer for the bank and any bank officer on his toes will readily answer frankly—and also be quick to solicit your banking business.

Call the Better Business Bureau about the builder.

Get the names of other buyers of the builder's houses from the builder or on mailboxes of other houses in the same development, and see a few. Nearly everybody loves to talk about his house, but be wary of the reverse English syndrome: people who blast a builder because he never came to replace a rusty nail, though all else in their house is shipshape. Others will praise a builder excessively but are really covering up their own bad judgment in buying a poor house. Probe a little deeper and ask specifically why the house is really good or why it is not.

Call the local home builders association, usually a member branch of the National Association of Home Builders, check with the local Chamber of Commerce and the nearest Federal Housing Administration office. Don't necessarily expect meaty facts from such sources, but this call could trigger a flow of peripheral facts of interest.

Is the builder listed in the local telephone book? A surprising number of builders are not, which could be a red flag sign that's not good. How do you get in touch with him later? Of course, there's probably a telephone number, given to you when you see his houses, but that could be a temporary number later disconnected and useless. It's best if the builder's home telephone number is listed, a sign that he's in business permanently with no reason to hide.

Checking on the builder cannot be overemphasized. It takes time and stamina that most of us tend to shrug off and avoid. Look at it this way. For every hour or so spent on checking a builder, you could well save yourself days and weeks of headaches, trouble, and repair expense later. Somewhere along the line the evidence will add up for or against the builder and you'll know whether or not to buy a house from him.

Of course, the structural integrity of a new house should be checked, though an intensive check may not be necessary with a good builder. But know your limitations. No one but an expert is capable of examining the structural worth of a house any more than a nondoctor is capable of giving you a physical examination.

Hire a home inspection consultant. He is a comparatively new breed of expert, usually an engineer, whose business it is to inspect houses and other buildings for potential buyers. His charge generally runs from about $50 to $125 for a house inspection; the larger and more expensive the house, the higher the charge. You get a report on the condition of the structure from foundation to roof (and for an old house such additional things as a termite inspection). Though not yet found throughout the country, home inspection consultants are listed in the telephone book classified pages under "Home Inspection" or "Building Inspection Firms."

Or hire a local builder or architect, one not associated, of course, with the house you're buying. Another possibility is a real estate appraiser who is familiar with house construction, not the typical appraiser with experience only for evaluating the market value of a house and not its structural bones and organs. Ask around for the names of local people capable of inspecting a house. A new-house inspection may not turn up serious defects (more likely in an old house) but it can tell you of the presence of new but low-quality or inadequate equipment (such as an undersize furnace) and also turn up inadvertent construction mistakes. A builder is more likely to make amends before the sale than afterwards, not to mention those who couldn't care less once the house is sold.

New-house warranty. Many builders will give you a warranty but it's only as good as the builder. Request a written warranty covering defects found within one year to be corrected at the builder's cost. A few top builders will make it five years.

Checking a used house. A general idea of the physical condition can be had by a personal inspection, by you, indoors as well as all around outdoors. If less than an hour or two is spent on this, forget it. Check the condition of the kitchen and bathrooms, two of the most common sources of obsolescence in used houses. Remodeling may be desired, if not essential. Is repainting needed, a new roof, or obvious repairs or renovation elsewhere? Then call in an expert not only to size up the structural condition, but also to give you an idea of the cost of repairs or replacement parts. Ask for special attention to be given to the following common causes of problems in used houses:

Wiring	Water heater
Heating	Termite damage
Plumbing	Structural dry rot and wood decay
Insulation	Air conditioning
Septic tank (if present)	Basement (for dryness)

The real cost of a used house is its sales price plus the cost of essential repairs and renovation. Put the other way, the sales price should be adjusted downward to allow for necessary renovation and repairs. A home inspection report from an expert not only can pinpoint essential repairs, but also can be excellent bargaining ammunition for you. Shown to the seller, it provides proof that his house is not worth as much as he may think, and therefore justifies a reduced sales price to compensate for needed repairs. It can also serve as a face-saving device for the seller to lower his price. That brings up the technique of negotiating for a house.

11

how to **negotiate** the lowest price for a **house** you're buying

A typical negotiation · Bargaining techniques · Bargaining for a used house · How to tell what a house is really worth · Negotiating for a new house

Much money can be saved—sometimes thousands of dollars—by knowing how to negotiate for a house. Call it bargaining, haggling or anything else. No matter what it's called, it's an accepted custom, though usually more accepted in the buying and selling of used houses than for new houses. And two to three million used houses are bought and sold each year for every million new houses built and sold. Consider what goes on when an experienced buyer decides to launch his negotiations for a house he'd like to buy.

How to negotiate for a house*

Jack Briggs and his wife had been shopping for a house for three months when they found the one they wanted. It was an older house owned by a man named Wilson, for sale at $38,500. Jack doubted that it was worth that much, so he hired a real-estate appraiser to appraise it. The man

* Reprinted from, *How to Avoid the Ten Biggest Home-Buying Traps,* by A. M. Watkins, copyright 1968, 1972, by A. M. Watkins.

78

figured that the house was worth $35,850, its current market value, he said, and charged Jack a fee of $60.

Jack was a thorough guy—he had learned from past experience. He called a professional engineer who inspected houses to check the structural condition of the house. This cost $75, which was worth it in terms of insurance.

The engineer's report cited a few flaws but nothing very serious. A new furnace might be needed in a few years and the house was not insulated. Some rewiring would be needed, and the foundation needed a little shoring up in one place. The house would also need a paint job, and Jack's wife figured on a certain amount of kitchen modernization, though not a whole new kitchen. In all, Jack calculated that about $3,000 would be required ultimately for repairs and improvements, though he could move in right away.

The house was overpriced, but how much could he get it for? Armed with facts about the house, Jack and his wife decided they would pay $35,500 or $36,000, their absolute limit. Jack told his wife he would tell Wilson he would give him $33,500 for the house, his first bid.

His wife practically screamed with alarm. She said Mr. Wilson would be insulted. "He won't speak to us anymore!"

"Hold on," Jack said. "He'll probably turn it down, but we've got to start low to leave room for negotiations." She continued to object, and Jack finally said reluctantly that he'd make it $34,000, but not a penny more on the first go-around.

Jack called Wilson and said he liked the house a lot. Exaggerating a little, he said it needed about $3,000 to $4,000 worth of improvements—painting, insulation, and so on. Therefore Jack simply could not pay $38,500, the asking price. Jack took a deep breath and told Wilson he would give him $34,000 for the house.

Wilson laughed. "I'm sorry," he said, "You'll have to do better than that."

Jack told him, "Think it over and let me know. If you want to come down, give me a call." They left it at that.

Jack waited a few days, and, sure enough, Wilson called back. He told Jack, "Look, I'd like to sell the house fast. If you want to do business now, you can have it for $37,500, a thousand dollars off the price. Another family is interested, and a broker is bringing them over this afternoon. I like you and your wife, so I thought I'd call you back and let you know. Thirty-seven five, that's the best I can do."

Jack said he'd talk it over with his wife and call back.

Jack's wife began to panic. "We'll never get the house now," she said.

"Especially if somebody else is seeing it."

"Don't worry," Jack said. "There's always another buyer in the wings. They always say that."

But Jack was concerned, too. Suppose there was another buyer who offered more?

Jack told his wife, "I'll call him back in the morning. Besides, I've got an idea. Two can play the game. I'll just tell him that we're considering another house."

Jack added, "Luckily we're dealing directly with him. He won't pay a broker's commission if he sells to us. If there's really another guy in the picture with a broker, it's going to cost Wilson six percent."

Jack did some figuring on a piece of paper and said, "If the other guy pays the full price, thirty-eight five, the broker gets his cut, and Wilson ends up with thirty-six, one ninety net for the house."

His wife said, "That's still more than our offer. We have to meet that."

"No," Jack said. "Chances are the other guy will offer less, too. So Wilson probably won't get more than about thirty-six thousand net. Probably less."

Jack called Wilson back the next day and said he and his wife would like another look at the house. Jack really wanted to make his next offer face to face with Wilson, rather than on the phone.

At the house Jack and his wife checked a few things and then sat down with Wilson. He braced himself as he prepared to make another offer. He said finally, "We still like the house, but the best we can offer is thirty-five five." Jack waited a moment and added his kicker: "We've been looking at another house we like a lot. But I thought we'd come over here once more and give our last offer. That's the best we can do." He would like to make it higher, he said, but he simply could not.

Wilson said, "I'm afraid that's not enough. I've already come down a thousand dollars, and I'm just not prepared to sell for less." He proceeded to recount all the special features of the house and the things he had done to improve it. He all but said that Jack's offer was unthinkable. They parted amicably.

Wilson had deliberately feigned unconcern. After Jack and his wife left, however, he began wondering if he would ever sell the house. The couple the broker had brought over turned out to be duds. The man had offered a mere $34,000 flat, that was all. Of all the nerve, Wilson thought. And the broker would get 6 percent from that. Well, maybe he could come down to $36,000 and Briggs would buy. Who knows?

If not, however, he might not sell the house for months. The market might get tighter, and there weren't many buyers. Was Briggs kidding about buying another house? He would wait a few days and maybe Briggs would call. Or else maybe he should phone and come down another five hundred, maybe even a thousand.

He decided to stall a bit (a standard technique). But he did not want to stretch his anxiety too far. If he held firm too long, he might see his only good prospect take off and buy another house.

Jack and his wife were also suffering nerve pangs. They were par for the course during such negotiations, he reminded himself. You need a stout heart and a firm hold on your nerves.

Fortunately, Jack and his wife were not compelled to leave their present house. They could take their time. He thought that if he held off a few days longer, he might save another five hundred or thousand dollars. He would pay up to $36,000 for the house, but no more unless perhaps Wilson really would not come down.

Things stood that way for several days. Both men fought off the temptation to call the other. Wilson called the broker to see if any other prospective buyer had shown up, but the broker said no. But if Wilson came down in price, the broker said he might be able to stir up new interest. As of now, he had exhausted every prospect for the house.

Wilson called Jack the next day. He could not hold back any longer. He said, "My wife wants to sell right away, and maybe we still can get together. If you really want the house, you can have it for thirty-six five. How's that?" Wilson said.

Jack avoided a direct answer. They talked for a while, each feeling out the other. Jack's wife, standing at his elbow, urged him to accept Wilson. "I just don't know what to say," Jack said.

A pause. Then Jack said, "Make it thirty-six even and it's a deal."

Another pause. Wilson said, "Okay, you've got yourself a house. I'll take it."

Jack confirmed his bid in writing and bought the house for that price, an even $36,000, or twenty-five hundred dollars below the original asking price. Clearly, Jack Briggs would have paid too much had he bought the Wilson house at $38,500, the first asking price.

Bargaining techniques

With a few exceptions the price of a used house is flexible and subject to bargaining. There are no set rules to the game and fantastic things continually happen. Some houses are priced high and later sold for as little as 50 percent of the initial asking price. Others priced too high go unsold for several years. Many are deliberately priced high with a cushion allowed for bargaining, as an eager buyer (sucker, perhaps?) may come by and pay the high asking price, though the seller is prepared to come down in price.

A house in a posh suburb was put on the market for $150,000 and later sold for $110,000, much closer to its actual value. A retired school principal put his house up for sale at an excessively high $55,000, nearly four times its cost when he bought it in 1950. He and his wife planned to retire in Florida but they were in no hurry. He figured he had time to wait for someone to pay his price and he brushed aside lower offers. His price remained firm for nearly three years. He finally got itchy to go south and sold the house for $44,000.

It happens the other way, too. A house on splendid riverfront property in a lovely midwestern suburb was worth $75,000 but its owner, out of touch with real-estate values, priced it at $52,000. The first lucky prospect knew house values and snapped it up. What a bargain, he thought, accepting the price with nary a thought of getting it lower. Bargaining might have blown the deal, he figured, and the price was already ridiculously low.

How much is a house really worth?

Thus, buying a house at a reasonable price requires knowing pretty closely the value of the house. If you're dealing through a real-estate broker, he might give you an indication of the real value. But generally you can tell more from his tone and what he doesn't say, since he's the seller's agent, too, and you don't necessarily know whose side he's on.

The worth of a house, its current market value, can be determined for you by a real-estate appraiser. You simply hire one to give you a professional appraisal of the house. A good appraiser figures this by knowing local property values, knowing what other comparable houses recently sold for in the area, and then mixing his brew of values with known facts about the house (square feet of living space, structural condition, lot size, etc.). This is always done, by the way, by an appraiser for the mortgage lender to determine the top allowable mortgage to be given on the house. (The maximum mortgage for a used house is usually pegged at no more than 75 to 80 percent of the *appraised value* of the house, no matter what the sales price. Hence, the amount of mortgage obtainable for a particular house is indicative of the real house value. Thus, a small mortgage in relation to house price generally indicates an overpriced house; more on this in a moment.) The names of appraisers can be obtained from local banks. The fee paid to one—about $50 to $100, more or less—depends on the house, and it's a small price indeed for knowing the value of a house you may buy.

Then negotiations can get under way in earnest. The twists and turns that follow will depend on the seller's flexibility, how quickly he must sell and how long the house has been on the market. The longer it has been, the more inclined the owner may be to reduce his price. It also depends on the intensity of your desire for the house and how much you're willing to pay. Your first offer usually can range from 10 to as much as 30 percent below the asking price, depending on what you feel the house is worth and how much cushion you wish for increasing your price with a second or even third offer. If you're adverse to bargaining, let a broker do it for you. Or make one tentative offer below the price you'll pay and then give your final price, and that's it. Your bargaining position is strengthened if you have checked the house carefully and know the cost of essential repairs and improvements.

If you really want a house at a time when the used-house market is boiling over, you'll very likely have to pay a higher price than you wish. Get a feel for the current activity in the house market by talking to brokers and others when you're shopping. To get a good house that you really want, be prepared to act fast but not hastily. The best house bargains are bought by buyers who retain their cool, know what they want and the top price they're willing to pay. They bide time, divorce emotion from their bargaining, and know also that to get a house at the best price they must be prepared to lose it to a higher bidder. Or, knowing what a house is worth, they are willing to buy it at that price with a minimum of bargaining. All of this is what a good real-estate broker can and should do for you, but that depends on the broker.

Negotiating for a new house

With a few exceptions the price of a new house is firm and not subject to much bargaining. A builder may make concessions in the form of a few extras tossed in at no charge, but that's usually it, particularly in a new-house development. If you desire extra features, such as storm windows, screens, an additional bathroom, extra appliances or anything else, you must pay more. Buying them from the builder can be advantageous because their cost ordinarily can be included in the mortgage and doesn't require additional cash expenditures by you. The price of an extra is, however, subject to bargaining. A builder generally puts a high price on them partly because the work must be done outside of his regular construction schedule and partly because, like an automobile dealer, options are an opportunity for a nice profit. The builder should justify the extra cost options, but by all means try to get the cost down.

The price of a new house is sometimes subject to a reduction by bargaining, when it is one of the last houses built in a development and it is standing there unsold. It is also subject to bargaining if it is a speculative house, usually put up by a small builder, particularly if it has been completed for a while and not sold. Every month the house goes unsold costs a builder money (because of capital tied up and interest paid each month on his construction financing). Then a builder often will be amenable to an offer of 5 to 10 percent or so under his asking price.

As in all bargaining, it depends on supply and demand and how much the builder needs to sell it. If he's in a bind and needs the money, it's often surprising how low an offer will be accepted. One speculative builder completed three $60,000 houses in early fall and sold two quickly, but the third had not been sold by Thanksgiving. He said, "Christmas was coming and nobody buys houses then. I didn't want to carry that house through the winter because it was costing me $200 a month in addition to the capital invested in it. I was ready to sell it at cost just to get out. A couple offered me $55,000 and I was delighted. I hemmed and hawed a while, let them come up to $56,500 and sold it at once."

12

how to **finance** a **house** and get a good **mortgage**

How much down payment? · The three main types of mortgages · Interest rates · Special features to request · Special mortgage features · "Closing costs" · And a summary checklist for buying a house

By no means are all mortgages the same. Moreover, the one you get to buy a house determines not only how much money you must repay the bank each month for the next 20 to 30 years, but also how and when you may repay earlier, and how much extra cash expense you must lay out right then and there just to obtain the mortgage (which is money in addition to the house sales price).

Since mortgage terms—in other words, the price paid for the mortgage itself—vary from lender to lender, shopping for a mortgage is recommended. The usual advice given by that friendly neighborhood bank mortgage officer is to gather up every last dollar of cash you can squeeze together, borrowing from friends and relatives if necessary, and then to use it to make the absolutely largest possible cash down payment for your house. And repay the mortgage as swiftly as possible, taking a 20-year mortgage, for example, rather than a 25-year one. That will make you a splendidly patriotic all-American mortgagor client for his bank.

Nonsense. The smallest possible cash down payment could make better sense, since you may require cash reserves for other important needs. And some people retain all possible cash reserves because they would rather invest the money elsewhere and earn a greater return on it than the interest saved on their house mortgage. Besides, most mortgages can be whittled down at almost any time later with extra cash when and if you wish it that way.

Obviously, the smaller the cash down payment for a house, the greater the mortgage loan required to pay the rest of the house price. The important point is to opt for a mortgage with monthly repayments that you can comfortably support (and remember that on top of your monthly mortgage payments there will also be property tax payments). Stretch the mortgage out as long as possible—25 to 30 years, if necessary—to cut the monthly payments to a figure you can afford. Sure, the total long-term interest paid on a 30-year mortgage will be greater than that for the same size mortgage repaid in 20 to 25 years. That's all right. For one thing, and as we just noted above, a long-term mortgage can be whittled down with extra payments after the children have grown or when your salary increases. (On the other hand, however, large monthly payments for a short-term mortgage cannot be reduced very easily if you find them too burdensome.) For another, the longer you take to repay a mortgage, the more the likelihood of repaying it' with increasingly cheaper dollars each year in the future because of inflation. And, of course, interest paid on a mortgage is tax deductible.

You will not need a mortgage, of course, if you can buy a house with all cash. That could save a lot of money, although 90 percent of all home buyers need mortgages. Sometimes, however, it is indeed best to put down the largest possible cash payment you can afford to get a small mortgage. If that's for you, fine. Decide for yourself what you can afford and don't be flimflammed into a mortgage you cannot afford just because somebody else says it's the thing to do.

The three main types of mortgages

If you're a veteran, try for a Veterans Administration, also called GI, mortgage. It's unbeatable but given only to veterans of World War II or later who meet certain requirements. Next best is a Federal Housing Administration (FHA) mortgage, available to anyone. VA and FHA mortgages generally offer the lowest down payment, the lowest interest rates, and the best small-print protection for the home buyer. Except in special cases, both VA and FHA mortgages are obtained, not from the government, but from a local bank or other mortgage lender. The government insures the lender against loss if, for example, he lends money to a veteran to buy a house and the veteran cannot repay. One exception is when you as a veteran cannot obtain a VA loan from a local mortgage lender, particularly in a small town or rural area. Then go to the VA and sometimes they will make a mortgage loan directly to you, a veteran.

The drawbacks with VA and FHA mortgages are that they can involve red tape and delays, requiring a frustrating wait to get one, and sometimes they are difficult to obtain because many mortgage lenders simply will not issue them.

There is also the "conventional" mortgage, the most common type. It embraces all other mortgages offered by private lenders. A conventional mortgage may require a higher down payment and stiffer terms than can be had with a VA or FHA loan, but it is usually easier and quicker to get and involves less red tape than a government-insured VA or FHA mortgage.

Where to get a mortgage loan

They're given by mutual savings banks, savings and loan associations, commercial banks, mortgage broker firms and insurance companies, and generally that's the best order in which to try them. If you're buying a house from a builder or through a real-estate broker, either one can generally help to arrange the mortgage (many builders have them set up in advance for the buyers of their new houses). Nevertheless, you should also check the competition, including your own bank.

Sometimes, in fact, banks and other lenders are loaded to the gills of their vaults with piles of money begging to be put out in house mortgages, and then you'll be welcomed (if not roped in from the street) by every mortgage lender in town, each one eager to sell you one of his mortgages. Concessions are often made at such times to get your business. At other times, however, obtaining a mortgage from the very same lenders can be harder than pulling teeth. The lenders couldn't care less. It depends on the state of the mortgage market at the time you're buying a house.

The interest rate you must pay will also vary according to the national money market at the time you need a mortgage. Interest rates for consumer mortgages reached all-time record highs, over 9 percent, in 1969 and 1970, and soon afterward fell somewhat. Calls to a few banks and other lenders will tell you what they are at any time. Local fluctuations in interest rates generally range from $\frac{1}{4}$ to $\frac{1}{2}$ percent, depending on the lender. Sometimes the interest rate will be lowered a little for you if you make a larger-than-minimum down payment.

The down payment may range from 5 to 10 percent up to about one-third of the house price depending not only on the house (lowest for new houses), but also according to the type of mortgage, the mortgage lender and the house location. In certain states, savings banks and savings and loan associations may by law lend up to 90 percent of house value (in other words, 90-percent mortgages), and 10 percent is made up by your down payment. In other states, the mortgage loan for certain houses cannot exceed 80 percent of the house value.

Remember that the mortgage offered and the subsequent balance covered by your cash down payment is not necessarily related to the sales price of the house. It is based instead on the appraised value of the house, which may be something else again. Shopping for a mortgage, Bob Adams and his wife were told that they could get an 80-percent mortgage for a $40,000 house they wanted to buy; thus a down payment of $8,000, they figured. Not so, they found out later. The maximum mortgage they could get was $28,000, which meant a down payment of $12,000 ($40,000 minus $28,000). Jack blew his top, claiming that the bank had reneged. Actually, it had not, though its mortgage officer could have made things clearer to Jack in the beginning.

After calming Jack down, he explained, "Unfortunately, the house was appraised at $36,000, and we can give you a mortgage of no more than 80 percent of that, thus a $28,000 mortgage, tops. You must make up the difference between that and the sales price."

That's how a high down payment and comparatively small-percentage mortgage required for a house, particularly a used house, can indicate that the house sales price is higher than the house is worth. The appraised value of the house is the vital figure. As a rule, the appraised value of a new house is close to the sales price and sometimes it's the same figure. But no generalization can be made for used houses.

Mortgage repayment terms. The accompanying table shows how monthly payments come down as the time to repay increases. Thirty years to repay is usually the longest term offered, though some lenders permit no more than 25 years; in a few cases others go up to 35 years. (The repayment period may be extended to 35 or 40 years by more lenders in the future.) The monthly mortgage repayment divides into two different categories. One portion goes toward interest on the loan, and a second portion goes to pay off the mortgage principal. As the mortgage loan (principal) is whittled down, the interest portion of each payment is reduced and more of each payment goes toward paying off the house. This, in effect, is money in the bank for you as it builds up your equity in the house.

How the interest rate of a mortgage affects your monthly payment

The accompanying table shows the monthly payments for mortgage loans of different interest rates.

A portion of each payment pays the monthly interest due on the loan; the second portion reduces the loan itself.

6% mortgage

	20 years	25 years	30 years
$ 1,000	$ 7.17	$ 6.45	$ 6.00
5,000	35.83	32.22	29.98
10,000	71.65	64.44	59.96
20,000	143.29	128.87	119.92
30,000	215.00	193.30	179.87

7% mortgage

	20 years	25 years	30 years
$ 1,000	$ 7.76	$ 7.07	$ 6.66
5,000	38.77	35.34	33.27
10,000	77.53	70.68	66.54
20,000	155.06	141.36	133.07
30,000	232.60	212.10	199.60

8% mortgage

	20 years	25 years	30 years
$ 1,000	$8.37	$ 7.72	$ 7.34
5,000	41.83	38.60	36.69
10,000	83.65	77.19	73.38
20,000	167.29	154.37	146.76
30,000	251.10	231.60	220.13

The open-end clause. Though not always available, this can be a great help in time of need. It lets you borrow, in effect, against your mortgage if you need money to finance a big home improvement, to meet a large medical bill or send kids to college. Your mortgage is refinanced, in other words, and you may borrow back a sum equal to what you have repaid. Most mortgages can be refinanced, but an open-end clause permits it to be done quickly, easily and at the lowest cost.

Skip-payment feature. Also called an automatic grace period, this permits you to skip one or more payments, if necessary, after a certain period of time, a good thing to have.

Taking over an existing mortgage

This could save you money when you buy a used house. You simply take over the mortgage that the seller has on his house. It's advantageous when it carries a lower interest rate than obtainable on a new mortgage. You must make up the difference between the sales price of the house and the balance due on the mortgage with cash, your down payment. If it's a comparatively old mortgage, quite a large down payment may be required. But its interest rate, pegged on the low rates of the past, may be so low that the mortgage lender will not permit you to take it over.

If it's a mortgage of comparatively recent vintage, all might work out nicely—attractive interest rate, attractive down payment, and you save money on the closing costs (described below). Ask about the existing mortgage and consider its merits. But you and a lawyer should check it before acceptance.

Closing costs

Be prepared to spend from $250 to $1,000 or more, in cash, on the day you close for a house. This is to pay a variety of bills that have to do with the buying transaction and preparing the mortgage. The total cost varies according to the mortgage and customary local fees for title insurance (about $100 to $500, sometimes more), mortgage origination or processing charge ($\frac{1}{2}$ to $1\frac{1}{2}$ percent of mortgage amount), tax stamps, recording fees, property survey, credit report and appraisal and legal fees. These bills can come as a shock because they are in addition to the price of the house. Determine them when you're shopping for a mortgage and request a full breakdown.

Title insurance is usually mandatory and you usually pay it, which is ironic and tough to swallow since it's protection against a flaw in the title to the property being transferred to you. By rights, the seller should guarantee that he's transferring to you a house and property that is free of legal entanglements (such as a previous owner's heir showing up out of the blue to claim that he is the true owner). The seller does provide it in a few areas, but in most places you, the buyer, pay. There are two kinds of title insurance, a mortgagee policy which protects the mortgage lender only, and a second, optional mortgagor policy, which will protect the buyer. This second policy ordinarily can be had by you for a comparatively small extra charge on closing day and can be good to get.

Some closing cost charges are subject to negotiation. If, for example, the bank requests a property survey, the seller may have one that should be accepted or you can request that, after all, he should pay for a new one. Some sellers will even try to bill you for fuel oil still left in the oil tank when they leave (even though you plan to convert to gas). Stand firm against such nuisance charges, small and large, especially when they weren't cited earlier, and often you can avoid them.

Other unavoidable charges are actually not closing costs. One is reimbursement of the seller for property taxes he has paid for the coming year. Whatever he has paid covering the time from when you buy the house to the end of the next tax year, is repaid to him. Additional tax "escrow" money is often also required from you, by the mortgage lender. That's an advance to cover the annual property taxes due for your first year in the house. Find out about these and any other charges when you shop for a mortgage.

Insurance

Naturally, the mortgage lender and you want protection if the house catches fire or is otherwise damaged. But you will usually save on its cost by arranging for it before closing the deal for the house. You may be expected to take over insurance that exists on the house. But you may not want to, desiring instead to provide your own. This is your prerogative, especially if you want better insurance arranged through your own insurance broker.

Legal protection. When you initially clinch the deal for a house and shake hands with the seller, you may sign what is sometimes called a "binder," and give the seller a good faith deposit of perhaps $50 to $100. A little paper with a few seemingly innocuous words is signed. It may be on the back of an envelope, but it can be as binding as the strongest steel. Tread carefully here.

It is generally best to sign nothing without checking with a lawyer. Oh, still another charge, you may say, groaning at all the expenses. This is one expense that's often avoided, many buyers choosing to be their own lawyers. If you're a reasonably cautious and a careful person with a legal bent of mind, that's all right—perhaps. You'll have to read every bit of small print carefully and know what should and should not remain in the standard contract. Also, know what often should be added for your protection. For example, the binder and the conditional sales contract of a house should be so worded that any deposit or down payment by you is returnable in full if something goes wrong. That's if, for example, you're unable to obtain a satisfactory mortgage, or an inspection of the house shows up a serious defect, or a new house is not completed and ready to move into by a certain date. Other small-print clauses could hook you, so maybe using a good lawyer is better.

A lawyer will cost from a few hundred dollars up to about 1 percent of the house price, depending on local fees. Choose a bona fide real estate lawyer—not all lawyers know real estate—and ask about his fee in the beginning. It's important to line him up early, which means before you enter the final negotiations. If, in fact, you wait till the last minute and hire a lawyer after having signed a lot of papers and closing day is upon you, a lawyer then may be too late. Mistakes he might have prevented may have been made, and the money you pay him now is for questionable services consisting of no more than officiating at your funeral.

Now, all the ins and outs of buying a house aren't always as mind boggling as they may sound. Everything can go off quickly and cleanly with no complications and no cause for headaches later, particularly if you've done a little homework. All those different expenses—for a home-inspection expert, appraisal of a used house, lawyer and so on—may sound burdensome but are really not. In all, their cost should add up to no more than a few hundred dollars. Consider them part of the home-buying cost, and the service purchased in each case could save you much more than its price.

Talk to friends and relatives about their home-buying experiences. Even if you've bought a house before, don't figure you know everything and need no further advice. Get a good book on home buying from a library or in a low-price paperback edition from a book store. Naturally, we recommend *How to Avoid the 10 Biggest Home-Buying Traps*, by A.M. Watkins (author of this book), $2.95 in paperback in book stores or available for that price plus 35 cent postage and handling from All About Houses, 855 River Road, Piermont, N.Y. 10968.

HOME-BUYING CHECKLIST
Use when you're shopping for a house.
1. Is the house located in an attractive area where
   you will like to live?   _____

2. Is the house conveniently located in relation to stores, schools, church, shopping center, other such needs? Will you be satisfied with the quality of each?   _____

3. Design: Is the house attractive and of good architectural design?   _____

4. Is the house well located on its lot? Can you enter it conveniently? Is there a pleasant outdoor area for private family use in summer? How much maintenance will it require?   _____

5. Is the interior well planned and designed for convenient living?   _____

6. Construction: Is the house well-built and in sound physical condition?   _____

7. Will special improvements, remodeling or repairs be required? How much will they cost?   _____

8. What are the annual property taxes? What is the cost of heating, air conditioning, other ownership costs?   _____

9. What kind of a mortgage can you obtain? How much down payment? What are the monthly mortgage payments?   _____

10. How much cash will you need for closing costs?   _____

11. How much money will be required for new furnishings, appliances, storm windows, screens, landscaping, or anything else needed, in addition to the moving expense?   _____

12. Now reconsider: Is it a house of good value and one you really want to buy and own?   _____

13. Can you afford it?   _____

how to cut the monthly cost of **owning** and **operating** your **house**

That means those inevitable bills for electricity, gas, water and especially the telephone, the cost of heating and cooling a house, appliance service and home repairs and, of course, one of the largest and most resented, those annual property taxes levied on your house. We usually take such bills for granted (not without a groan or two) and figure that nothing can be done about them. Why fight City Hall (or the local utility)? You can't win. That's not necessarily so. Often something *can* be done about reducing the high cost of operating and running a house and cutting household expenses, right down to cutting family postage and mailing costs.

13

little-known ways to reduce your **telephone bills**

Dial direct for major savings · Know the best time period
for low-cost long-distance calls · Why person-to-person calls
should be avoided · Reduce monthly rental charges
for unnecessary devices

Start with the telephone bill because government figures say that it is now the largest single utility bill for the typical American family. (An exception would be in the cold north where family heating bills get high and exceed all other utility bills.) Telephone bills have increased sharply because of the large increase in long-distance calls in recent years and because telephone rates, after long being fairly stable, have risen sharply in recent years. However, telephone bills are also higher than they need be for many a family simply because many of us do not use the phone efficiently. There is a right way and a wrong way to make many calls.

    1. *Dial your own calls whenever possible.* This can cut the cost of a phone call from 20 to 60 percent. The typical savings possible on a three-minute call between San Francisco and New York can run to over two dollars, as shown in the accompanying table.

    The important point to remember: Any call an operator helps you with costs more, as do credit-card, collect, person-to-person calls, and billing a call to a number other than the one from which you're dialing. Dial your own daytime call, for example, from Chicago to New York, or the other way, and the three-minute rate is $1.05. Ask the operator to

97

get the number for you and the price of the same call automatically jumps to $1.45. (The specific charges for telephone calls cited here and elsewhere are those at the time of this writing and could change in the future.)

There's one exception. You're not required to pay extra if you ask the operator to complete a call that you tried to dial but couldn't get through to. Be sure, though, that you tell the operator what happened.

2. *Save your long-distance calls for bargain time periods.* Long-distance telephone charges are based on airline mileages and on the time at the calling point. The cheapest time to make most long-distance calls is after 11 P.M. any night, any time on Saturday and on Sunday up until 5 in the afternoon, as shown in the table. After 5 P.M. on Sundays the cost goes up a notch. These bargain time periods, also shown in the table, apply only to interstate calls; the cheapest time periods within a state vary from state to state. If you can't put off a long-distance interstate call until late at night or the weekend, at least try to make it after 5 in the afternoon, when the first of the two cost reductions goes into effect.

3. *Take advantage of the one-minute, late-night rate for long-distance calls.* Dial the call yourself to any part of the continental United States after 11 P.M. and it can cost you no more than 35 cents, the maximum charge for a one-minute, late-night call. Each additional minute will cost you no more than 20 cents. As a rule, you automatically pay the full three-minute rate (in a few cases, two or four minutes) on all calls, even if you complete the call before the allotted time is up. But with this new late-night rate you pay only for the actual time spent talking. It applies to any interstate call covering 926 miles or more; for shorter distances, it's even less. It holds good until 8 A.M. the next morning at the call's point of origin.

4. *Get credit for wrong numbers and cutoffs.* If you get a wrong number after you dial a call, the computer automatically charges you for the minimum three minutes (or whatever), even though you hang up right away. Redial the call and you'll be charged again, unless you call the operator, report the wrong number and ask for a credit. The same applies when you're cut off in the middle of a telephone call and must make it again. Tell the operator and ask for a credit. The only time there's no point requesting a credit is on a call within your local calling area when you have unlimited local service.

5. *Cut down on person-to-person calls.* As the accompanying table shows, a three-minute, cross-country person-to-person call costs $3.55, or nearly three times the cost of making the same call during the day by dialing it yourself station-to-station ($1.35). What's more, the

cost of a three-minute interstate person-to-person call isn't reduced at night or on weekends. (*Within* some states, the cost may go down.) By and large you'll save money by calling station-to-station, even if you have to wait a few minutes for the person you want to get to the phone.

6. *Cut down on expensive rental equipment.* Telephone extensions, fancy phones and other optional equipment can cost you from about 50 cents to as much as $1.50 *per month* for each item. If you're in doubt about how much you're paying for an item, call the company to find out. Some things—a colored telephone, for example—don't entail a monthly rental charge. You pay a one-time installation fee, and that covers it.

How much are you paying extra now, every month, for rental equipment that you do not need or want? An extension, a Princess phone or other monthly-cost feature is easily eliminated. Call the telephone company, and your monthly bill goes down.

7. *Know the cheapest time periods for making calls within your state.* Each state has its own rate schedule. The rates for a long-distance call within a state can be quite different from a call of the same distance to another state. Within New York State, for example, the cost of certain long-distance phone calls drops twice. There's a reduction at 6 P.M. and another at 8 P.M. These reductions apply only to calls to more than 71 miles away, however; shorter-distance calls will cost the same. Check your directory for the rules and rate reductions that apply.

8. *Take advantage of special billing plans.* Various arrangements are offered in different cities and states. In general, you may pay a small extra charge for a large number of extra calls within a certain area. In Virginia, for example, this is called a "Circle Plan," offering an unlimited number of calls within a 20- to 30-mile radius of your home. Because such plans vary considerably, you must check with your local telephone company for information.

9. *Check your phone bills every month.* The telephone company has been known to make mistakes, so if you are ever billed for a strange call, don't hesitate to ask for an explanation. Keep a record of credits due you, particularly on expensive long-distance calls, to make sure you're not charged for wrong numbers or cutoffs.

10. *Use your phone efficiently.* If you make a lot of long-distance calls, get yourself a telephone timer. It's amazing how a timer can help you keep your calls short. Before making an expensive call, organize your thoughts so that you can say what you have to say as briefly as possible. Prepare your own reference table of charges and lowest-cost time periods for those long-distance calls you commonly make.

How long-distance telephone charges vary

Here is the cost of a long-distance interstate telephone call between New York City and San Francisco, or between any other two points 1,911 to 3,000 miles apart. Charges are less for shorter distances.

Time at originating phone	Station-to-station call dialed yourself		Operator-aided or coin phone call		Person-to-person call	
	First 3 minutes	Each additional minute	First 3 minutes	Each additional minute	First 3 minutes	Each additional minute
DAY Mon. to Friday 8 A.M. to 5 P.M.	$1.35	.45	$1.85	.45	$3.55	.45
EVENING 5 P.M. to 11 P.M. Sun. to Friday and all day on holidays	.85	.25	1.40	.25	3.55	.25
LATE NIGHT 11 P.M. to 8 A.M. Every night	.70, or .35 for 1st minute	.20	1.40	.25	3.55	.25
WEEKEND Saturday all day; but only 8 A.M. to 5 P.M. on Sunday	.70	.20	1.40	.25	3.55	.25

NOTE: The above rates were those in effect when this book went to press but they could change in the future.

14

save 25 to 50 percent on **postage** and **mailing** **costs**

It used to be called the penny postcard and it's now six cents. First-class letters not too long ago required a mere two-cent stamp. Mailing costs have climbed more than 500 percent in recent decades, much faster than ordinary inflation, and just since 1970, U.S. postage rates have climbed by 25 to 50 percent or more, depending on the kind of missive being mailed. It's time to reverse the cost spiral and here are 15 specific money-saving tips. The rates cited may be different later since postage schedules are subject to change.

1. Stock up on postcards for short, nonprivate messages at 25 percent less cost than a first-class letter. If delivery speed is essential, use them for air mail, too, overseas as well as domestic, at good savings. You may make your own postcards, in fact, using plain white cards up to 4 x 6 inches in size and adding the required stamp.

2. Use first class rather than air mail for any destination within approximately 250 miles of your home, since air mail is generally no faster within that radius. Even for longer distances, first class is often almost as fast, if not equally fast, since first-class mail is often sent by air on a space-available basis.

3. If speed is essential, mail before 4 P.M., and this applies to both first-class and air-mail letters. Air-mail letters sent before 4 P.M. on weekdays are supposed to be delivered the next day to most cities in the U.S. if they're dropped into one of those special air-mail mailboxes.

4. Don't waste money on air mail on Fridays or any day preceding a

holiday, unless you're mailing coast to coast. First class generally goes just as fast at such times.

5. Use "aerogrammes" for letters abroad. They're available at any post office for 15 cents each and mailable to anywhere in the world at savings of up to 28 percent compared with regular overseas air mail. Air-mail postcards for overseas are even cheaper and fly just as fast.

6. Cut down on special delivery costs. This service is usually unnecessary except for mail that is picked up after regular delivery hours or on weekends. Special delivery often goes no faster than first class to the destination post office, and only then gets special hand delivery. It is recommended only for urgent mail and only when prompt delivery is essential.

7. Never send special delivery to a post office box number. No delivery time is saved and it's money wasted.

8. Use "special handling" for third- and fourth-class packages, where faster-than-usual delivery is desired. It speeds packages along almost as fast as first-class mail and at much less cost than first-class or special-delivery rates.

9. Don't waste first-class postage on packages; that's especially expensive. Paste a letter on the outside of a package or put it inside. Say on the outside, "Letter Enclosed" and merely add one first-class stamp for it.

10. Don't overinsure letters and packages, a common mistake. No matter how much insurance is bought, you will not collect any more than the actual value of the mail lost.

11. Avoid spending extra for registered mail unless essential. Use certified mail instead at big savings for proof of delivery or a return receipt. Registered mail at a higher cost is necessary only if the contents of a first-class letter are to be insured.

12. Get a "certificate of mailing" for a few cents if all that you want is legal proof that the letter was mailed.

13. Use the low-cost book rate or special "educational materials" rate for books, records, manuscripts and other educational items mailed. At 14 cents for the first pound and 7 cents for each additional pound, it offers big savings compared with regular third-class and parcel post rates. Mark the package clearly and also add at bottom, "Return postage guaranteed," in case delivery cannot be made.

14. Weigh your mail and don't waste postage. Buy and use a good mail scale, which can be had for a few dollars at a stationery store. If your postage is inadequate, your mail is either returned to you for the additional postage required or the recipient pays the extra postage.

15. Use light materials especially for air mail and for parcel post

packages. Even an ounce or two of weight saved can add up to nickels and dimes regularly saved.

Other tips

Use zip codes for packages as well as letters. Mark clearly the mailing method desired on letters and packages, such as "air mail," "first class," "special handling," and so on. Get postage rate information pamphlets for domestic and international mail from your post office. They contain mailing facts and rates. If in doubt about postage rates or rules, telephone or see your friendly local postmaster. (Most are friendly.) He can be particularly helpful if you do a lot of mailing, since the post office offers a variety of different services at varying rates.

15

how to avoid home
repair bills

*What to do before calling a repairman · Preventing common
breakdowns and service · Avoiding structural problems
in a house · Buying appliances and household equipment that
need little service*

There are more than one *billion* different household appliances in use
today in America and they cost us more than $500 million a year to
service and repair. On top of that, we spend another $2 to $3 billion a
year for service and repairs on our houses.

Individual repair bills are often high because of their emergency
nature. The furnace breaks down in midwinter, or the refrigerator goes
on the blink. Even when the TV stops working it can be an emergency
for children who don't let up till it's fixed. Service costs are then high
because there's no time to shop for the best price, and often the work
must be done at night or over a weekend. Most household breakdowns,
in fact, occur at night or on weekends because most people are home then
and subject household equipment to the greatest stress.

A little knowledge and ounce-of-prevention care can, however, minimize if not prevent such troubles. It's really a game directed at knowing
when and where the enemy, a mischievous tribe of gremlins, is likely to
strike next with their sabotage crews. You outsmart them with, among
other things, coddling (also called oiling and lubrication) of your kitchen

and other appliances, a periodic check or two of the major equipment and appliances in the cellar, and the same for key parts of the house which, like a valued employee, require personal attention off and on to continue to function efficiently. Most women as well as men can provide the usual attention required without anybody's having to be a mechanical genius.

Before you call a repairman

Consider household appliances first for they are by far the most frequent cause of home service and repair bills. When one stops working, pause for a moment, since it's often a problem that's simple and easy to fix. As many as one-third of all service calls are unnecessary, says a spokesman for the Association of Home Appliance Manufacturers. Sometimes the electric plug is dislodged so that it's not making contact. Merely push the plug in firmly and fully. Be sure that there's electricity at the outlet. Sometimes a fuse or circuit breaker has blown. Check this at the main house electric board, and then plug a lamp or other device into the outlet to be sure there's power.

If the fuses or the circuit breaker continue to blow when the appliance is replugged stop right there. Unplug the device and examine it (but don't necessarily start taking it apart).

Get out the manufacturer's instruction booklet, go down the list of likely problems usually mentioned and read what can be done about each. Sometimes one of the controls is turned the wrong way. Merely checking the controls will unearth this problem and put you back in business. If you don't have a copy of the manufacturer's instruction booklet, write for one, giving the model and serial number of the appliance. In a pinch, call the repairman for checklist advice over the phone.

Nearly every mechanical device requires periodic tightening, cleaning, readjustment, and, if there are moving parts, a drop of oil here and there. Only a caveman would expect otherwise. Like an annual physical checkup, such checks can pay off handsomely in longer equipment life. The specific things to check and do are noted in the instruction booklet.

Know your warranty terms

Many people pay unnecessarily for repairs or parts covered by the manufacturer's warranty which should mean no charge, but it's up to you to substantiate this. The trend toward longer warranties can save you money for as long as 10 years and sometimes longer.

In addition, new appliances may continue to give trouble after their warranties have expired. Many manufacturers will, nonetheless, still honor your warranty and provide repairs at no charge. That's when a problem should have been corrected for you before the warranty expired and they'll make it right for you afterward. Remember, though, that the manufacturer's liability is usually limited only to faulty parts. If you manhandle or abuse a new device contrary to operating instructions, you must pay the bill even if the warranty period has not expired.

Specific appliance tips

The automatic clothes washer, probably the biggest single cause of service calls, is often overloaded or operated with the wrong detergent or too much detergent, or its guts are stricken by a loose coin, bobby pin or other hard object left in a clothing pocket. So we repeat, *don't overload,* even if it means an extra wash or two (that cost is peanuts compared to the cost of a new pump or motor); use the proper type and quantity of detergent; and clean out pockets beforehand.

The dishwasher, another major cause of repairs, also requires proper loading and proper use of detergents. The silver basket in particular should be loaded so that a knife or fork can't flip out and jam the drive mechanism.

Your TV set, particularly a color model, should be placed so that it has proper ventilation. Intense heat is built up inside and the vent holes— at rear, sides or top, depending on the model—must have access to free air circulation. Otherwise, the big heat build-up inside could burn out an expensive part. The TV set should be located at least six to 10 feet away from other electric equipment (to prevent magnetic field disturbances). Because a color set contains exceedingly fine tuning, a firm and stable table or floor mounting is necessary.

The rear coils of a refrigerator also need to be ventilated and should be cleaned and vacuumed periodically. Defrost a refrigerator before frost accumulates to avoid reduced operating efficiency and high electric consumption.

As for other appliances, remember that the dryer's lint trap should be kept clean. The dryer should be vented outdoors not only to keep down air-conditioning bills in summer, but also because its heat and humidity let loose indoors can cause moisture problems in winter, too. Be sure that you properly set the controls on the kitchen range; remember that the automatic oven clock often causes trouble and requires servicing.

Know thy house

The plumbing and the heating are two of the biggest causes of problems and repair bills but these, too, can be greatly minimized or eliminated. Plumbing drains, which often clog up, should be given a periodic dose of drain cleaner. Drain off a gallon or so of water from the bottom spigot of the water heater every month. This will minimize the build-up of minerals, rust and sludge at the bottom of the heater tank. Keep the kitchen sink and bathtubs properly caulked around the edges and especially at the floor to prevent water seepage into the walls and floor and major water damage later.

Learn how to replace faucet washers and repair a faulty toilet-tank mechanism, two of the most common kinds of plumbing troubles (as well as high water bills). Only a few simple tools are needed and the repair parts are cheap and available at any good hardware store. And before winter cold comes, turn off the outdoor spigots to avoid the possibility of freezing and burst pipes.

The air filter in a warm-air heating system and in an air conditioner should be cleaned or replaced periodically, not just to let the blower work more easily and keep down operating costs, but also to prevent costly furnace damage caused by a neglected, badly-clogged filter. Since the same equipment breakdown could result with an oil-burning heating plant if the oil burner is neglected too long, having it cleaned and adjusted at least once a year can prevent serious trouble as well as reduce fuel oil bills.

Have your chimney cleaned occasionally. This can prevent "blow-back" (which sounds like an explosion and causes a sudden black cloud of filth from the chimney to rain dirt and soot throughout the house). Cleaning the chimney periodically is particularly important with oil heat.

Regardless of the kind of heat you have, also remember that motors and other moving parts, such as an air blower or a circulating pump will appreciate periodic cleaning and attention. A little oil once or twice a year is ordinarily all they request to go on working for you with renewed vigor.

Other tips

Know where your main house water valve is and tag it. Then you can turn it off in case of a burst pipe. It's usually in the basement where the water-supply line enters the house.

Keep the earth around the foundation sloped away from the house so that rainwater may drain away. Otherwise, it can seep into the ground and get into the basement. That's usually the most common cause of wet basements. Sometimes the faulty drainage is from a bad roof downspout. Check these, too, off and on, for good drainage and be sure that the water is discharged well away from the house structure.

Anticipate service

Ask about its likelihood and also whom to count on to do it before you buy appliances and equipment for your house. Cultivate good dealers and repairmen. In nearly every area there are dealers and repairmen noted for good service and dependability. Find out who they are and patronize them. In some cases, however, it's best to use a manufacturer's service outlet or his franchised serviceman for repairs. These men are usually noted in the manufacturer's literature with a new appliance or in the telephone book's yellow pages under the kind of appliances involved.

When all else fails and repairs are inescapable, you usually can keep down the repair cost by taking an appliance that's portable to the repair shop. That will save you the cost of a repairman's travel time to and from your house, plus the cost of his $10-an-hour truck.

To play safe, always get an estimate before a man starts repairs. An estimate may cost a few dollars, but it's worth it. If repairs will cost more than one third to one half of the price of a new device, it's often better to junk it and buy a new one. The deciding factor is the age of the device and approximately how much more life it has.

You'll get the longest life and best performance, of course, from well-made, high-quality appliances and equipment, though some people don't believe this. Or why are so many junky, poorly-made appliances continually manufactured and sold? Because they're cheap in price, of course, compared with better-made appliances of the same type. We know of a water heater for houses that sells for $140 with a one-year guarantee. We know of another model, exact same type and capacity, but better made and sold with a ten-year guarantee for $180, or $40 more. Both cost the same to install. Which should you buy?

The higher-priced, ten-year model will almost certainly last longer than the cheaper model. Say it lasts for 14 years, a good estimate, while the cheaper model breaks down after eight years. Over 14 years, therefore, the better model will cost you $12.84 a year ($180 divided by 14), compared with a cost of $17.50 a year for eight years of service from the cheap heater. The answer is obvious.

Not necessarily, you may say. Why spend more for the better unit if you arc likely to move after a few years? The answer to that is that an expensive breakdown is less likely with the better-quality unit. Only one breakdown and one service call could cost you more money than you saved on the purchase price. (There's another reason, too. When you sell your house, the presence of high-quality equipment, pointed out to a potential buyer, could help get a better price for your house.) More and more home buyers are sophisticated shoppers and know about such things, since they have had houses of their own. Conversely, the mere presence of just one or two cheap, low-quality pieces of equipment in a house can cast doubt on the quality of the whole house.

Get a copy of a good home handyman repair book and refer to it whenever a problem comes up. See them in a bookstore or borrow a few from your local library, and then buy the one that will be most useful. Some good ones are published in a low-cost paperback edition, though a few can be had only in a more expensive hardcover. In either case, a good one will still pay for itself. We recommend: *America's Handyman's Book*, by the staff of *The Family Handyman*, Scribner's, $8.95; *The New York Times Complete Manual of Home Repair*, by S. Gladstone, Macmillan, $7.95; *How to Fix Almost Anything*, by Stanley Schuler, Evans, Lippincott, $4.95.

CHECKLIST

1. Stop, look and think through a repair problem before you reach for the phone to call a repairman. Half the time it's likely to be easy for you to fix. Refer to the device's instruction booklet for trouble-shooting help.
2. Develop the habit of checking on your appliances and equipment, off and on. Inspect them for loose parts, clean and adjust them and keep them in good operating condition; i.e., practice preventive maintenance.
3. Provide the same preventive maintenance checks for your house structure.
4. Buy high-quality appliances and equipment.

16

how to reduce your monthly
utility bills

*Reducing house heating bills · Determining the cheapest
energy in your area · Reducing operating costs of major
appliances · Cutting air-conditioning costs · Light bulbs
and lighting bills · Stopping common water leaks*

Utility bills

Nearly everyone has heard about the energy crisis, but not everyone may
realize the high price each of us pays for it in increased monthly utility
bills. As a nation, we have been using up electricity, gas and oil faster
than new means of producing each can be created. Result: climbing costs
and higher household utility bills than ever before.

Household electric rates in the U.S. had been declining for nearly 50
years until 1970 when the energy crunch forced a turnaround and began
pushing up the cost of electricity for the first time since 1925. Just since
1969 the cost of coal, which produces much of our electricity, has gone
up by close to 50 percent. Prices of household gas and oil fuel have also
been going up. The average price of residential fuel oil, for example, has
risen by one-third in recent years, from about 15 cents a gallon in the
late 1960's up to 20 cents a gallon in 1973. Moreover, the price you will

110

be paying each month for household energy, whether you own or rent your housing, is likely to continue rising.

If you haven't noticed how much your utility bills have increased in recent years and how high they are today, compare a few recent ones with your checkbook records for the same bills four or five years ago. If you're typical, your utility costs have gone up by 10 to 20 percent, if not more. Many families' bills have increased more because of the accumulation of new appliances and equipment, like color TV or a combination refrigerator-freezer, which consume from 50 to 100 percent more electricity each month than the standard old black-and-white TV sets and conventional refrigerators replaced. New models of other devices also contain special new features, which are nice to have, but which in similar fashion also mean higher energy consumption, thus another boost in your monthly utility bill.

That monthly bill often can, however, be reduced in ways that now give you greater dollar savings than ever before, if only because you're chopping away at higher bills than before. Reduce your monthly energy consumption and you also strike a blow for conservation and reduced pollution, albeit a small contribution per family, but something which can add up and which all of us may have to do if we are to avoid future brownouts and blackouts. Your contribution also earns you a personal reward in money saved each month.

Reducing winter fuel bills

Because home heating is usually the largest single energy cost for most families (except in the warm South, of course), it is the obvious place to start. Even if you rent a house or apartment and the landlord pays for your heat, you can still benefit by improving the efficiency of your heating system; it can mean increased comfort and fewer chilly drafts and cold spots within your living quarters during winter weather.

An attack on high heating bills is made in two main ways. The primary way is to slow down the leakage of expensive house heat from inside the house to the cold outdoors. The heat you have created and enjoy indoors is continually leaking out through your walls, ceilings and window glass and directly out through cracks and openings in the house shell. It's a thermal process that goes on continuously, every minute, every hour, day and night, when the outdoor temperature is a fraction of a degree or more cooler than the temperature of your living quarters.

It's inexorable and as fundamental as Newton's First Law, with heat flowing always from hot to cold.

That heat leakage from your house, however, is reduced greatly with well-insulated walls and ceilings, by putting up storm windows and storm-doors and by putting simple hardware-store weather stripping around window and door frames. It's comparatively easy and inexpensive to insulate a new house and thereby reduce winter heating (and summer air conditioning) costs, but not necessarily easy after a house has been built.

The attic floor of an existing house should be insulated with at least four inches thick of mineral wool insulation (like the fiberglass type); six to eight inches if you have air conditioning or electric heat. That generally can be done quite inexpensively on a do-it-yourself basis. The cost of insulating the walls of an existing house and adding new storm windows and storm doors (at least on the cold north exposures) generally will not pay for themselves in lower fuel bills, however, unless you stay in the house for at least six or seven years. The walls of virtually any existing house (brick, stone or wood) can be insulated by a professional insulating contractor (who blows insulation into the walls under pressure) at a cost for a typical one-family house of about $600 to twice that, depending on the wall area. This alone should reduce your winter heating and summer air-conditioning bills by about 20 to 30 percent a year. Money spent to insulate your house and reduce your monthly energy consumption may be tax deductible on your income tax returns in the future if proposals before the U.S. Congress, introduced in 1972, are enacted into law. (Also, because of the energy crisis, President Nixon in February 1972 directed that all new housing built with federal financing, including FHA and VA mortgage financing, must be insulated in accordance with stiff new insulation standards.)

The second way to lower fuel bills is by increasing the efficiency of your heating system. Get it to give you better mileage, or more heat for less fuel. If it's a gas-burning furnace, have it cleaned, adjusted and tuned by a good serviceman at least once every three to five years. If you burn oil, the oil burner should be cleaned and adjusted at least once a year. This is important with fuel oil because the nature of oil combustion causes fouling-up relatively quickly, with combustion efficiency falling off, thus increasingly wasteful oil consumption. The necessary check can be done by a good oil burner man at reasonable cost—no more than $15 to $20 usually—especially if you use the man who supplies your oil. A house with electric heat generally requires the least periodic checking because electric heat involves no combustion and generally has no moving parts.

Other heating tips: Coddle the heating system. Keep moving parts, like the air blower or water-circulating pump, clean and lubricated; each ordinarily requires a drop or two of oil once or twice a year. If you have room radiators, tack a sheet of stiff aluminum foil on the wall behind each to reflect heat back into the room, thus preventing the cold outside wall from drawing off radiator heat.

With a warm-air heating system, dirt-clogged air filters are a frequent cause of poor heating, and they are also, according to heating experts, the largest single reason for warm-air service calls. So, with warm-air heat (and central air conditioning), vacuum clean the filters or replace them every two to three months, more frequently, if necessary.

If, by the way, you suffer poor heating with warm-air heat, have the blower adjusted for what is called "continuous air circulation," a common cure for sick warm-air systems. The furnace fan-control switch is turned to the "continuous" setting; or from "fan" to "automatic," or the "summer-winter" switch is set permanently on "summer," even in winter. The fan then operates all the time, when the furnace burner is off as well as on, and air circulates through the house all the time whether or not the thermostat is calling for heat. That produces a more uniform air-temperature level throughout the house. Even though your electric bill for the fan goes up slightly, the better heating can reduce your fuel consumption, which will offset the increased fan electricity cost. If you're unsure about the furnace switch setting required to give you "continuous air circulation," ask your heating dealer.

The heating thermostat

The most economical setting is, as you might guess, the lowest house temperature at which you're comfortable. For every degree you can lower the thermostat and maintain a comfortable interior, fuel consumption is reduced by 2 to 3 percent. Your should be comfortable within a house with the thermostat, and house temperature, at 70 to 72 degrees. If you require a higher temperature, particularly 75 degrees or more, it's a sign that your house is inadequately insulated.

You can save up to 15 percent on overnight fuel consumption by turning your heating thermostat down six to seven degrees, but no more, at bedtime, up again in the morning. But the savings depend on the temperature outdoors at night and your house must be insulated. You save the most at an outdoor temperature at night of 30 degrees, and the savings gradually diminish down to none at all when the outdoor temperature hits zero degrees or lower. The colder the outdoor temperature, the more fuel required to reheat the house the next morning, which offsets the nighttime fuel savings. Fuel savings accrue only if your house is reasonably well insulated (so that heat inside is conserved when the indoor temperature is reduced at bedtime). If your house has little or no insulation, forget the whole matter—turning your thermostat down at night will do you no good.

The cheapest heating fuel?

It's usually gas or oil for house heating. If low-cost natural gas is piped into your area, it is usually cheaper for house heating than oil. A 1970 survey of ten different areas of the U.S. by Consumers Union, the non-profit publisher of *Consumer Reports,* shows that piped-in gas was "generally less expensive" than oil. The cost of each was about the same in the Seattle, Washington, area, and oil was cheaper only in the Boston area.

To determine the cheaper fuel in your area, ask the local utility plus a few heating dealers and fuel-oil suppliers. An engineer at the local utility will generally tell you frankly which it is, even though his energy may be more expensive (and then he'll probably add why *its* special features make it better even though it costs more).

Suppose you now heat your house with an expensive fuel locally, oil, say, though gas is cheaper. Ordinarily, you can convert an oil heater to gas, or vice versa, for several hundred dollars. The resulting fuel savings should repay that cost within a few years and after that your savings are all gravy.

Heating a whole house with electricity generally does not pay unless you live in an area with very low electric rates, such as the TVA region or certain parts of the Pacific Northwest, or if electric rates are low locally for houses with electric heat. You can determine this by a call to your electric company, but before installing electric heat ask for a written estimate of its annual cost. A house with electric heat also requires beefing up with extra-thick insulation throughout.

Converting a gas or oil heating system in an existing house to electric heat generally does not pay, however, because it's quite difficult to insulate an existing house as thoroughly as electric heat requires. An exception is in an area with a mild winter climate. On the other hand, electric heat can make sense and indeed be economical in an all-electric house—no other energy used—and particularly if you also have electric central air conditioning in summer. That's because concentrating all your household equipment and appliances on one energy, electricity in this case, can mean a lower cost to you per unit of electricity consumed, as described below.*

Reducing appliance operating costs

After heating, appliances are the next largest cause of high utility bills. The accompanying tables show that the electric water heater, electric range and electric clothes dryer are the most expensive appliances to operate. But each also comes in a gas-burning model which can be less expensive than its electric counterpart. Therefore, when one of these big-energy-appetite appliances is being bought for the first time or an old one is being replaced, consider a gas model for lower operating costs. An electric model generally will cost less to operate only in an area where low-cost electricity is sold or in an area where natural gas is not available and local gas rates are high compared with moderate local electric rates. That means, too, that gas cooking, by and large, is cheaper than electric cooking. Of course, you may have personal reasons for choosing an electric appliance over gas, or vice versa, though the other may be cheaper where you live. Then you simply acknowledge that you must pay more for personal preference.

If you are unsure about which energy is cheaper locally for you, for cooking and other household use, call both the local gas and electric companies, plus possibly a dealer or two who sell appliances for both types of energy. Although gas has generally been cheaper, especially where natural gas is piped in from the Southwest, electricity has been getting more competitive in many areas where the electric companies offer special low rates for electric water heaters and even more so for electric house heating.

The greatest savings on utility bills are possible if, first, you use the cheaper energy where you live—gas or electricity, whichever it is—for all three of those major appliances, the water heater, the range and the clothes dryer. That's because both electricity and gas are each billed on a sliding scale, the more you use, the lower the unit cost of each. And,

* Since the above was written, the energy crisis has made fuel shortages more acute in the United States. Thus it is difficult to predict which fuels will be best and cheapest in the next 15 years. Gas prices are likely to rise faster than oil prices and electric rates, however. Above all, thick, heavy house insulation will be more important than ever.

second, if these three major appliances also use the same energy that heats your house. Concentrating on that one energy should get you down to the lowest-cost rate block each month. Look at the rate tables for your gas and electricity and you'll probably see that the low-cost block for each can cut your energy costs by 50 percent or more, compared with the high initial rate paid for each every month.

It does not make sense, however, to junk an existing water heater, range or dryer, and replace it with a new one using another energy just to concentrate all three appliances on one energy. Wait till a replacement is required, and then buy the new model for the cheaper energy.

Average operating costs for electric appliances

	Average annual kilowatt hours used	Average annual operating cost
1. Water heater, quick recovery	4,811	$101.11
2. Water heater, standard	4,219	88.60
3. Refrigerator-freezer, 14 cu.ft. frostless	1,829	38.41
4. Room air conditioner, ¾ ton	1,389	29.17
5. Electric kitchen range	1,175	24.68
6. Clothes dryer	993	20.85
7. Color television	502	10.54
8. Dishwasher	363	7.62
9. Television, black and white	362	7.80
10. Auxiliary room heater, radiant kind	176	3.70
11. Electric blanket	147	3.09
12. Electric iron	144	3.02
13. Electric coffeemaker	106	2.23
14. Automatic washer	103	2.16
15. Portable broiler	100	2.10
16. Hot plate	90	1.89
17. Radio	86	1.81
18. Vacuum cleaner	48	1.01
19. Toaster	39	.82

NOTE: The operating costs above are based on the average national cost for household electricity of 2.1 cents per kilowatt hour in 1970 (the last year such figures were available at press time). Costs for your family will run higher or lower than average depending on your local electric rate and family usage. A kilowatt hour (kwh) is the standard measurement of electric consumption, one kwh being the quantity of electricity used by a 100-watt bulb turned on for ten hours.
SOURCE: Edison Electric Institute.

Average operating costs for common gas appliances

	Average therms used per year	Average annual cost
Water heater	270	$28.62
Kitchen range	105	11.13
Clothes dryer	90	9.54

NOTE: Above costs are for an average family based on a national average cost for household gas of 10.6¢ per therm in 1970 (the last year for which such figures were available at press time). A therm equals the heat energy content of 100 cubic feet of natural gas. Costs for a particular family may be higher or lower depending on local gas rates and family usage.
SOURCE: American Gas Association.

Operating techniques

A few examples show how your appliance energy consumption can be reduced with the cumulative savings adding up to a nice profit. The thermostat on your water heater—usually located at the base of the unit—should be set down to the hottest water your hands can tolerate and no hotter. The dishwasher may require hotter water, but most dishwashers contain their own built-in heater for that.

The clothes dryer—and clothes washer, too—should get a full load whenever possible. A partial load consumes almost as much energy. But don't overload, as this can cause a premature breakdown. Overloading also causes clothes wrinkling (by preventing free clothes movement). And clean the dryer lint trap regularly.

Efficient energy use in the kitchen will keep down utility costs especially with an electric range. Obviously, burners and the oven should be turned off after use. Remember that flat-bottomed, straight-sided pans give the most efficient cooking on the range top. And don't overcook. For example, avoid violent boiling. A slow, rolling boil usually cooks as quickly with less heat (with exceptions like spaghetti and other pasta which need fast boiling). Avoid frequent oven peeking, as much heat can escape when the oven door is opened.

Defrost the refrigerator regularly to avoid excessive frost buildup. Thick layers of frost cut down operating efficiency and push up the electricity demand. Keep the rear cooling pipes on a refrigerator vacuumed and free of dust to maintain high operating efficiency. Refrigerator and freezer door gaskets should be checked periodically and fixed or replaced, if necessary. Leaky gaskets are another common cause of high electric consumption (and poor refrigeration inside).

Reread the operating instruction booklet that came with each of your appliances, especially those for the high-energy consumption appliances shown in the table. You may be reminded of money-saving techniques that you've forgotten.

Buying efficient appliances

Certain brands of appliances require more energy to operate and hence mean higher utility bills than other brands of the same appliance. Some refrigerator-freezers, for example, use a third more electricity than others of the same size. Some automatic clothes washers use twice as much water per clothes load as others with the same capacity. Some home air conditioners use over 50 percent more electricity than others with the same total cooling capacity.

Like automobiles, in other words, some appliances give you more— or less—mileage from the same energy input. So check on the power ratings when you shop for a new appliance. The rating is usually noted on the nameplate or in the attached booklet. You may pay a little more for a high-efficiency appliance model, but its lower operating costs will soon repay you that extra cost and save you money from then on. Besides, the most efficient brand and model of a particular appliance also tends to be the highest in quality and therefore should give you the best performance and the longest life.

Cutting air-conditioning costs

In 1972 close to 20,000,000 American families had one or more room air conditioners and over 7 million had houses with complete central air conditioning. The fundamental principle of economy for both is this: The greater the inside heat load is reduced, the less the work load on the equipment and the lower your operating bills.

Thus:

Don't let direct sunshine pour into your house through window glass. Draw shades or blinds over windows exposed to the sun, including east windows in the morning. Exterior shades, awnings or shade trees will keep out twice as much fierce sun heat, an immense load on air conditioning, as indoor blinds or shades.

Cut down the entrance of roof heat through the attic, as sun on the roof is the biggest heat source and thus the biggest single cost factor in air conditioning. (The sun pours down on the roof all day but only on one or two walls at a time). The attic floor should be insulated heavily with up to six inches of insulation (more with electric heat, as we mentioned), and the attic also should be well ventilated with screened vents, usually one at each end.

Keep doors and windows in an air-conditioned house closed, though a window can be left open a little in a bedroom at night, for example, without sabotaging the air conditioning. Use a kitchen exhaust fan to blow cooking heat and fumes outdoors (but only where you're cooking).

Leave storm doors and windows on in summer to slow down heat entry into the room from outside. (A few can, of course, be replaced with screens so that you can open them when the weather is nice.) Don't let moisture build up inside the house, including the basement. A clothes dryer should be vented outdoors even if it's in the basement or laundry area. That's to keep its big steam and heat load from infiltrating the house and loading down the air conditioner. A wet basement is hard on air conditioning, as water vapor from it inexorably rises and puts extra load on the air conditioner—and on your bills.

Operate an air conditioner in accordance with the manufacturer's directions. As in warm-air heating, keeping the air filter clean and unclogged is important for efficient operation and low power consumption.

Light bulbs and lighting

A few individual light bulbs left on at night don't cost you much, but a whole battery of bulbs left on can indeed increase your electric bill. A 60-watt bulb burning all night—10 hours, say—will use about 1.2 cents worth of electricity; a 100-watt bulb, 2 cents worth of electricity. That's with an electric rate of 2 cents per kilowatt hour. Your cost may run higher or lower depending on your local electric rate. Ask the electric company for a rate card if you don't have one.

Not too much can be done to reduce lighting bills other than turning off lights when they're not in use and not leaving them on overnight. And it doesn't pay to skimp on light and use a lot of little 25- and 40-watt bulbs when you need bright light for seeing and reading. The very small savings don't justify inadequate illumination and the eye strain that can result. Money can be saved, however, by using good-quality "long-life" electric bulbs. They give up to four times as much bulb life (up to 2,500 hours) as regular bulbs (750 to 1,000 hours) at about twice the purchase price. Long-life bulbs are recommended especially for hard-to-reach locations.

Fluorescent bulbs are the cheapest of all, giving up to five times as much illumination per watt of electricity, and one will last substantially longer (up to 18,000 hours) than a comparable incandescent bulb. Fluorescent bulbs are therefore excellent and cheap where a lot of continuous light is required for long periods, such as kitchen ceiling light or a desk-study lamp. Their main drawback is their cool glow, which not everyone likes.

Reducing monthly water bills

Common causes of high water bills are drippy faucets and leaky toilet tanks. Almost any man or woman who can read a few lines of printed instructions can cure a leaky faucet and stop an insidious toilet tank leak. See a good home handyman's book. That could save you a $10 to $20 plumber's bill each time, as well as eliminate an excessive water bill. A toilet tank leak is spotted by the sound of water leaking from the tank into the bowl, or by a continuous little swirl of water moving in the toilet bowl; the bowl water should be calm except when flushed. It is caused by a faulty float-ball inside the tank (which requires a new ball mechanism from a hardware store for a few dollars), or the water level is too high in the tank (which requires lowering the water level by gently bending down the float arm).

Water consumption also might be reduced by using a more economical shower nozzle than you have now. Shower nozzles spray as little as two gallons of water a minute up to about ten gallons a minute, sometimes more. The rating should be noted on the nozzle head. Try for a nozzle with the lowest output that will give you the maximum spray desired. An adjustable head is usually best, since you can turn its volume up when desired, down at other times. Shower nozzles can be bought in a hardware store for as little as three to four dollars, and are easily installed. You merely unscrew the old nozzle and screw on the new.

CHECKLIST FOR REDUCING UTILITY BILLS

1. Winter fuel bills, the largest annual utility cost in a cold climate, are reduced the most by insulating your house shell and using storm windows and doors and weather stripping.
2. Keep your heating system operating efficiently by having the system properly tuned and maintained. Moving parts require

periodic lubrication, air filters periodic cleaning, and the whole oil system should be cleaned and adjusted at least once a year.

3. Save fuel overnight by turning down the thermostat at bedtime, but only if your house is insulated.

4. Determine the cheapest heating fuel for you locally, and if you do not now use it, consider the economics of switching to it.

5. When you must buy a new water heater, clothes dryer or kitchen range, aim for ultimate use of all on one energy— either gas or electricity. It is cheapest of all when the lowest-cost energy in your area is also used to heat your house.

6. Review your appliance operating habits, especially for those appliances with the greatest energy appetites.

7. Buy efficient appliances. Check on the power consumption before buying and choose a high-quality model that costs the least to operate.

8. Cut air-conditioning costs by reducing the interior heat load: by shading window glass from the hot sun, insulating the house well, ventilating the attic, keeping the house free of water and moisture, and by operating the equipment efficiently.

9. Save on lighting costs with long-life bulbs and fluorescent lights.

10. Avoid high water bills from leaky faucets, leaky toilet tanks and high-flow shower nozzles.

17

how to **sell** a **house**

*Pricing your house properly · Preparing the house for
sale · Where to advertise · How to show a house to
prospects · Negotiating the sale · The best time to sell · How a
lawyer can help · The case for hiring a real-estate broker*

The idea, of course, is to pocket the highest possible price for your house
and also sell the house quickly. The longer a house stands unsold, the
harder it is to sell and usually the lower the price ultimately obtained
for it.

A real-estate broker can sell the house for you and take 6 percent of
the sales price, the usual broker's fee (up to 10 to 12 percent for farms
and rural properties). Thus a house sold through a broker for $40,000
earns the broker $2,400; you, the seller, keep $37,600.

Sell your house yourself and there's no broker's fee to pay, and you
keep the full price, $40,000 in the above example. That is, however, if
everything goes right for you, but "everything" means quite a few things
that can go wrong when an amateur sells his own house. You might not
sell the house for months and then be compelled to sell at a lower price
than a broker would have sold it for. A good broker also can save you a
lot of time. Some people should call in a broker with no question about
it. That's especially if you're not sales-minded, and neither willing nor

equipped to undertake the effort and work often required to sell a house at a good price. It's no picnic and a certain talent is required.

On the other hand, you need not be a sales genius to sell your own house, and besides, you may well be better able to do it than a lot of brokers. Take on the sales effort yourself, do it successfully and you will deservedly earn the broker's commission, with several thousand dollars or more extra ending up in your pocket. But know what's involved.

Price the house properly

Overpricing is the most common and widespread mistake made by people selling their own houses. It's because many people hold wildly inflated notions about the value of their houses, or they confuse the high, dream-like figure that they would like to get for their houses with what the house is worth, which is more than a little lower. That's all right, you may say. If the house doesn't sell for awhile, you can always lower the price later. Those are famous last words because things don't work that way in real estate. For example:

Harry Eberstone and his married sister inherited their parents' nice little two-story house in a New England suburb. It was the place they grew up in, and they put it up for sale a few years ago for an outlandish $47,500 because they had heard that a house nearby had recently sold for $45,000. They figured they had all the time in the world to sell the house and they might as well begin at a nice high figure. Their parents' house, however, had smaller rooms, and was in ancient condition compared with the nearby house that had sold for $45,000. Nobody would pay the price asked for their house and it went unsold for three years. They finally sold the house for $34,500, one of the few bids they had received.

While the house stood unsold, they had to pay taxes for it and they also lost three years of interest on the capital they would have received if they had priced the house properly in the beginning and sold it then. In all, a loss of over $8,000 as a result of overpricing the house. Thus, they ended up with less than $27,000 net received for the house.

On the other hand, if they had initially priced the house in the mid-thirties and sold it at, say, $34,000, they would have ended up after three years with close to $41,000 and a total of as much as $14,000 ahead! That's compared with the $27,000 net received for the house and takes into account a reasonably quick sale for $34,000, which, put in the bank, would have earned 5 to 6 percent a year for three years, plus the three years of property taxes saved. They almost certainly would have sold the house at that price initially because at the time the housing market was boiling over with prospective buyers who far outnumbered the houses for sale. By reaching for the moon, much too high for the house they had to sell, they not only sold it for less later, but the long time it took to sell the house cost them dearly.

Why overpriced houses don't sell

A house usually stirs up the most interest when it is first put on the market, the most likely prospective buyers being flushed out to see it, just as the arrival of new-model cars stirs up big interest in automobile circles each year. But if the price is too high, potential buyers are turned off and lose interest permanently. A seriously interested buyer may consider giving you a much lower bid, though this is problematic. Hold your ground or close to it at an unrealisticly high price and perhaps there's a long-shot chance that a foolish buyer may pay it. What generally happens, however, is that the overpriced house stands unsold, like passed-up merchandise and, like the Eberstone house, it is viewed with growing suspicion. Rumors arise that something's wrong with it. A stigma grows around the house, and ultimately it is sold at a substantially reduced price. In addition, the owner has had to carry the house, paying taxes, among other things, for all the time it went unsold.

How to price a house for sale

The sensible way is to determine its market value. You find out what houses nearby like yours have recently sold for. You look into the prices of similar-size new houses going up nearby to estimate the cost of building a house like yours today. You determine local land values to figure what your lot is worth. Mix factors like these together and you will come up with the approximate value of your house. It can be quickly done for you, however, by a good real-estate appraiser hired to appraise your house (as Jack Briggs did, Chapter 11). That will cost you about $50 to $100, more or less. Get the names of recommended appraisers from local banks and mortgage lenders.

Then you will know what your house is worth, the approximate price that it should bring on the market today. You generally set the asking price for your house at about 5 to 10 percent, perhaps up to 15 percent, above that figure. As a rule, the higher the value of the house, the greater the percentage markup. There's no set rule on this, however, especially with very high-priced houses and luxury estates where the asking price depends greatly on the local market and customary practice. It also depends on the speed with which you must sell your house and the tempo of the housing market at the time. Obviously, with more buyers in the market for houses than houses available things are working for you and you might get a nice high price. If the opposite is true—a strong buyer's market—you should tread lightly in pricing the house.

On the other hand, don't be timid like Erik Philthrop who was transferred and wanted to sell his house quickly. It was worth about $40,000. The time was June, 1971, and good houses were scarce with plenty of eager buyers looking for houses. He was a supposedly bright professional person but would neither seek professional advice nor spend a few dollars for a professional appraisal. He knew it all and put his house up for sale at $35,000, a price he figured he could get quickly. The house sold instantly to a buyer who privately said later that he would have paid $40,000 for it. Erik's timidity and refusal to seek professional advice cost him at least $5,000.

Clean up and fix up

Put your best foot forward. A broken window, creaky steps, a busted door knob and a drippy faucet should be fixed or replaced. Such expenses, by the way, are tax deductible. The property should be cleaned up, the lawn mowed and the shrubbery trimmed. No need, however, to spend a fortune on fixup and repair expenses. About the only major expenditure that generally will pay is, if necessary, repainting the exterior of a house for sale. Interior repainting, extensive redecorations and money spent for almost any other major repairs or fixup work is generally unwise. For one thing, nearly every person has his or her own ideas about interior painting and redecoration. Thus a new interior paint or redecoration can put off a potential buyer; most people prefer an existing interior as is and consider it a waste to see a freshly repainted interior which they do not like.

Advertise in the right outlets

Pass the word to friends, neighbors and business acquaintances that your house is for sale. You'll probably put a notice in your company house organ and tack a card or two on community bulletin boards. You'll probably have to run a few paid advertisements in the newspaper, but limit these to where serious house hunters will see them. That might be the classified ads in a suburban newspaper, where rates are low, or a large metropolitan newspaper. Where do most of your neighbors and local homeowners come from? If they're chiefly from the local area, a local newspaper is probably your best bet. If they are chiefly professional people or white-collar corporation types from everywhere, then one of your large metropolitan newspapers will probably be your best bet. It's generally best to advertise near the end of the week or over a weekend, preferably in the newspaper with the largest local real-estate coverage and especially in the weekend edition that carries the most real-estate advertising. Plan the advertising effectively because its cost in a large newspaper can get expensive.

Prepare a fact sheet on your house

This can impress home shoppers. You simply put down a list of pertinent facts and information about your house and the neighborhood, such as size of house, lot size, annual taxes, cost of heating, and location of the local schools, shopping centers and so on. Put in special features about the house that may not be obvious, such as new furnace or water heater recently installed or an ample attic that can be converted easily to additional rooms.

Present the facts as they are, and don't go overboard on fanciful or imagined features which you may think are great but which leave others cold. Your presentation will be especially effective if you also list an obvious drawback or two, such as the need for new wiring, a garage door that eventually must be replaced, or a dying tree that, alas, must come down before it falls down. No house is perfect and being honest gains the confidence of a potential buyer. You may have allowed for a reduction in your house price to pay for the necessary repairs and you say this. This may not be believed, but at worst you may make a sale at a cost of a few hundred dollars reduction in price for your honesty, the alternative being no sale.

Financing the purchase

Few people selling a house check on the mortgage financing necessary to buy their houses, though virtually every new-house builder does so. Builders know that the financing can make or break the sale. With them, the down payment and the monthly mortgage payments required to buy a house are often more important than the house price. Call a few local mortgage lenders (see Chapter 12), including the lender who holds your mortgage, to get an idea of the financing available to buy your house.

The cash down payment required can be crucial. If a large cash down payment is required, investigate the possibility of a buyer's obtaining your house with an FHA mortgage and its lower-than-average down payment. Knowing facts about the financing and especially the down payment required also can help you qualify buyers and save a lot of time otherwise wasted on people who may like the house but cannot afford it. This is second nature to a real-estate broker, who obviously has no wish to waste time showing a champagne house to a beer-income couple.

Show the house with restraint

Next to overpricing, overselling loses more house sales than anything else (except for people viewing your house being greeted by a termite convention in the basement). Let the house speak for itself.

Show the house by appointment only and evacuate kids, grandparents and everyone else before viewers are due. Hang back when you show people through the house. "Keep your mouth shut," an expert says. Home buyers resent being told what they can see for themselves. Of course, you should answer questions, but briefly, and discreetly point out inconspicuous features, such as the built-in privacy of the master bedroom or shade trees that cool the house in summer. But don't expand proudly about the large new furnace you've installed, since a buyer's mind immediately thinks of large fuel bills.

Almost anything else like that you may say can be interpreted the wrong way. For example, writer Chris Welles recently told, in a *Family Circle* article, about the owner who proudly opened a closet door to point out an expensive new burglar system he had installed. A prospect for the house fled in alarm, "scared to death" with worry about why a burglar alarm was needed.

Instead of talking, listen for revealing comments. Occasionally, you may want to correct a misimpression, but never argue, a cardinal rule. Welles says, "If you win, you lose." Inevitably, some prospects can be chalked off as mere lookers. Your house simply will not charm everyone. The serious shopper, on the other hand, may say little but will return for a second or third look. That indicates real interest, especially when the man wants to check the furnace in the basement and the woman takes measurements for her furniture.

The woman, by the way, generally chooses the house, or so real-estate brokers say. A wife does the scouting for a house because she generally has more free time than her husband. She narrows down the choice to a house that she likes before hauling her husband out to see it. But if a woman does the initial choosing, most men have a decided veto power over the choice. At buying time, the man generally steps forward and takes over. That's when things heat up.

Selling the house

You may never hear again from the couple you thought were your hottest prospects, whereas the unlikely couple will want your house. Home buying is charged with emotion, and at this stage the voltage steps up. Generally, the first bid you get will be lower than you asked. How much lower depends on how much your asking price is higher than the house is really worth. Some people will made a ridiculously low bid deliberately because they'll take your house only if they can obtain it at a bargain basement price. If you receive several very low offers, your asking price may indeed be too high. Assuming your asking price is not too high, you probably will get bids within 10 to 20 percent of it. Occasionally, one who really wants a house will pay the asking price or bid close to it.

Reducing your price during the negotiations depends on the minimum price you will accept and on how quickly you want to sell. Ordinarily, you should be prepared to come down in one or two steps, but generally that's it. An exception is a serious buyer who likes to play games, stays interested and will buy only when he obtains the satisfaction of having you reduce your price enough to make him feel triumphant. If you negotiate carefully, dropping your price just enough to satisfy him, you can be triumphant, too.

The best time to sell

Things are working for you if your house goes on the market in late spring or early fall, the two peak home-buying periods of the year. The greatest number of buyers generally enter the market in the spring, as the weather warms up drawing people outdoors (except in a warm climate), and also as the school year approaches its end. Most people don't like to move and transfer their children to a new school before the school year is over. They begin looking for a house in April or May, which allows time to buy and move before the next school year starts in September. Thus, home-buying figures hit their annual peak in May through July. They tail off a bit during the summer vacation period, heat up again in September and October and then fall off sharply as Christmas approaches.

Hence, the very best time to put a house on the market is usually in April to June, and second best is right after Labor Day. Houses can be sold at other times, of course, and a good house at the right price can be sold almost any time. Nevertheless, take into consideration when you wish to sell your house, weighing the number of likely buyers around against how much hard bargaining you are prepared to do.

Get a lawyer

Know how to sign up a buyer and clinch the sale. If you're not using a broker who knows such things, you'll generally want legal guidance from a lawyer. Consult one early and he can tell you the kind of "binder" that a buyer signs initially to seal his intention to buy your house. Since the wording is important, you'll want a good *real-estate* lawyer, not any lawyer, remember, but one who is active in and knows real estate. A conditional sales contract comes next, and a lawyer is often mandatory for it, followed by the house closing. A lawyer's fee generally will run from about $100 up to 1 percent of the house price, depending on the customary legal fees in your area. Determine the fee in advance.

How should you use a broker?

Selling your house by yourself will not necessarily save you the full 6 percent broker's fee because of the money you must spend to advertise the house, hire an appraiser and retain a lawyer. A good broker can save you each of these expenses, in addition to finding prospects, showing your house and negotiating the sale.

Take everything into consideration and now decide if you need a broker. If you must move quickly and leave your house, a broker can be invaluable, since he will be there to sell it, if necessary, after you've moved. Then it's good to deal exclusively with a single broker. He and no one else is entitled to sell the house, and the exclusive agreement usually runs for 90 days. An exclusive gives him incentive to put special effort into selling your house because another broker may not sell the house out from under him. It may also call for the broker to be paid his fee even if you sell the house by yourself. This depends on the wording of your agreement with the broker. Dealing exclusively with one broker, however, doesn't necessarily limit your market to one broker's prospects. Choose a broker who belongs to the local "multiple listing" system, and he will generally list your house with other brokers in the area. If another broker sells the house, the fee is shared between the two brokers involved.

How to choose a broker

There are more than 600,000 licensed real-estate brokers in the U.S., including taxi drivers, store clerks, and hacks of every description. It is best to choose a licensed real-estate broker who is also a "realtor," the registered trademark for brokers who are members of the local real-estate board. The 90,000 or so realtors in the country are, by and large, the full-time professionals in the business, the most qualified and generally the most ethical brokers. There are some good nonrealtor brokers, too, and, on the other hand, some realtors who are not as good as they would have you think. So don't necessarily choose a broker only because he's a realtor. Shop around, find out about local brokers and choose a good one.

You might list your house with a few brokers and also be selling it yourself. One or more brokers are given the house to sell on a non-exclusive basis. A broker will not be charmed by this arrangement but it occurs frequently. If your house is attractive and properly priced, he will try his best prospects on it and perhaps achieve a sale. If you sell the house first, you do not pay any broker a fee. Talk to a few brokers before you decide to sell and then act accordingly.

If you like the idea of saving the broker's fee and earning a few thousand dollars or so more by selling your house yourself, don't underestimate the work involved to do it. You could indeed save yourself money, and more money at one crack than possible at any other time in your life (with the exception of when you turn around to buy another house and begin negotiating from the other side). Because housing shortages in many parts of the country are not expected to be relieved quickly, small supply and large demand could be working for you when you sell a house nowadays. The services of a broker may be unnecessary, assuming that you have a good house in a desirable area and you don't overprice it.

REVIEW

1. Determine the value of your house realistically and don't overprice. Hire a real-estate appraiser to do this, if necessary.
2. Show the house to its best advantage. Fix up and clean up, repaint the exterior, if necessary. But, by and large, spending a lot of other money to fix up a house for sale does not pay.

3. Prepare a fact sheet about your house. It can be excellent sales literature.
4. Advertise the house where the most likely buyers will read about it.
5. Determine the financing available to buy your house. Helping a potential buyer with it can help you.
6. Show the house like a professional. Don't be overaggressive and don't oversell.
7. Be prepared for heady negotiations and bargaining. The alternative is simply putting a firm, no-compromise price on your house and saying that's it. This is occasionally done, though it goes against the grain of many buyers. But the house should be worth the price.
8. Hire a lawyer for legal advice and services.
9. Or hire a good real-estate broker to sell the house. Then you may forget about virtually all else above except the second and third points above.
10. In your local library, consult books on real estate and selling a house. For a broker's hard-sell views on selling houses, get *The Number One Success System to Boost Your Earnings in Real Estate* by Edward F. Rybka, $8.95, from Prentice Hall, Englewood Cliffs, N.J. 07632. Also, you will find a special chapter on how to sell a house in *The Home-Owner's Survival Kit*, by A. M. Watkins, a book on how to beat the high cost of owning and operating your home, published by Hawthorn Books, Inc., $6.95, also available by mail postpaid from All About Houses, 855 River Road, Piermont, N.Y. 10968.

cutting the high cost of
transportation–
your car

According to the U.S. Department of Transportation, a typical one-year-old car of standard size costs its owner $1,467 a year. or $122 a month. The largest single portion of that ($583) goes for "depreciation," an unfamiliar term to many car owners who nevertheless pay dearly for it. Next largest car expenses are gas and oil ($233) and between $100 and $200 apiece for insurance, service and repairs, parking and tolls, and automotive taxes.

That typical $1,467 bill can be cut sharply by buying the smallest car suitable to your needs and perhaps a good used model, keeping it longer than usual (to reduce depreciation costs) and by knowing the kind of upkeep maintenance that cars require for maximum performance and longest running life.

18

buying a **new car**

*Small versus large cars · How depreciation costs you
money · Shopping for a new car · Best times of the year to
buy a car · Common car dealer tricks and how to avoid them*

In 1969 small cars—compacts, subcompacts and all other economy cars, including imports—accounted for 30 percent of all new-car sales in the U.S. In 1970 that figure climbed to 40 percent, and soon afterward the small car had taken over more than 50 percent of the total new-car market. The small car is not only cheap but it's easy to drive, especially in a city and by a woman shopping, and a stigma is no longer attached to ownership of a small car.

Small car owners formerly were considered screwballs and nuts, while for years Americans had a love affair with the biggest, longest dreamboat car that money could buy. Such a car was expensive, but parked in front of your house it made you look like a million dollars—or so many people thought.

Times have changed. The small car, compact in both size and price, has become more and more the status symbol in automobiles. Parked in front of your house, it marks you as a wise and prudent person who knows how to get the most for your money.

And it can cost you from $1,000 to $2,000 under the price of a standard, full-size dreamboat car because, like steak, car prices are pretty much tied to the weight you buy. Cars cost about $1.00 a pound, down to 90 cents for some and up to $1.10 per pound for others. Thus for every 500 pounds of additional car you buy, you must spend another $500, more or less.

Recently, for example, a popular new economy car from Detroit weighed a little over one ton—exactly 2,202 pounds curb weight—and was priced at $2,200, or almost exactly $1 a pound (plus factory to showroom transportation and sales taxes). A larger, standard sedan from the same Detroit maker weighed almost 4,000 pounds and was priced at almost $4,000, or also close to $1 a pound.

The larger car not only costs twice as much to buy, but it also costs up to twice as much to finance and to operate as the smaller car. It must be fed more gas to keep its two tons of weight moving and it contains 2,000 more parts to maintain and service than the smaller one. Thus, one of the best ways to cut your transportation cost, one of your five biggest costs of living if you're reasonably typical, is to think small.

Choosing a car

A good rule is to shop for the smallest car that will serve your needs and if necessary work upward. A large, high-powered car makes sense if you indeed require a car to climb mountains, or for hard, long-distance driving. But if your car is chiefly for short-haul traveling and only an occasional long trip, an economy car could serve you well.

What kind of driving is your car most used for? Commuting to work, short-trip or long-distance family driving? How many people ordinarily ride in your car? If you think you need a roomy family car, ask yourself why. If you do much hauling of kids or household equipment, a station wagon may be the answer. Remember, though, that station wagons are also available in the compact size and price range as well as in giant luxury models.

Engine size also makes a difference

Most small cars can be had with either four or six cylinders; large cars with six or eight. A four-cylinder engine is the most efficient, though you might need the extra power six cylinders can give you. If you have a choice between six and eight cylinders, however, the six will usually save you money and serve well. A six-cylinder engine can save you from $100 to $250 on car price, compared with an eight, save $40 to $50 a year on gas, and cost less to service. Except for a large, heavy car, the six will usually deliver all the power needed. Some sixes in fact, deliver more horsepower than higher-cost eights.

That's all very good, you may say, conceding that sheer logic calls for an economy car to economize on car costs. But logic doesn't always prevail and, as we mentioned earlier, many men in particular will pay extra, sometimes considerably extra, for a big, powerful car that fulfills a special emotional need (and repent later). Many a woman who has fought such purchases unsuccessfully can tell you how strong that need can be.

The urge to buy a big expensive car can be fought off in two ways. First, figure out on paper, in black and white (if not red, too), just how much extra a big car will cost you in monthly payments, as well as gas and upkeep. Second, and perhaps more important, probe your motives and determine exactly why a big car and nothing but a big glamorous car is for you. Whom are you trying to impress? Do you really need a big car? Perhaps you do for practical reasons, or the personal glory of owning and driving a big car is especially important to you. Or perhaps not, and that's up to you.

Depreciation

Suppose you buy a car for $3,000 and sell or trade it in a year later. You would get no more than about $2,100 for it—30 percent less than its original purchase price. If you keep it two years, its value will have depreciated still another 20 percent, down to $1,500. In other words, if you keep the car for only one year, ownership alone costs you $900. That does not include gas, service, repairs, insurance and other expenses. In two years, even if all you do is keep the car in your garage, it will have cost you $1,500. That's depreciation, usually the biggest single cost of owning a car.

The value of a new car automatically begins to depreciate the moment you get in and drive it away. It's a used car instantly, and never again will command a new-car price. Its value falls 30 percent, more or less, at the moment next year's models are introduced, usually the fall of each year. You may have bought your car only a month or two before, in the summer, for example, but nonetheless when next year's models are introduced the value of your car automatically falls in value by the full first-year depreciation rate. Depreciation falls off to about 20 percent during a car's second year, and then by a smaller annual toll year by year, as follows, according to Merle E. Dowd, author of *How to Save Money When You Buy and Drive a Car:*

Average annual car depreciation rate

Car age, years:	1	30 percent off new car price
	2	20
	3	15
	4	10
	5	7
	6	5
	7	4
	8	3
	9	2
	10	1

The above depreciation figures are averages for most cars. In general, the greater the popularity of a particular car and model, the lower its annual depreciation. Yearly depreciation is therefore somewhat lower than in the above table for prestige cars like the Cadillac and for certain imported cars in demand, like the Volvo or Volkswagen which retain value well. Depreciation tends to be higher, thus less value retained, for other imported cars, particularly the kind favored by sports car buffs (since parts for them can be difficult to obtain).

But the longer you keep a car, the lower its annual cost for you, regardless of make or model. Consider two neighbors, Harry and Tony, each of whom bought a new $3,600 car a few years ago. Harry is a salesman and he and his wife like new cars. They traded their car in a year later, getting $2,500 for it toward a new car. It therefore cost them $1,100 to own the car for a year, a 30-percent depreciation loss. That cost them $92 a month, basic ownership cost (plus insurance, gas, operating and other expenses).

Tony is an engineer and he and his wife like to milk maximum value from their car. They plan to keep their car five years and figure they can trade it in then for about $650. Then the car will have cost them a total of $2,950, its five-year depreciation, or $590 a year. That's $49-a-month basic ownership cost. Compared with his neighbor, Tony and his wife will have a clearcut, money-in-the-bank savings of $43 a month and $516 a year for every year they will have had their car.

Of course, the longer you keep a car, the greater the cost of service and repairs, but this is less than many people think. You will have to buy new tires, a new battery and other items along the way. Nonetheless, the U.S. Department of Transportation says that such expenses don't make that much difference as a car gets older if you keep the car properly lubricated and serviced. In spite of the cost of the inevitable repairs and replacement parts as a car ages, you generally will be financially ahead of the game by keeping a car as long as it will run well for you.

This puts special emphasis on buying a well-made car that will hold up over the years. How do you find one? Ask friends and neighbors about their cars. Ask automobile servicemen. Read up about cars and car buying in books and magazines. A particularly good and up-to-date source is *Consumer Reports'* annual roundup feature on new-car buying usually published in April and its *Annual Buying Guide,* both available on newsstands or together with book issues available in libraries. Any reasonably good car should last as long as eight to ten years, assuming it's given a little care and regular attention. All that you need do is keep it properly serviced—and start with a good car, of course.

Shopping for a low price

You'll often find that the price of a car, or a comparable model, varies from showroom to showroom. Although by law the "suggested list price" of every new car must be posted on the car, that list price is by no means sacred. Nearly every new car dealer, at one time or another, will reduce that price to sell a car. A survey by the Federal Trade Commission showed that most car buyers bought new cars at 5 percent or more under the sticker price, with over 50 percent of all buyers getting their cars at 10 to 20 percent under list.

Play it cool, and a dealer may reduce the sticker price to sell you a car. The greatest discounts are generally found in large cities and metropolitan suburbs where competition among automobile dealers is stiffest. If your dealer takes a hard line on price, there's nothing to stop you from going elsewhere.

Do, however, be wary of the large-volume, cut-price dealer who may offer great discounts off his car prices. He is a breed, however, who is likely, literally, to tell you to get lost if the car has a defect, special repairs are required or you want him to make good on the warranty. In other words, don't shop with a singleminded passion aimed solely at getting the lowest possible sales price. It's also important to buy from a reputable car dealer. Even though he may not offer you the lowest price available, buying from him can still be worthwhile because you know you are getting a well-prepared car and can rely on him later for dependable service.

Bargaining and haggling

Like buying a used house but even more so, bargaining can save you money when you buy a car, new or used. It's a reality of life with most though not all car dealers. If you dislike bargaining, simply ask a few dealers for their lowest price and accept what is best for you. Or brace yourself, quietly mention the highest price you're willing to pay and leave it to the dealer to accept or not.

By and large, the higher the price on a car, the greater the likelihood that its price is subject to a reduction by bargaining with the dealer. The smallest price reductions are obtainable on small economy cars, including certain imports, where the dealer markup is not large, so that he can't give away much. That means cars chiefly in the $2,000 to $3,000 price range and some in the $3,000 to $4,000 price range. Above that, most car prices are greatly flexible with the exception of a big prestige car at a time when it is selling well for dealers.

Four best times of the year to shop for a new car

The best time of all is before you need a new car. Not under pressure to buy, you may take your time and pick carefully. This also lets you choose a time when dealers offer the best breaks on car, which can mean savings of from 10 to 30 percent. Supply and demand at the time you're shopping determine how much a dealer is likely to reduce his price. When buyers are flocking into his showroom, checkbooks clutched in hands, there's small chance that he'll take a soft line on price. But if he has more cars than buyers, he will often come down in price to make a sale.

One of the best times to buy at a discount is during cleanup season at the end of summer just before next year's models are due to arrive from Detroit. Many car dealers then reduce the prices of the last cars in stock to make room for next year's models. They will take less profit, and often the manufacturers will give them incentives (cash rebates) to unload such cars. A new car often can be had at savings of 20 percent or more, a $3,000 car for $2,200 or less.

But tread carefully here. Though it's a spanking new car at at a big initial saving, when next year's models arrive from Detroit the same new car becomes last year's model and declines approximately 30 percent in value. If you keep the car for no more than a year or two, that walloping initial depreciation loss can cost you dearly when you trade in the car.

If you buy an end-of-the-year model, you'll be ahead of the game only if (1) you keep the car for at least three years, preferably longer, or (2) you can buy the car for at least 20 to 25 percent below its sticker price.

A second time to save is a little later in the fall after the new models have been introduced and a dealer still has a few of last year's models, still new. Some dealers will unload them at discounts of 20 up to 40 percent off list price, and you get a new car. Actually, the real "list" price of such a car is 30 percent below the sticker price because it has just fallen in value by that much depreciation; it's already last year's model. It's a bargain only if it can be bought at a 30-percent discount at least or if you keep it at least three to four years. Another drawback is that your choice is limited to whatever cars happen to be left.

The third best time to buy is after New Year's Day in January or February when the winter doldrums hit new-car sales. This, of course, is chiefly in a cold climate when icy weather puts a damper on sales, and dealers get hungry. One dealer says, "The best time to make a good deal is to walk into my showroom the day after a blizzard. Practically no buyers are around. We're so delighted to see anyone that we'll often make it worthwhile to buy." Special sales are often held during this slow period and manufacturers offer dealer incentives to move cars. To a hot dealer and salesman, this can mean anything from a cash rebate to a Caribbean vacation for each car sold.

Imported cars, incidentally, don't go through the same sharp seasonal sales patterns as domestic cars, except for the winter doldrums. It's because imported cars don't undergo pronounced annual model changes, new models aren't introduced on a group basis and consumers tend not to buy imported cars as much by season. Thus, the most likely time to buy a desirable imported car at a discount is during the winter doldrums.

The fourth best time to save is late March to early April, give or take a few weeks, before the high tide of spring car sales begins. Again, manufacturers give incentives to sell cars and build up sales momentum as they enter the big spring sales season.

One other good time to buy at a saving varies from dealer to dealer. It's when sales slow down for a dealer and he's in a financial bind and needs the cash. As a result, he's often willing to move cars at almost any price to get money flowing in. He may advertise a special sale or simply be receptive to giving you a good price break if that's necessary to get you to buy.

How much savings?

As we noted, the percentage discount a dealer might give you is generally less on a small car than on a big car because he gets a lesser discount on small cars. You can get an approximate idea of the dealer's cost for a particular car, thus how much leeway he has for bargaining, in this way:

Start with the bottom price figure on the window sticker of a new car and subtract the transportation charge (usually listed), and dealer's preparation cost. What's left is the car's basic price.

The dealer's cost (or wholesale price) of a compact or subcompact is usually about 15 percent less, or 85 percent of that basic sales price. For a typical intermediate model, it is about 20 percent less; for a full-size car, about 22 percent less; and for a luxury model, about 25 percent less.

Not all of that difference, however, is pure profit. Part of it obviously goes to pay the dealer's overhead, operating expenses and the salesman's commission. In general, dealers in a highly competitive metropolitan area may settle for as little as $100 gross profit per car; less discount in a less-competitive city or town; and least discount of all in a small town or rural area where a dealer must charge pretty close to the sticker price to stay in business. The wholesale values of cars are published in automobile pricing publications available at most newsstands.

How a dealer cuts car prices

He can do it in one or more of four ways:

1. Reduce the list price and take a smaller markup.

2. Reduce the list price by getting a rebate from the manufacturer, which in effect means a lower cost for him.

3. Toss in optional extras free at a time when the manufacturer gives a special discount on a set package of options, or because a car in stock that you want is already equipped with options that you do not want.

4. Give you a higher trade-in allowance on your old car than it is worth. Ask dealers what they will give for your old car. Also determine the current wholesale value of your present car from one of the trade periodicals that furnish such data. Some of these, like the *Customart Monthly Used Car Prices*, are sold on newsstands, or ask your neighborhood bank loan manager to let you see his copy of the National Automobile Dealer's Association (NADA) *Used Car Guide*, or the *Red Book, Official Used Car Market Values*, or send $3.18 for this to National Market Reports, 900 South Wabash Avenue, Chicago, Ill. 60605.

Don't go overboard for extras

What you can save on the list price you could lose several times over by paying extra for a car loaded with expensive options, like a deluxe "Super-Eight" engine, power seats and windows and so on. These can hike the cost of a car as much as $500 to $1,000—sometimes more. You may want one or two of these extras. In that case, remember that the price of each option is, like the car itself, subject to "negotiation," which means that you can often get the price reduced if you bargain.

Bargaining here is important because the human tendency is to strive for savings on the base price of a car and then wearily accept a lot of extras at their full cost. That's especially when the car you want is in stock equipped with extras and you're eager to drive away in it. As much as 30 percent can be saved on the total sticker price of a given car merely by asking for the car itself, stripped of all options.

You may have to wait up to a month or so for delivery of a simple, stripped-down basic model, since most new cars on showroom floors are usually—and deliberately—loaded with extras. Don't be bamboozled into paying for extras—a little patience can save you a lot of money. Sometimes, if you stand firm, refuse the showroom model full of extras and start for the door, it's amazing how quickly a dealer will remember that there is a low-priced, stripped-down model for you back in the warehouse after all.

Of course, some extras are desirable, such as a radio, a heater, automatic transmission (though this is often overrated, since it cuts your gas mileage and is expensive to service), and power steering and power brakes on large, heavy cars. Other things, such as power windows, power-operated seats, and air conditioning not only cost dearly in initial price but also in high operating and service costs. Some of these optional features could mean higher value for you at trade-in time, but do you really want and need them? Or should you spend your money for other things more desirable?

Profile of a car dealer

However jolly and friendly he is, never forget that the dealer and his salesman are hard-headed professional businessmen. They have the edge on you because they know all the tricks and learn new ones every day. You're a neophite playing the game only infrequently. Their goal is to sell you a car at the highest possible price. Not all dealers are the same, however. Many are civilized, honest and straightforward, particularly those in a small town whose long-term business profits depend on maintaining a good reputation. Others, however, may not be so straightforward, some are as crooked as a pretzel, and still others are perhaps in between, bending their morals as necessary according to how well or not so well business is for them when you walk in.

Most will negotiate a price, making a concession or two depending, again, on how much they want to make the sale. A typical hard-line dealer often will feign absolute firmness, indicating he sells at just one price, "The figure on that window sticker." But if you maintain your ground, he will come down in price quicker than you can open that door and leave. Some dealers strive for profits through volume sales and will sell cars at almost any price to keep sales moving. Walk around the place and notice how many new cars are in stock to be sold. More than a few on hand from the factory can indicate that a dealer has cars coming out of his garage ears and will sell low. Ask about the delivery date. If the model you want is for immediate delivery, that could be another indication that a dealer is eager to sell and if necessary, lower his price.

By all means visit several dealers and get a price from each for the car you want, and get them in writing. If you're trading in a car, get the trade-in figure, in writing, too. Try to determine what type and model of car you want, its dealer cost plus the lowest price you're likely to be charged for it. But don't close your mind to other suitable models. If you're sufficiently aggressive, simply state your price to the salesman and ask him if he can meet it. You may be surprised at the swiftness of the salesman in accepting it.

Dealer tricks

Beware of two common tricks: "low-balling" and "high-balling." Though these two deceptive practices are not as common as they formerly were, they are still good to know about. The first is illustrated by a young friend of ours, Jim Harlevan, who told us, "I really liked that new car, and the salesman offered it to me at a very low price. I test-drove it, and it handled just swell, so the salesman wrote out the order. Everything was all set and the salesman left for a moment to get the sales manager's okay.

"Well, he came back looking glum. (What an act, I realized later.) He was sorry, he said, but somebody had made a mistake and he had given me the wrong price. The sales manager refused to approve it. The real price was $600 more, and there was nothing he could do about it.

Either I paid more or didn't get that swell new car just waiting for me to drive off in."

That's low-balling, a ploy made when a used car is not being traded in. You're given a very low price, impossible to resist, to keep you from going elsewhere and to set you up for a sale at a higher price. But at the crucial moment, the sales manager refuses to approve the deal. "There was a misunderstanding," or "the auditor gave me the wrong price."

"High-balling" occurs when there's a used car to trade-in. A former car salesman says:

"A guy would drive in with an old heap and talk about a new car. The sales manager gives me the wink and I was off. The old heap wasn't worth more than $400 at most. I didn't even have to look it up. But I could tell this guy was a hot customer, and we didn't want him going all over town shopping for other prices. He really wanted that super-eight on the floor, so I high-balled him. I told him that we could do business and I'd give him twelve hundred bucks for Old Firesides. He practically flipped with delight. We set an appointment for him to come in and buy the car in a couple of days, and we would prepare the car for final delivery.

"The guy showed up right on time, and I had all the papers ready to sign. I could hardly keep him from signing. First, I put him in the car again for a short drive. Back in the office, I had to tell him that there had been a mistake, and just that very morning the boss had said no more trade-ins. We were overstocked and didn't want his trade-in any more. I was sorry, I said.

"But since we had aranged a deal, I said, I didn't want to go back entirely on my word. I told him I thought I could get him at least $300 for his old car. His face dropped half a mile, but I expected that. So I raised it to $400, the book price. I told him how awfully sorry I was, but that's the best we could do. It took him a few minutes to absorb the blow, but he was so eager to get that new car that he sat down and signed the papers—and I had a sale."

That's high-balling, a wildly high trade-in figure offered on a used car to neutralize the customer. The customer knows that his car is not worth anything near that much. He figures that the dealer has made a mistake, and he's so flabbergasted that he tries to conceal his delight.

That's how he's supposed to react. Sometimes there's a delay of a few weeks or so until the particular model being bought is delivered from the factory, and the customer is getting increasingly anxious for it, particularly since he's getting such a high trade-in for his old car. The trap is sprung when he arrives to consummate the deal. The customer's response is one of shock. The salesman pours on his sympathy, and the customer resigns himself to the inevitable. He figures that he probably couldn't do any better elsewhere, so he capitulates and buys the car at the dealer's price.

A dealer has the right to reappraise a trade-in car before delivery of a new car, to be sure no damage occurred since he first saw it. If your old car is in the same condition, the original trade-in quote should hold. You can avoid being high-balled only by getting all prices put in writing and signed not just by the salesman but also approved by the sales manager or dealer, as called for in the estimate form you're given. Usually, a deadline date, saying how long the offer is good, also will be stated. Remember that the purpose of high-balling is to stop you from shopping elsewhere. The idea is that when the new car is ready you'll be so anxious to buy it that you may be disappointed, but things have gone so far that you will accept a lower trade-in price for your old car.

The same precaution applies to avoid being a victim of low-balling. Get the offer in writing, clearly and unmistakably, and have it countersigned by someone in authority. Though a minority of dealers may practice such tricks nowadays, if you have reason to suspect that a dealer is doing either or is otherwise unreliable, go elsewhere. If, despite all precautions, you find yourself caught up in the final act of a high- or low-balling scheme and the dealer will not stick close to the original price quoted to you, walk out and chalk it up to experience. You may be in desperate need of the car but you probably could rent one to tide you over and still end up financially ahead.

Financing a car

Roughly 60 percent of all car buyers finance their purchase, but many of them lose money by signing all the loan papers right there and then in the showroom at the time of purchase. Without knowing it, such buyers may pay more and sometimes considerably more for such financing than they would if they got an installment loan elsewhere. Some dealers, on the other hand, do offer reasonably low-cost financing.

Figure up the total cost of the car dealer's financing, and then figure the cost of arranging for your own financing by one of the five good ways to finance anything that we presented in Chapter 3. That's the only sure way to determine the lowest-cost method of financing a car.

Saving money on a second car

Do you really need a second car? More than 20,000,000 American families have a second car, but for many it drains off far more money than they realize. The transportation it offers often could be had cheaper in other ways. Right off the bat, a typical second car costs as much as $500 to $600 a year, or up to $50 a month even if it's just parked in your driveway. That's its basic, inescapable cost for annual depreciation and insurance, and then there's also gas, service and repairs to pay for.

Figure its total cost to you, and then ask yourself whether it's really worth it. And can you afford it? That's an individual decision. A frequent response is, "How will we ever do without it?" You may indeed need it, but often there are good alternatives at considerably less cost. In a pinch and even occasionally as a convenience luxury, you could call a taxi or rent a car for up to a month or more. The $50 to $75 a month saved on a second car could pay for quite a few taxies and car rentals and still leave you ahead of the game. If you're financially fastidious, instead of buying a second car put half of its cost in a special account to draw on for taxis and car rentals. At the end of a year the chances are that money will still be left in that special kitty. The trick is to realize that spending money occasionally for a taxi is no idle luxury, that you may do it when necessary, and while you're sitting in the taxi with the meter going you know that you're still saving a dollar for every dollar turning up on the taxi meter.

Also consider a bicycle, for commuting to the station or for a woman's shopping. That not only saves money but it can be great for your heart and your figure. Look at all the people, including grandmothers, who are taking to bikes and love them. Of course, there are rainy days and stormy times that rule out using a bike. But then the number one car might be available or you dip into that special transportation fund for taxi money.

If you live in a city where a car is desired chiefly for summer, even a first car may be an unnecessary expense. Consider the cost of renting or leasing a car just for summer and using cabs at other times. If you're a typical family, that could sharply reduce the 10 to 15 percent or so of annual family living expenses that go into owning one or more cars.

Before accepting delivery of a new car

Test drive the car before you sign the last paper and pay for the car. Inevitably, a certain proportion of new cars come through with bugs, missing or misaligned parts or other small or large flaws. Sometimes they are serious, but the dealer balks at making the necessary repairs under the warranty, often saying it's up to the manufacturer; but when you call the manufacturer he says it's the dealer's responsibility. You're caught in the old run-around. This and other new-car problems can be avoided by a test-drive prior to final acceptance of the car to be sure that everything is shipshape. If something is wrong, the dealer generally will make the necessary repairs fast (to clinch the sale), or you simply refuse the car and get another one.

According to the National Automobile Dealers' Association in Washington, D.C., most new car repair problems today involve three main systems: the carburetor and gasoline supply system, the electrical system and the braking system. Put special emphasis on these when you test drive a new car. The engine should purr like a baby when idling, hardly to be heard, and react smartly and powerfully up a steep hill; the electrical system requires turning on every electric device in the car to be sure each works properly; and the braking system requires hard stopping under severe stress, but work up slowly to this.

CHECKLIST FOR BUYING A NEW CAR

1. Shop among different car dealers and get the prices available for the car you want, plus the trade-in allowance for your old car. But low price alone should not be the sole influence on your purchase.
2. Do business with a reputable dealer. Call the Better Business Bureau about him. What kind of record do they have for him?
3. Accept only those optional features you really want. Remember that the additional cost of extras is also subject to negotiation.
4. Arrange for your own financing, if necessary, and for your own insurance beforehand. Compare different rates and insurance coverages.
5. Road-test the car before completing the purchase. Be sure everything operates smartly. If not, have anything wrong corrected before you sign.
6. Read the contract carefully before signing, the same old advice but always important. Special conditions covering the sale should be written in.
7. Be sure the guarantee is clearly understood and in writing.

19

buying a **used car**

How to check the condition of a used car · Vital parts
to inspect · Determining used car value · Where and when
to buy a used car · Used-car warranties

The best used-car buy is generally a car two or three years old. At this time
a used car usually can be bought at a price 50 to 60 percent under its
new-car price because of depreciation and it is still likely to have a lot
of driving life left in it.

The big problem with a used car, of course, is that it could be a very
chancy purchase. This is no longer so true because a thorough examination of the condition of a used car now can be done quite easily and
inexpensively in one of those automobile diagnostic centers that have
sprung up throughout the country. For a mere $10 to $15, more or less,
a diagnostic center with a laboratory full of electronic test equipment can
give you a thorough report on the condition of almost any car. Just take
a used car you may buy to the center for the complete treatment. Most
car dealers will permit this, though some private sellers may balk. Anyone who balks could have good reason for doing so and then it's a car
you probably don't want.

If you think there's no diagnostic center near you, you may not have
looked hard enough. Or take the car to a good automobile service center
such as those run by Sears, Penney or one of the major tire company

chain stores, which usually have the electronic test gear needed. Make an appointment in advance.

What to check

Before spending money for a professional check, do a few simple tests of your own. Check the lights, windshield wipers, turn indicators, heater, horn, the dashboard gauges and all powered parts (radio, air conditioning and so on). Open and close the doors and windows all the way. Are new tires needed? There should be sufficient tread on each tire so that a penny inserted in each tread reaches down to the Lincoln's head, at least.

Start the engine, of course, and listen for odd sounds and clunks. Test drive the car a mile or two, checking brakes and acceleration. Be suspicious of any repainted parts and of excessive interior wear in the carpeting, around arm rests and light switches. Be suspicious, too, of such reconditioning tricks as brand-new floor pads, new rubber pedal pads and a new trunk mat (often put in to hide a rusted-out trunk, so look underneath). Check for worn shock absorbers with the old ritual of bouncing up and down on the back bumper. If the car rocks at all after you've hopped off, new shocks are needed.

From there on, however, don't trust yourself (unless you're a whiz mechanic). Get the car checked by one of the professionals we mentioned above, and specifically ask for, among other things:

- Engine efficiency and compression check.
- Visual check of engine mounting, undercarriage and engine compartment.
- Front-end alignment.
- Check of transmission, suspension, steering, shocks, brakes and other such items, though these generally require a short road test.

Armed with a report on a car's condition and the repairs that are necessary, you have good reason for a price reduction by the amount required for repairs, or have the seller make them. If the seller makes them, be sure they were made properly, which may require a return trip to your test mechanic.

What is a used car worth?

What should you pay? Almost never the initial price. With rare exceptions, nearly every used car is subject to a price reduction. Used-car dealers are notorious for pricing cars higher than the lowest price they will accept. Nearly every one will come down at least 5 percent without blinking an eye, and sometimes down considerably more. A private seller may be less prone to negotiate a compromise price, because of the wild hope of getting big money for his car.

Protect yourself by determining the approximate value of the car you want. This can be done by subtracting the amount of depreciation (from the table on page 138) based on the age of a car. The age to use should be based on the model year of the car, which is not always the same as its actual age. Remember that, like a new car, a used car bought in late summer will be subject soon to a depreciation loss when the new models from Detroit are introduced.

If possible, consult your banker's copy of the NADA *Used Car Guide* or his *Red Book* on used-car prices or get one of the periodicals cited earlier that gives current used-car prices. The value of a particular car may be adjusted up or down to allow for its condition or special features it has that you do or do not want. You might inform the seller that you know the car's value in the used-car market and this might soften him. Like buying a used house, effective bargaining generally calls for your first offer to be lower than you expect to pay and allowing yourself room to raise your price and let the seller save face.

Where to buy a used car

A good new-car dealer with a used-car department and his own service department generally offers the best balance between a broad selection of used cars and the safest buys. He generally gets rid of the worst trade-in lemons he has received (to the wholesale market) and generally backs up his used cars with some guarantee. You may have to pay a few dollars more for a car from him but it's often worth it.

A car from a private seller may be great or not so great, and you're on your own here. No guarantee is generally given and even if it was you generally have no recourse in case of trouble. Do watch, however, for a good car you know owned by a friend, relative or neighbor who plans to trade it for a new car. You could get it at or near its wholesale value, the highest trade-in price he's likely to get. Beware of a car advertised by a "private party" who "must sell." Some used-car dealers use this method to palm off lemons, with the dealer or a friend taking it home to sell.

The used-car dealer with the garish lot and no service facility is a breed of man who demands the caution reserved for a king cobra. Most such used-car lots contain a plethora of wrecks each given surface treatment to look presentable. Finding a good one at a good price requires hard looking and a thorough check before buying. Avoid the used-car dealer with the characteristic come-on signs, "No one undersells us!" or "Fantastic Savings!"

The lemons to avoid

Worst of all are the ex-taxis and many former fleet and rental cars, which have been driven hard and long in a year or so and then dumped into the used-car market. They don't of course, carry big signs saying, "Beware— I'm an Ex-Taxi," or "Watch out—Driven hard as Rental Car." In fact, they're given a fast face lifting, touched up by nimble hands and the odometers generally turned down to a low mileage. A new federal law that will outlaw odometer tampering is, by the way, expected to be enacted soon.

What you see is a fairly attractive used car for an unbelievably low price for such a late model, only a year or two old. You deal with that kind of used car in the same way you deal firmly with any other used car you might buy—have it checked thoroughly at a diagnostic center or comparable service shop. That kind of car, by the way, will break all the records in reverse for low engine compression, high oil consumption, and other poor performance.

The best time to buy a used car

The used-car market brims over with the most cars and the best buys in late spring and in fall following the high tide of new car sales each year— in other words, when many cars have been traded in for new cars. The next best time to buy is during the winter doldrums when the demand is low for all cars, new or used. Used cars are, of course, available at other times when the in-and-out tempo of supply and demand largely determine availability and price.

Guarantees and warranties

A 30- to 60-day warranty should be expected from a dealer, though sometimes it's a 24-hour guarantee or a car is sold "as is." The "as is" clause, buried in the contract's fine print, is typical for worn-out cars. The word "guaranteed" by itself means nothing. Your contract should specify what it means and for how long. Used cars are often sold with a 50-50 guarantee, which means that the dealer will pay half of any necessary repairs within the time specified and you pay the other half.

Try for a 100-percent guarantee covering both labor and materials. That's to avoid the shifty dealer who will insist on making repairs in his own shop and overcharge you so that the 50 percent that you pay actually covers the whole cost. A 100-percent guarantee for a shorter period is better.

You may be told that a warranty is unnecessary, "After all, the car just passed inspection," a salesman may say, pointing to a recent inspection-passed sticker on the windshield. That means nothing. Assuming that a car is in good condition because it displays an inspection sticker is a common mistake. That sticker generally means only that the lights go on and the wheels turn. The engine could be an arthritic wreck, a heartbeat away from total relapse even though the car has just passed inspection.

Summed up, *should* you buy a used car? The big carrot offered is a potential savings of $1,000 to $2,000, perhaps more, on the purchase price compared with buying a new car. But to earn that carrot, you may have to expend a little time and effort shopping for a good value. Is it worth it for you? That's up to you, of course.

CHECKLIST

Most of the same checks for buying a new car apply, as given in the preceding chapter. In addition:

1. Know the current dollar value of the car you may buy. Consult the used car book figures when you go to a bank to prearrange the financing, or obtain a copy of one of the used-car publications sold on newsstands.
2. Have the car checked thoroughly at a diagnostic center or by a good mechanic with the necessary equipment.
3. If service or repairs are required, have the price adjusted accordingly. Be prepared, however, to spend up to $50 to $100 to put a used car in really good condition. That's considered part of your purchase cost.
4. Be prepared to bargain, the customary practice with used cars. Set the highest price that you're willing to pay and stick to it.

20

cutting the cost of **owning** and **operating** your **car**

The importance of proper maintenance and service · Why frequent oil changes are important · A three-stage do-it-yourself program

True, some cars are not made as well as others, and off and on some individual cars come through with mysterious defects that can drive an owner to distraction. On the whole, however, most cars are ruggedly built and will take an enormous amount of hard wear and tear with one proviso: that you give it a little love and attention in return to minimize the wear and tear.

The extreme opposite attitude is the resentful person who is determined to exact the absolute last bit of performance from his car with a minimum of grudging attention and sympathy. That's obviously asking for trouble and the person usually gets it.

A growing number of people are, on the other hand, taking over both minor and major servicing of their cars, not just to save money but also to be sure that the servicing is done right. They've been forced into it because of the growing shortage of good mechanics. That includes a growing number of women who never before held a wrench in their hands.

If you dislike such do-it-yourself work and wish only for a car that will provide dependable transportation and not hound you with the need

154

for repairs, get your car to your neighborhood garage on schedule, regularly, and have it checked and lubricated according to the manufacturer's instruction book. If you want to save money and also get maximum performance and satisfaction from your car, go a step further and get a complete service and maintenance manual for your car. This generally can be had in a book store for a few dollars or ordered from a mail-order house like Sears or Montgomery Ward. You'll get that money back many times over. Such a book, for example, usually contains a list of common problems encountered with the car plus the probable cause and the remedy. Often the remedy can be applied by any reasonably intelligent car owner. You save the time and expense of a special trip to a garage for repairs.

Saving on gasoline

The kind of gasoline fed to your engine depends on the engine and its compression ratio. Whether it requires high test (premium) or regular gas at 10 to 15 percent less cost should be stated in the instruction booklet. That depends on the gasoline octane rating required for your car engine. Regular gas generally has an octane rating of 90 to 95, premium gas about a 100, more or less. Put gas with a lower octane rating than needed in your car and you'll hear about it fast in engine-knocking pings. About the only time that you can get away with regular gas in a high-compression engine is after the car has been driven about 50,000 miles or more. Then the engine, a bit worn here and there, sometimes will settle for cheaper, regular gas.

Not all brands of gas are the same, however, so it may pay to try different brands. You may find a brand with lower cost regular gas that will perform well in your engine, while another brand of regular with a slightly lower octane rating leaves your engine knocking. The time to save money on gasoline is when you're initially buying a car. If low gas bills are important to you, buy only a car that will accept regular gas.

The savings possible on gasoline are not necessarily all that impressive, however. The average driver buys about 800 gallons of gasoline in a year. Assuming a saving of up to 4 cents a gallon on regular, versus premium, gas, that will mean savings of up to $32 a year, or $2.67 a month. Does that make a difference to you? More important, however, is to use the recommended gasoline so that your engine will run well and not break down prematurely, which could cost you considerably more than $32 for repairs.

Use the best engine oil

And change the oil frequently. Oil is the heart blood of a car engine, and high-grade oil, as necessary, is essential for top engine performance and long engine life. It's simple-minded, penny-wise and pound-foolish to stretch out the intervals between oil changes in order to squeeze the very last bit of lubrication from tired old oil.

Ordinarily, oil should be left in a car engine for no more than 60 days or 4,000 miles, whichever comes first. That's usually the outside limit; more frequent oil changes are recommended for hard driving—see your car manual. On the other hand, some car manufacturers recommend an oil change every six months or 6,000 miles, whichever comes first. To play safe, use the 60-day, 4,000-mile yardstick, since after that time the usual engine oil tends to thin out with absorbed engine muck, sludge and dirt; it just can't lubricate as well any more. An exception is top-grade "extended service" oil which is specially designed for the long-term oil use recommended by those six-month oil change car makers.

The type of oil for your engine will also be stated in the car's instruction booklet, and this, too, depends on the kind of driving you do. The toughest driving on a car engine is not long, fast cross-country driving, as some people believe, but is frequent short-trip, stop-and-go local travel, particularly during cold weather. Thus, a car used for commuting or by a woman for frequent local shopping trips subjects the engine to the severest strain. That calls for the most frequent oil changes and top-grade MS oil; the "S" stands for severe driving conditions, the "M" for motor. There is also MM and ML oil, for medium and light driving.

High-grade oil can be bought in bulk from an auto supply store or a wholesale parts distributor for 30 to 40 percent less than the usual one-quart gas station price. Get it in multigallon cans or in a 24-quart case and add oil yourself when necessary. That will get you high-grade $1-a-quart oil for as little as 60 cents a quart, 40 percent saved. Pulling the dipstick from an engine and checking the oil level is absurdly simple; any reasonably normal individual can do it. Don't overfill, however, and don't mix different oil brands in your engine. Stick to the same brand of oil because different brands mixed together could cause a bad chemical reaction inside the engine.

To save real time and money, you could change your own oil and oil filter when necessary. A couple of wheel ramps may be required to raise the front of your car—they're obtainable at auto supply stores—and an oil-plug wrench will also be required. The job takes a little care and caution, naturally, and if your car must be propped up in front so that you can get under it, be absolutely sure that it cannot topple down on you accidentally. The author of this book spends less than $18 a year for top-grade oil bought in bulk for his car, and changes the oil and oil filter himself every two months. That not only saves money, but, equally important, the job is done in less time than otherwise required to drive the car to a local service station and wait for the work to be done there.

A three-stage do-it-yourself program

You need not be a French chef to make an omelette, and you need not be a master mechanic to service your own car well and inexpensively. In addition to checking your oil, the routine checks include checking and replenishing the radiator and battery water, checking tire pressure (get your own gauge for this, as many service station tire-pump gauges are incredibly inaccurate), refilling the windshield washer tanks as necessary, and, depending on the car, other basic checks. These ordinarily should be done when you get gas or when your car is left for a lubrication, but nine out of ten times a careless or harassed mechanic will overlook one or more. Thus you have to take on such maintenance yourself simply in self-defense.

Next step upward is changing spark plugs, installing your own antifreeze and battery and keeping your engine tuned. Good savings are possible here because the parts required often can be bought on sale or from an automobile supply store much below the usual prices charged by a local service station. Spark plugs, for example, often cost about $1.25 or more from the serviceman who installs them, but the same plugs often can be bought for as little as 50 to 75 cents. You pay more for oil, plugs and almost everything else bought at a service garage largely because you're a captive customer and because the price is higher to compensate the dealer for the labor to install them. The parts for most cars can be had at any good automobile parts supplier, or at savings by mail from Sears, Montgomery Ward, or a national mail-order automobile supply house, such as J. C. Whitney, 1917 Archer Ave., Chicago, Ill. 60616. Each has a parts catalogue for domestic and foreign cars obtainable by mail.

The third and final step up is turning your garage into a full-fledged automobile service center. You must spend up to $100 for the essential tools and you should also arm yourself with the basic full, thick service manual for your car (obtainable from a new-car dealer of your brand of car). A pretty penny can be saved and many people get much satisfaction out of doing their own work and feeling that it's done properly. It's recommended, of course, only if you have the aptitude and ability for it.

Special caution: Regardless of how highly you value your mechanical skills, don't tackle any serious maintenance or repair on a car unless you know what you're doing, or unless you're willing to learn first. Even deceptively small work, such as changing the spark plugs in some cars, requires special knowledge or tools. Spark plugs, for example, may require a torque wrench and a specified pressure fit or you're in trouble. You find out things like that from the service manual for your car.

Getting good repairs

Get an estimate on work to be done before it's done. Depending on whom you're dealing with, it may be important to get it in writing. You may be told, "Oh, we can't tell you the cost till we take it apart and see what's wrong." Nonsense. Any good mechanic can give you an approximate estimate based on what is likely to be needed plus the possible additional cost if extra work is required.

Sometimes a mechanic will frankly be stymied; he just doesn't know what's wrong with a car and as a result he will have to try one thing after another to correct a mysterious ailment. This is par for the course, especially since not all automobile mechanics are as smart as they might be and, in addition, many gas stations simply don't have the sophisticated test equipment to track down a complicated trouble.

Here is when taking your car to an automobile diagnostic center could pay off. A thorough examination of the car there could turn up what's wrong—and what's right—quickly, thus tell you the specific repairs necessary. As a matter of fact, having your car checked out in a diagnostic center once a year or so is a good idea. The check could point to weak spots or areas of potential trouble that can be corrected easily at low cost before they cause a major breakdown.

Don't necessarily decide to get rid of your car just because it has a chronic ailment that your local mechanic cannot cure, especially if the car is only a few years old. Yes, again, take it to a diagnostic center, which usually can pinpoint the problem and inform you whether it is really serious and something that justifies getting rid of the car, or something that can be replaced or repaired quite easily.

Honor thy mechanic. Finding a good one is increasingly difficult because there are fewer to go around. A quarter of a century ago, following World War II, there was one mechanic for every 75 cars. Today they're spread twice as thin, one mechanic now for every 150 cars. You find a good one the same way you look for and find a good repairman of any kind (Chapter 1). Once you've got a good one, pet him and be nice. Smile when you go by and never fail to ask about his wife and family. Deal fairly and honestly with him, which also means you probably should buy parts and tires from him even if at a higher cost than at a cut-rate supply store. But that's the price you must pay to count on him in a pinch, and for reliable service and repairs.

Drive sympathetically. That's important for the hundreds of moving parts in a car. Let the engine run for a few moments up to a minute or so before driving off when starting from cold and particularly during cold weather. That gets the oil loose and circulating before you push the pedal to the floor. With a regular gear shift, depress the clutch before starting, and to conserve your battery don't turn lights, radio or anything else on till after the engine is started.

Avoid sudden, sharp starts and stops. Start up slowly and slow down in anticipation of stops. Don't press going up hills and don't hit top speed until the engine is warmed up. Keep the tires inflated to the recommended pressure and check the pressure regularly (when car has been at rest and tires cold, since hot tires give erroneous pressure readings). These and other care and sympathy for a car not only will prolong its life, but will also increase your gasoline mileage.

CHECKLIST FOR OWNING A CAR

1. Take the service recommendations in your car manual seriously and have the car checked and serviced accordingly. Have you reread the manual recently?
2. Use the recommended gasoline for your car, regular or premium, whichever is needed. Trying different brands could pay off in good gas at a lower price.
3. Don't skimp on engine oil. Use high-grade oil and change your engine oil as frequently as required for the car and your type of driving.
4. Save money by buying replacement parts at automobile parts stores and install them yourself.
5. Service your own car but only up to the stage that you are capable of handling.

how to **stay healthy** and spend less for **medical care**

In recent years medical bills have skyrocketed faster than any other regular item in the U.S. cost-of-living index. Our country's total health bill now averages about $300 a person, or over $1,000 a year for the average family with two or three children. It's more for the one out of seven Americans who ends up in the hospital each year, particularly since hospital bills are up to $100 a day in many areas and sometimes higher. Hospital bills account for our biggest single medical expense item (about 35 percent), followed by doctor bills (20 percent) and drugs and medicine (14 percent).

The obvious conclusion is: Stay out of the hospital—unless you're a visitor—and don't get sick. Since that's not always easily done, the second thing to do is to have good health insurance for paying a big medical bill.

161

21

the 12 best ways to **save on medical costs** and **doctor bills**

Preventive medicine for you and your family · Avoiding a big hospital bill · Saving on prescription drugs · Using community health facilities · Insuring your blood supply at no cost · Stress and what to do about it

The very best way to stay well may be easier than you think. A study of hospital patients by the Massachusetts General Hospital with the Harvard University Medical School shows that three out of every five patients could have stayed out of the hospital and kept healthy if they had followed the ounce-of-prevention adage.

Many failed to consult a doctor in time or scorned a regular checkup (which could have detected their incipient problems before things got serious). The study also showed that heavy smoking and overweight are characteristic of many people who end up with a serious illness and hospitalization. This is additional evidence that reduced smoking and a reasonably lean figure can help you stay healthy and save you a potful of medical money.

Actually, it isn't necessarily all that easy, as many a heavy smoker who has tried to quit but cannot well knows, and as many a heavy eater who has tried to lose weight but cannot also knows. A growing body of medical evidence suggests, in fact, that cigarette smoking, a fatty diet loaded with cholesterol and lack of proper exercise do not necessarily

163

pose the great perils to our health and well-being that we have been led
to believe. It is workaday anger, emotional tension and anxiety or, in a
word, *stress* that can be the really great peril, a growing number of medical researchers say. They say that stress is really the underlying cause
that compels many people to overeat, oversmoke and, among other things,
overdrink, so it's a vicious circle.

Medical science has long known that certain stress due to worry or
anxiety often plays a contributing role to such chronic ailments as gastric
ulcer, eczema, diabetes, arthritis, migraine, asthma and ulcerative colitis.
On top of that, many doctors say a high proportion of day-to-day ailments
brought to them show no organic basis and are due to "nerves," or,
again, stress. Strong links are also being found between stress and our
two most fearful medical plagues, heart disease and cancer. Not every
case of these or the other ailments just cited can be connected to stress,
and it would be silly to say that stress is at the bottom of all human
ailments, small or large. Nevertheless, coming to terms with emotional
stress could well be as important as any other single factor, if not more
so, in staying healthy and saving a lot of money on medical expenses and
doctor bills. But before getting into what might be done to alleviate
personal stress, let's first take up some practical, proven ways to reduce
medical expenses, one of the American family's five largest annual living
expenses.

Reducing doctor bills

1. *Use the telephone.* Often a doctor can give you advice on
the phone and save you, and him, time and money. If you must see him,
visit his office rather than paying extra for a house call. Besides, a house
call is sometimes ineffectual because the doctor may not have the essential diagnostic equipment he keeps in his office. Save the house call for
a real, flat-on-your-back emergency.

However, don't put off seeing a doctor just to save a few bucks. Some
people, to be sure, have lived to 100 without ever seeing a doctor, or so
they claimed. But you don't hear much about many more people who
do not live so long and wish—often too late—they had seen a doctor in
time. Putting off a visit to the doctor for a minor, if not chronic, complaint just to save the money is a widespread malady of itself. That's
silly, because it permits a small initial ailment to gain headway and grow
into something serious, including the size of the medical bill later, compared with the small initial bill required to trap and eliminate a few small
bugs at the beginning.

Don't, however, put blind faith in every doctor. No doctor knows everything and there isn't a doctor alive who is infallible. If you have a persistent problem and nothing your doctor recommends seems to work, consult another doctor, and even a third one, if necessary. That's also recommended when a serious decision must be made, about a major operation, for example. As a matter of fact, a good doctor, treading uncertain terrain, will by himself consult another, such as a specialist who is more familiar with a specific problem.

2. *Have your own family doctor.* This is particularly important today as our national supply of family doctors has shrunk to an all-time low (fewer than 70,000) while our population has soared. The result: In an emergency more and more people find that doctors are unavailable. "Try the hospital emergency room," they're told.

A family doctor not only gives you personal service, but often can save you time and money by knowing your medical history and being armed with your family's medical record. This can mean a speedy diagnosis as well as sometimes avoiding expensive tests. A family doctor is unnecessary, however, if you belong to a good prepaid health group (described in the next chapter).

3. *Get a regular medical checkup.* This is more stock advice, true, but preventive measures are more important than ever in these days of fewer doctors, crowded hospitals and soaring medical costs. An annual checkup is especially recommended for small children and everyone over 35. The cost is small—usually $35 to $85—and the benefits are large, since early detection of incipient trouble, especially with heart, lungs and other vital organs, often can mean quick and relatively inexpensive control. It could even save your life, as in the early detection of cancer of the breast or prostate, two of the most common cancers which show remarkable recovery rates if found early. Cancer is our second biggest killer, with heart disease first.

4. *Discuss the fee before the bill comes.* Most doctors welcome this. Determine what special treatment or an operation will cost. If you're financially strapped, tell the doctor so. In some cases, he'll reconsider his fee. Also ask what you can do to keep down the cost. To check on typical fees for a specific operation or treatment, call your local medical society. That's also where to call if your bill seems high or if you have a complaint (though not all medical societies will necessarily respond satisfactorily). The best medicine for inflammation of the bill—still another widespread medical problem—is to discuss the charge beforehand.

5. *Keep down hospital costs.* If you must go in, get out fast. The sooner you're out, the greater the relief when the bill comes, espe-

cially since the bill can hit the $100-a-day level; that doesn't include doctors' fees, by the way. What's more, much hospitalization insurance nowadays pays only part of the bill; you pay the rest.

Discuss the choice of a hospital with your doctor. A large medical center or university hospital may offer the most modern facilities and services, but it's usually necessary only for special treatment or a really serious condition. You often pay considerably less in a perfectly good community hospital offering excellent, if not top-notch, facilities for routine operations and hospital care. Also ask your doctor about the available choice in community hospitals, considering the best for your purpose, as well as for price and convenience.

Don't check into a hospital early on a weekend, when few staff people are there. Most serious tests and other work are not done till Monday morning, but you still pay the full rate every day. Check in between Sunday evening and Friday morning, if possible. Schedule a hospital stay for summer or before Christmas, when most hospitals are not crowded and the economical rooms are most likely to be available. You may also get the most attention at such times.

Then tell your doctor you want to get out fast, and you generally can return for a special check or test on an outpatient basis. If you require extended hospital convalescence, inquire about being moved to a "halfway house," such as an accredited nursing home or a motel-like, intermediate-care convalescent hospital section. You get all the necessary professional care at 50 to 75 percent of the daily hospital rate, sometimes less. More and more hospitals provide such highly sensible facilities.

Room charges will run somewhat higher than above in a big city, somewhat lower in small towns for each state noted. Above fees do not include fees for doctors and surgeons.

How hospital charges have zoomed:

Average recent daily charges for a semiprivate hospital room in random states:

California	$85.53	Illinois	$70.29
Florida	68.14	New York	80.14
Hawaii	67.19	Pennsylvania	65.82

6. *Before checking into a hospital, ask about Pre-Admission Testing, PAT.* This can reduce the number of days spent in the hospital and reduce your bill considerably. With PAT certain patients scheduled for hospitalization receive routine tests prior to their admission. The tests are usually done in the outpatient department and can mean a postponement of your in-hospital care until you're ready for that stage. Your health insurance may or may not pay for PAT, however, so check on this beforehand. Even if yours does not, PAT still could conserve your in-hospital coverage for benefits you may need later.

7. *Don't get private-roomitis.* The deluxe status of a private room can cost you dearly. For one thing, hospital insurance often covers only the cost of a semiprivate room; you pay the difference. For another, a private-room patient is often the target for the custom deluxe bill from doctors, surgeons and other consultants who equate a private room with a private fortune. A semiprivate room, usually for two to four occupants, not only costs less but is eminently satisfactory for most people.

8. *Be a "vertical" rather than a "horizontal" patient.* More and more medical tests and treatment that formerly required hospitalization are now done on an out-patient basis in a hospital, clinic or doctor's office. Even tonsils are being removed that way, thus eliminating the time and cost of a hospital stay. Talk this over with your doctor. Formerly, this was unwise financially because insurance generally covered only treatment in a hospital, but more insurance plans now cover the same treatment done in a clinic, doctor's office or at home. Check your policy on this.

9. *Save on drugs.* Don't be "drug happy" and don't insist that the doctor give you fancy medicine you don't need. To save on this category of medical costs, shop among drugstores for the lowest prices, particularly for nonprescription drugs. Take advantage of low-cost drug rates offered by certain health plans, unions and such groups as the American Association of Retired Persons. Ask your doctor to specify a good "generic" drug on your prescriptions rather than a higher-priced brand name. Remember, however, that a special brand-name drug sometimes may be better or have greater strength and therefore be worth its extra cost.

10. *Use your community health facilities.* They often offer free chest X-rays, vaccinations and other free or low-cost services, and this is not charity. Such services are especially notable for handicapped persons, mental illness, alcoholism and drug addiction. They can do much good at great savings when your medical bills would otherwise skyrocket. Get details from your public health department.

11. *Insure your blood supply.* In a real emergency, such as an open-valve heart operation, you might need as much as 30 to 40 pints of blood at $25 to $35 a pint. Give a pint of blood a year to many blood banks, however, and you and your family later get all the blood you need at no charge. Call the Red Cross or your local hospital about this.

12. *Take all allowable tax deductions for medical expenses.* Not everyone does. Eligible deductions people often miss on their income-tax returns include: travel cost to and from the doctor's office, hospital or any other place for medical reasons; medical bills paid for dependents, such as a child away at school; money spent for orthopedic shoes or other physical support or garments; hearing aids; and dental costs.

To be deductible, however, all your medical bills must exceed 3 percent of your income with one exception, which also is often missed. That's your medical insurance premiums, half of which up to $150 is deductible. That's for Blue Cross, Blue Shield or other health insurance. The other half of such premiums is deductible when your total medical expenses, including health insurance, exceed the 3 percent level. (More on income tax savings in Chapter 31.)

Other tips

Always check your medical bills. Everybody (or nearly everybody) is human and makes mistakes and so do nonhuman computers. Be sure that you don't pay for an item covered by your insurance. Don't go overboard for unnecessary private nurses; use part-time visiting nurses for at-home nursing care. And don't panic if you're hit with an astronomical medical bill. Talk it over with the doctor or hospital people. Nearly all such people will usually work out a payment schedule that you can meet over a period of time.

Of course, you probably should have health insurance, but much health insurance today pays according to preinflation medical costs, such as a mere $10 to $20 a day for hospital rooms that cost considerably more today. Up-to-date health insurance is virtually essential today and it is dealt with in the next chapter.

What about stress?

It could be a splitting headache, a pounding heart, severe cramps, even a rash or backache, but nothing the doctor does seems to help. Often it's just feeling tired all the time, being unable to sleep or eat and feeling nervous. Sometimes there is no blatent symptom that drives one to a doctor, but nevertheless subconscious stress is taking a toll. It could lead to a sudden breakdown, a heart attack being the price often paid by certain stress-prone people.

Many other examples can be cited of people suffering from emotional stress that have led to a variety of real live ailments. But doctors still don't know for sure why stress can strike one in the stomach (via ulcers), another in the back (via backache) and still another person in the heart. Each of us is apparently more vulnerable in certain parts of the body than in other parts, and the way we react to stress determines the ailment that results.

Two California cardiologists, Drs. Meyer Friedman and Ray H. Rosenman, are leading students of stress and they believe that people can be divided into two major types, the Type A person and the Type B, with A being far more prone to heart disease than B. Type A, the coronary-prone person, is characterized by intense drive, aggressiveness, ambition, and a fierce competitiveness. Type B may be equally serious but is more easygoing, less competitive, takes more time to enjoy life, seldom becomes impatient and tends to speak in a less hurried, more thoughtful manner. Many people are a mix of A and B characteristics, but one set or the other tends to predominate. Studies since 1955 by Drs. Friedman and Rosenman show that Type A is two to three times more likely to suffer a heart attack in middle age than Type B is. Dr. Rosenman also found that any Type B whose level of cholesterol and other fatty acids was within normal limits had "complete immunity to coronary heart disease, irrespective of his high-fat cholesterol diet, family history, or his smoking habits or his lack of exercise."

Heart disease is, of course, a dramatic example of the end-result of stress. Stress also can lead to less serious ailments and problems with no apparent organic cause. Thus, many of us go from doctor to doctor unsuccessfully seeking a cure for what bothers us and paying a mounting series of medical bills without being cured. That's when the chances are high that stress could well be the underlying problem. We have mentioned stress here because we believe it is a major cause of medical ailments and therefore a major cause of medical expense and doctor bills. Unfortunately, however, pointing a finger at stress is much easier to do than saying what can be done about it. If you are seemingly suffering from a medical ailment that is not cured or solved with conventional medical treatment, then it might be caused by an underlying stress problem. But don't jump to that conclusion. It's a tentative conclusion that can only be made by a good doctor and only after a thorough examination has disclosed no organic cause of the problem.

The next step is to explore possible causes of stress. "Open your heart to your doctor," the *Reader's Digest* says, but that, too, may be more easily said than done. More to the point, perhaps, is to consult a specialist, in other words a good psychiatrist whose specialty is dealing with the human mind and emotions. A few visits to a good psychiatrist sometimes can unearth the underlying crisis that has caused stress to rear up and trouble a person. Sometimes it's simply due to a constant daily confrontation with a conflict at work that a person is unable to resolve or live with and only a change of jobs can solve the problem. Sometimes it's deeper down and a full-fledged psychoanalysis may be required, though not everybody succeeds in analysis and not every medical analyst is as good as he might be.

Unfortunately, little else can be added here to the subject of stress because medical science still knows comparatively little about it. Because the research on the subject is relatively recent (other than the pioneering breakthroughs of Sigmund Freud), there is also very little practical literature on the subject that a layman can turn to. One excellent article, particularly for businessmen readers, is "What Stress Can Do to You," by Walter McQuade, in the January 1972 issue of *Fortune*, which should be available in the back-issue department of a good library. Also ask a librarian about new books on the subject.

Stress summed up: Unlike a flu bug, infected throat or broken arm, each of which can be quickly diagnosed, treated and usually cured in a short period of time, stress has now been identified as a real medical ailment, but is far more difficult to diagnose and cure. The underlying stress, however, can gradually build up and lead to a serious—and expensive—medical ailment, even though it may take years before it breaks through and cripples a person. That's shown by the growing number of middle-age heart attacks being linked to long-term stress.

A word to the wise should be sufficient. To stay healthy and spend less for medical care and doctor bills, beware of stress. Or call it, if you will, tension, anxiety, or "emotions." It's probably one of the biggest single basic causes of a wide variety of medical ailments from simple skin itch and/or just plain "nerves," across the spectrum to some of the most serious and ultimately deadly ailments of modern man today.

22

health insurance: how would you pay for a $15,872 illness?

Basic hospital insurance · Doctor-bill insurance · Major medical · Prepaid group insurance · Special features to have and blueprint pitfalls to avoid · Medicare and Medicaid

A quick way to go broke today is to be crippled by a serious sickness and have to pay for the cure yourself. Medical costs have risen so steeply that probably 98 out of every 100 people cannot afford extensive medical treatment. A good health insurance policy is virtually mandatory, as shown by these actual examples.

A two-year-old girl in Florida was stung by a bee and a serious reaction followed which, among other things, knocked out her kidneys. She has required special treatment and care to keep her alive for more than six years and is still not cured. Her total medical bill so far has been over $60,000, but her family's health insurance covered only a mere $15,000 of it. Her family was formerly well off but has been reduced to close to the poverty line in order to pay for her survival.

A New York couple was financially ruined by medical costs for a son paralyzed by a football injury.

A woman in Seattle, Washington, ran up an $18,000 hospital bill for treatment of an intestinal obstruction but she was covered by insurance that paid all but $527 of the total bill.

A heart attack hospitalized a young man in Chicago for 76 days, and his bill came to $15,872. He had basic hospital insurance plus a major medical policy which paid $13,052 of that cost. He paid the difference, $2,620.

How would you pay for a bill like that, $15,872? You probably have health insurance—six out of seven Americans do—but will it pay for a hospital siege at rates of $100 a day or more?

As we mentioned earlier, the chances are about one in seven that each of us will end up in the hospital this year. Putting it another way, you are likely to be a hospital patient once in the next seven years. The average hospital stay is eight days at an average bill for $758, which is a nearly threefold increase (from $285) over a decade ago. That's the average cost, however. If you're lucky, you may get out of the hospital quicker and at lower cost. If not lucky, there's no telling how long you may be hospitalized and how high your bill might go.

A Cincinnati study recently showed that hospital bills of $5,000 to $10,000 have increased by 1,000 percent in recent years. The Blue Cross people in Wisconsin had 808 insured patients each with hospital bills in a recent year of more than $5,000 and up to $35,000. If that isn't enough, a federal government study forecasts that medical care costs are likely to climb another 50 percent by 1975!

The likelihood of being hit with a big medical bill increases if you have children, if you are middle-aged or over, the older the age the more likely, and particularly if you are 55 or older. The likelihood is less if you are reasonably young, strong and healthy or married (preferably happily) with no children, especially if you are seldom sick and your parents lived long and healthy lives. But even if you are robustly healthy with the stoutest heart and likely to live to 100 with never a day of sickness, you are still not immune to a freak ailment or accident that could cost a pretty penny for medical treatment. So unless you're rich, having health insurance makes important good sense. As a matter of fact, without it you might not even get admitted to some hospitals today.

There are three main kinds of health insurance and ordinarily a combination of at least two of the three is recommended.

1. *Basic hospital insurance.* This is fundamental protection, sometimes called "first-dollar" insurance, and by and large most families should have it. It's the hospital insurance provided by Blue Cross and some 1,000 private insurance companies. But what you get varies all over the lot—even Blue Cross policies are not standard. Some Blue Cross plans give you terrific coverage, but others do not. For example, many Blue Cross policies in the New York City area cover you for only 21 days in the hospital, while others in the New York area, as well as elsewhere, pay your hospital bills for 60 up to 365 days in the hospital.

That's the first thing to check in a basic hospital insurance policy you may have or may buy: How long will it pay your hospital bills? Though the average hospital stay is eight days per person, insurance is not so much for an average stay as for the possibility of an expensive, prolonged stay. A good policy should pay all or most of your hospital bills for at least 60 days and preferably 120 days or more.

How much will the policy pay? It should pay the *full prevailing* daily cost in the hospital for a semiprivate room. That means $50 to over $100 a day or whatever the daily room charge is where you live.

Beware of the policy that pays only $10 to $20 a day toward your hospital room, as you pay the difference between that and the actual cost. Also beware of advertisements for insurance that say, "Pay up to $100 a week," or "$600 a month." This last—$600 a month—works out to a mere $20 a day for a month in a hospital. It may not even cover additional costs for X-rays, medicine, drugs, and so on. Insurance that pays, for example, $35 to $40 a day for your hospital room will be adequate only if hospital costs where you live are no more than that.

Does the policy cover both accidents and sickness? Some hospital policies go only halfway, paying only for care due to an accident, not due to sickness. Many cover both but pay less if you're sick than if you've had an accident.

Hospital insurance, including the Blue Cross kind, will not necessarily pay your bill unless it's in an "approved" or accredited hospital. A Washington, D.C., woman with Blue Cross insurance ran up a large bill in a private hospital, which, alas, she found out later was not a genuine accredited hospital, and Blue Cross would not pay her bill. Most hospitals are accredited for Blue Cross and other insurance, but before you enter a hospital be sure that your insurance covers you in that hospital. Of course, this may not be easy to do when you are being raced to a hospital in an ambulance. Better to check ahead of time when you're well, and read what your policy says on this score.

At group rates, a family hospital policy generally will cost about $10 to $25 a month, perhaps more in the future, depending on where you live and the coverage provided. The cost is more for an individual policy you buy yourself. But not all hospital policies pay the cost of doctor bills for your own doctor visiting each day, the cost of a surgeon if needed or any other doctor needed.

     2. *Basic medical insurance.* This is doctor-bill insurance and is provided by Blue Shield and many private insurance companies. Sometimes it's called surgical insurance and then pays only for surgery. Basic medical insurance should pay the prevailing doctor rates when you're in the hospital, just as a hospital policy should pay the prevailing room

rates. That means the usual fees charged locally for having a baby, a tonsillectomy, a hysterectomy and any other common—or uncommon—cause of hospitalization.

Like some hospital policies, however, some doctor-bill policies are laced with midget-low limits on their payments for doctors, compared with the prevailing rates where you live. The limits paid are listed in the policy and again it's up to you to determine their adequacy. Check them with your doctor or an official at a local hospital. Are they realistic? (We'd like to be more specific—and more helpful—in answering questions like this, but unfortunately no answer will apply for most readers. We are just as frustrated as you when we tell you that you must check your local costs yourself.)

Ordinarily, twofold health insurance consisting of a good hospital policy married to a good medical policy should provide adequate insurance for most families, particularly those with children. An example is a combination Blue Cross-Blue Shield policy where the Blue Cross portion of it gives you hospital coverage for at least 120 days up to 365 days maximum coverage. The doctor-bill coverage usually can be added to a basic hospital policy at family group rates for about $6 to $12 a month.

That kind of good double protection—hospital plus doctor-bill protection—can, in fact, pay for all or most of the largest potential bill you might have. A Massachusetts woman was hospitalized for eight months with a rare nervous disorder and her record bill was $85,500! The bill was paid in full by a 365-day Blue Cross-Blue Shield policy. Such insurance, however, does not necessarily cover everyone for everything that might be needed in the hospital, and it falls down when you may require special care outside of the hospital, at home or in a convalescent home, for example. That brings up the third main kind of health insurance.

3. *Major medical insurance.* Also called disaster insurance, this is designed to pay the lion's share of a big medical bill of from $10,000 to $20,000, sometimes more, but it is not total insurance. For one thing, major medical policies usually contain a "deductible" clause, which means that you pay the first $100, $250, up to $1,000 of a medical bill, and the insurance company doesn't begin paying until after the deductible has been reached. The lower the deductible, the higher your premium cost. Deductibles come in for criticism, but they serve a justifiable purpose. Because major medical insurance is intended, chiefly, to protect you against a really big bill, it has the built-in assumption that you can pay for routine bills. The greater the initial portion of a medical bill that you're willing to pay, the cheaper the cost for the insurance.

In addition, many major medical policies pay only 75 to 80 percent of the bill over the deductible limit and you pay the rest. Without this hedging clause, also called co-insurance, and without a deductible, a major medical policy would be prohibitively expensive.

The maximum coverage with major medical insurance generally ranges from $10,000 to $25,000, but some companies offer it up to $50,000 and sometimes $100,000. You choose what you want with coverage of at least $20,000 to $25,000 recommended. Though such a policy may be obtainable only with a deductible and even though the company may pay only 75 percent of the rest of the bill, you are still insured for a large portion of a potentially large medical expense.

Because most major medical policies in force today protect people for only $10,000 to $15,000, the insurance companies have introduced "excess" major medical insurance, which will cover you for a bill of up to $100,000 or more at comparatively low cost. It's designed chiefly to supplement a regular major medical policy, ride piggyback on a basic major medical policy, in other words. Jackson Halloran has a $10,000 major medical, for example, and after reading about the skyrocketing costs of medical care he realized one day that if he, his wife or one of his children needed a kidney transplant or was hit by a really big medical expense his $10,000 major medical policy would not be adequate. So he got an excess major medical policy with $100,000 coverage and felt reassured. This new policy has a $10,000 deductible, but that's all right with Jackson, since his regular major medical covers him for that much expense. His new policy costs $100 a year, and it will pay for virtually all medical expenses he has over $10,000 and with no co-insurance; i.e., it pays 100 percent of all bills over $10,000 within specific limits (such as up to $60 a day for a hospital room).

Excess major medical can be had with a deductible of $5,000 up to $30,000—you choose what you want depending on how much basic medical insurance you already have. Depending on the company selling it, you can be covered for up to $250,000 or $500,000. Naturally, the higher the coverage, the greater the cost.

Major medical insurance is also a good way to fill in common gaps in basic hospital and doctor-bill insurance. That's because most regular hospital and doctor-bill insurance policies do not pay for certain medical charges, such as not paying for blood transfusions, private nursing care in or out of a hospital, rental of certain sophisticated medical equipment, cobalt treatment, and not for convalescent costs at your home or a convalescent home. For complete health insurance, you then need a major medical policy in addition to hospital and doctor-care insurance.

A major medical policy with a $500 deductible clause and 75-25 percent co-insurance for a husband and wife in their mid-thirties with two children generally costs between $200 and $300 a year. That's an individual policy that you buy yourself; the cost is less for a group major medical bought at work or through another group.

An alternative, particularly for a single person or a couple with no children, is a good major medical policy by itself. That's if you can afford to pay small bills or a percentage of a major bill by yourself and you desire insurance chiefly for protection in case of a large bill. This is done by many a person today who is reasonably healthy and particularly if hospital and doctor-care insurance cannot be obtained at a low-cost group rate. Since the cost of basic hospital insurance bought individually can get expensive, such people figure that over the years it will cost them little or no more to pay for their own infrequent medical bills of small to medium size. But if they're suddenly laid low by a serious illness, a good major medical policy will pay the brunt of a really big bill.

Prepaid group health plans

This is how to get virtually complete health insurance at reasonable cost with such groups as New York's HIP (Health Insurance Plan) and the much-praised Kaiser-Permanente Health Plan of California, Washington, Colorado, Ohio and Hawaii.

In such a group you pay about $45 to $65 a month per family for health, hospital and medical coverage. It covers routine doctor visits and annual checkups, as well as the cost of a hospital stay, however long and expensive.

About 8 million Americans are covered by prepaid plans and usually have no need for any other health insurance. If you can join such a plan, by all means give it serious consideration. It can be unbeatable with a few exceptions. The nature of group medicine precludes your own personal doctor, with your care being rotated, as necessary, among member doctors of the group. And with some plans you may have to wait in line, for weeks or more, for a routine checkup.

Group plans stress preventive medicine and catching incipient problems before they become serious. As a result, members of the Kaiser plan spend less than half as many days in the hospital as other Americans, and their cost for Kaiser care is less than other comparable insurance. A list of such medical plans can be had from the Group Health Association, 1321 14th Street, N.W., Washington, D.C. 20005.

Special tips

Try first for health insurance that you can buy at a group rate, through an employer, a union, a professional society or other group affiliation you may have. Group policies are not only cheaper than a comparable individual policy you buy yourself, but a group policy generally gives broader coverage, too.

Seek insurance that is "guaranteed renewable" and gives "the right of transfer." The first prevents the company from cancelling you out if you have submitted several claims, for example, or for any other reason. The second gives you two other safeguards: With a group policy it gives you the right to continue the policy on your own if you leave the group (change jobs, for example); and if it's a family policy in the name of a husband or wife, it gives the other spouse the right to continue the policy when that may be desired.

How much of a waiting period is there before you are covered by a new policy? Virtually all hospital policies, for example, do not cover a family for birth of a baby until the insurance is more than ten months old. Many individual policies (as opposed to group policies) do not cover you for up to two years for a medical condition that you had before getting the policy. You may not collect from some companies even if you were unaware of the precondition; your claim is simply rejected if at the time of treatment it is determined that the illness stems from a pre-existing condition. And some policies pay no benefits until the policy is at least a month old.

These precondition and waiting-period clauses are understandable, since they're designed to guard the insurance company against a big claim by a person who scorns health insurance until the last minute, taking it out on his way to the hospital. On the other hand, they can leave a wide gap in your coverage.

Be wary of mail-order health insurance. Some of it is good and some of it is not so good, being downright misleading and fraudulent. An example is an insurance company whose national advertising is given the seal of approval of a well-known television star. The company advertises, "Collect up to $600-a-month extra cash!" But, as we mentioned, for a month in the hospital that will pay a mere $20 or so a day of your $100-a-day bill. Such insurance is really only supplementary insurance, though this fact is not prominent in the advertising.

Besides, if you have a claim problem with a mail-order company, your state insurance department people could be powerless to help you because many mail-order firms are not licensed in all states (but they can sell by mail virtually anywhere). Before buying mail-order insurance you must investigate exactly what you're getting, and you definitely should not buy from a company unlicensed in your state. Also check first on the availability locally from an agent of private company insurance. If you can't locate a good agent, write to the Health Insurance Institute, 277

Park Ave., New York, N.Y. 10017, for a list of companies that sell health insurance.

Insure your blood supply. This was also mentioned earlier but should be amplified. To review: whole blood by transfusion is not covered by the usual hospital insurance and it can cost you as much as $25 a pint or more. (It is generally covered, however, in a major medical policy.) A Rhode Island woman required $2,350 worth of blood during treatment of an abdominal abscess, which was the only part of her $21,000 hospital bill not covered by her hospital insurance. She could have had all that blood free if she had been a member of the Red Cross blood bank program. This is a national program available in most areas which calls for you to donate a pint of blood a year. In return, you are entitled to all the blood anyone in your immediate family may need, when required, at no charge. Donate more than a pint a year and you get additional blood rights for other relatives outside of your immediate family, such as an in-law or grandparents. The exact coverage can vary from one group to another, so check on this locally.

What about Medicare and Medicaid? Medicare is, of course, the federal government's medical insurance for people 65 and older. At this stage in life, it will handle a good portion of hospital and other medical costs. But it has gaps for which supplementary insurance is recommended. This often can be had for as little as $5 a month.

Medicaid is a federal–state program in most, though not all, states, which provides health and hospital care for low-income families and others such as blind and disabled people. Details on both programs can be had from your nearest Social Security office or by writing to the U.S. Department of Health, Education and Welfare, Social Security Administration, Baltimore, Md. 21235.

Health insurance summed up

Since a hospital bill and possibly a large one is the greatest peril, a good hospital policy ordinarily should be your basic health insurance. Married to a complementary doctor-bill (medical care) policy, which pays for the doctor, it can give you excellent insurance.

Major medical insurance is intended chiefly to plug gaps in the hospital and doctor-bill policies you may have, for instance, when your hospital insurance covers you for a limited 21-day period. Then a major medical policy is back-up insurance to pay for a longer stay in the hospital; it is also there to pay for certain other bills not generally paid by regular hospital insurance. A major medical policy by itself also can be good for a single person or a couple with no children who can afford to pay for routine medical expenses (including a short hospital stay) and figure that their chief need is disaster insurance. But then, your major medical should have a fairly high coverage, at least $20,000 to $25,000, if not higher.

A combination of all three kinds of insurance—hospital, doctor bills and major medical—will give you fairly complete health insurance, but try to obtain it at a low-cost group rate. About the only way to get virtually total medical insurance is by being a member of a prepaid group-health plan, which will pay for practically every doctor visit, as well as for a siege in the hospital, however long it may be.

Actual hospital bill for a 38-year-old man, husband and father of three children in Providence, Rhode Island

---

Diagnosis: Cerebral hemorrhage

Date admitted to hospital: 12/2/70; discharged 3/31/71
Intensive Care Unit 12/2/70 to 12/8/70

Cost of semiprivate room	113 days @ $65 per day	$7,345.00
Intensive care	6 days @ $110 per day	660.00
Operating room		615.00
Medical and surgical supplies		382.00
Drugs and medications		3,348.00
Laboratory examinations		2,383.00
Inhalation therapy		4,892.00
Physical therapy		350.00
Blood administration		57.00
* Electrocardiogram		15.00
* X-rays		472.00
* Electroencephalogram		30.00
** Whole blood		140.00

Total hospital bill	$20,689.00
Total paid by Blue Cross Hospital Insurance	20,445.00
Paid by patient	244.00

---

* Blue Shield items paid in part.
** Payable by patient.
NOTE: Not included in above is surgeon's bill of $750.00 of which $397.00 was paid by Blue Shield.

HEALTH INSURANCE REVIEW

1. Hospital insurance: A good hospital policy should cover you for the prevailing hospital room rates in your area, for at least 60 to 120 days in the hospital, if not longer, and for laboratory tests, X-rays, anesthesia and other related expenses. Does yours?

2. If your hospital insurance gives limited coverage, only 21 days, for example, consider supplementing it with major medical insurance for protection against a long hospital siege.

3. Medical care and doctor-bill insurance: Will the benefits pay the standard doctor bills and surgery charges in your area? But don't expect a policy to pay for every potential doctor bill in full.

4. Does your doctor-bill insurance cover special treatment and emergency care provided outside of the hospital, in a doctor's office or at your home? More and more such insurance pays for such treatment and care outside of a hospital, as well as in.

5. Major medical insurance: What's the coverage of your policy? At least $20,000 is the minimum generally recommended today (unless you also have a good hospital insurance).

6. How much of an initial deductible is made before you are paid? What percentage of the balance of the bill does the company pay? Do you pay?

7. Do you need an "excess" major medical policy?

8. For all medical insurance: Is there a waiting period before you are covered for certain conditions or reasons for treatment?

9. Can you renew the policy automatically? Must certain provisions exist before renewal?

10. What exclusions or limitations does the policy contain?

11. How does the cost compare with that of other policies?

12. Can you obtain health insurance through a group plan at work or elsewhere?

13. Write for the booklet, *The New ABC's of Health Insurance*, free, from the Health Insurance Institute, Dept. W., 277 Park Ave., New York, N.Y. 10017.

the **law** and you

The trouble with lawyers is that some of them charge a lot of money for questionable services so that many people just avoid lawyers. Yet a good lawyer can provide important help and guidance at an important time, but how do you find a good one? A lawyer might be needed to get a good lease on a new apartment, to buy or sell a house, or to settle a dispute with a neighbor or City Hall, for a major legal entanglement, or in a hurry when a teenage son calls for SOS help at midnight from the police station.

You often can obtain quick legal counsel from a lawyer for a few dollars—no more than $10 to $15 usually—which could save you many times that fee, plus much time and trouble. How to do that plus other facts to know about lawyers are given in the next chapter, followed by a chapter on one of the most essential legal services to obtain from a lawyer, making a will and keeping it up to date.

23

how to get low-cost
legal counsel

The Lawyer Referral Service · The most common legal needs · Using a family lawyer · Choosing a lawyer for a special case · No-charge legal services · Basic fees charged for common legal services

You can now get low-cost legal counsel for a fixed fee—usually $5 to $10—in some cities in the country. That's for a half-hour conference with a private lawyer member of the local bar association. The price is as low as $3 in some cities up to $15 or so in others, such as affluent Beverly Hills, California.

This legal help is provided by the Lawyer Referral Service (LRS), organized on a nationwide basis by the American Bar Association and sponsored locally by many, though not all, local bar associations and by a growing number of state bar associations. It's not charity, either. Its purpose is to provide a lawyer quickly and inexpensively for anyone who needs legal help but doesn't know a lawyer, or fears that a lawyer would cost a lot of money.

Another purpose is to introduce more people to lawyers and more lawyers to potential clients, and thereby bridge the gap between lawyers and a lot of people who could use lawyers but do not. Of course, there are also lawyers who may charge you an arm and a leg for legal services, sometimes questionable services, and others who just squeaked by their bar examinations and who are no credit to the profession of law. But nearly all of us will experience problems at one time or another when a good lawyer can be of help, if not essential for getting us through a legal thicket.

The Lawyer Referral Service can enable you to take the first—and often final—step in solving many problems. More than 300,000 people a year use it throughout the country. That includes men and women in private need of legal counsel, many involved in starting up or running a small business, and even many diverse people, such as members of church, social and community groups in need of legal advice.

More than half of all the people using the LRS have their legal problems resolved during a single visit. If you require more than the initial half hour, a full hour is often available for an additional small charge. If the legalities involved require intensive study and attention, you are referred to another lawyer. His charge should be based on the standard local fee for the work involved. At the first meeting he should state his fee and spell out what he'll do for you. If he does not, you should ask, preferably right at the start of your discussion. Studies show that the great majority (over 90 percent) of the people who use the LRS come away satisfied with the results.

The greatest number of cases brought to the LRS each year concern family law, marital and juvenile problems, alimony, adoptions, and even name-changing. Other common categories include accident and personal injury cases, buying or selling a house, zoning and property taxes, disputes with landlords or neighbors, trusts, estates, and wills, contracts, installment loans, consumer credit, and criminal law.

The nearest LRS office should be listed in the Yellow Pages of your telephone directory under "Lawyer Referral Service" or "Legal (or Attorney's) Referral Service." The organization is active in all states but Alaska.

The LRS is sponsored in eleven states by the state bar association. It's that way in Illinois, for example, where you dial a toll-free number (800-252-8916) from anywhere in Illinois to be referred to a lawyer in your area. The cost in Illinois for the initial half-hour interview is $10, and some 175 lawyers located in most areas of the state participate in the program. Other statewide lawyer referral services operate in Delaware, Florida, Hawaii, Maine, New Hampshire, Michigan, Oregon, Rhode Island, Utah and Washington, as this is written; others are expected to be formed in the future.

If you need a lawyer and no LRS operates in your area, call the local bar association for the name of a lawyer or two who can help you. Any lawyer in the telephone book can direct you to the head of the bar association. When you arrange to see a lawyer, any lawyer, including one you appoint to see at the LRS, ask in advance for one who is experienced with the kind of legal problem you have. This is a need not always filled by the rotating lawyers provided by the LRS, so check in advance. It could be a waste of time and money seeing a lawyer whose specialty is criminal law but who has had little or no experience with the feud you're having with a relative over Uncle Joe's will.

The family lawyer

Having your own family lawyer can make sense since, like a family doctor, he knows you and he's there for help in time of need. You avoid wasting time on preliminaries when you must act fast. Getting yourself a good family lawyer is the standard gospel handed out by "experts," but the standard response, not necessarily voiced, is the concern about paying a lawyer to be on call at all times. Actually, it need not be that formal or expensive. Merely find a capable lawyer whom you like and use him, off and on, as the need arises. That could be for a will or buying or selling a house.

No matter how good a family lawyer is and no matter how good a friend he may be, there are times, however, when he's not the man to handle a special problem and particularly a major legal case for you. That could be if you're hit with a big negligence case (which requires an expert negligence attorney) or if the Internal Revenue Service hauls you in over a major tax question which calls for an expert tax man. Few lawyers know everything about all phases of the law, so when you need a specialist get a specialist. In fact, a good family lawyer will tell you this himself and even help you find such an expert. Some, scenting a big fee, however, may volunteer for specialty work that they are not qualified to handle.

Finding a specialist can require scouting and asking the president of the local bar association, for example, or a local bank for the name of a good tax or real estate lawyer, or at the courthouse for the lawyer specialist you need. If no help comes from such sources, consult a copy of the Martindale-Hubbell Law Directory, published by Martindale-Hubbell, Inc., available in reference libraries. It gives facts about lawyers, such as years of experience, and the nature of their practice.

Never hire a lawyer you dislike or cannot confide in. The lawyer-client relationship is too close and sensitive to be handicapped by personal dislike or lack of confidence. Moreover, if you find a lawyer you have hired unsatisfactory or if you seriously question his course of action for you, don't hesitate to voice your doubts. Inevitably, some lawyers are unsuitable for some people, and some people are unsuitable for some lawyers. Then it may be time to call it quits, but this should be by mutual agreement. It's not advisable, however, to switch lawyers in midstream. Once you've gone that far with a lawyer, it's seldom good to leave him and start from scratch with another lawyer. Besides, quitting a lawyer could have him put a "retaining lien" on the case until he gets his full fee. The fee, we emphasize, always should be nailed down in writing at the start. If you believe a lawyer is neglecting your case or not giving you competent counsel, there are grievance committees in every state which will hear your complaint and, if warranted, prod the lawyer or even punish him.

If you need a lawyer urgently and lack the money to pay for one, call the nearest Legal Aid Society. There are about 500 legal-aid groups in the country which do not charge for legal services. You must prove, however, that you are financially unable to pay for a private lawyer.

Typical legal fees

Different lawyers charge different fees for similar services. The fee is determined by the customary local charge for legal work, the time and research required, a lawyer's status and experience and the amount of money involved in the case.

Following is the range of *minimum fees* charged by lawyers for typical services. It is based largely on a survey by the American Bar Association. Minimum fee means the lowest charge recommended by the local bar association for a particular service. The price will seldom be less than the minimum in your area or less than those given below, but it can be more, especially if you require special legal attention.

Generally, legal fees tend to be on the low side in small towns and rural areas, particularly in the South, and highest in big cities, particularly in large industrial states. Many local bar associations have a schedule of recommended minimum fees for a particular service, though the fees charged are often higher.

▪ Administering an estate: $35 to $500 except in Florida, where it can go higher. This fee range is, naturally, for the smallest estates; minimum fees increase with the size and complexity of the estate.

▪ Consultation and office work: $10 to $50 an hour; highest in California, Ohio and New York; lowest in Mississippi.

■ Contract (involving a simple agreement, bill of sale, power of attorney, etc.): $25 to $150.

■ Uncontested adoption: $25 to $350; highest in New York, New Jersey and Ohio, lowest in Nebraska and Tennessee.

■ Uncontested divorce: $75 to $750 minimum in most places, except certain rich California towns, where it can cost as much as $1,000.

■ Buying or selling a house: $50 to $250, or .5% to 1% of the price of the house.

■ Examination of abstracts: $10 to $125.

■ Clearing title to property: $100 to $500, depending to a large extent on the size and value of the property.

■ Trial practice: $75 to $500 a day; less in a few states, depending on the time the lawyer is required to spend in court.

■ Organizing a business corporation: $150 to $500, though sometimes based on a percentage of the corporation's assets. This does not include other charges made by a state for incorporation papers.

■ Contingency fees: 25% to 50% of the amount collected for an accident, condemnation or other award; there is no charge if you lose the case (other than lawyer's disbursements for bonds, court fees, etc.).

Money sometimes can be saved by discreetly shopping around for a good lawyer whose fees are reasonable. Such shopping is easier in large cities and for certain services, such as probating a will and administering an estate. Also inquire about paying a lawyer a straight hourly charge for the actual work performed when his fee would otherwise be based on a percentage of the total money involved. According to Murray Teigh Bloom, author of the recent best seller, *The Trouble with Lawyers* (available in a $1.25 paperback), paying a lawyer an hourly fee to handle a simple estate, for example, often will cost much less than the usual charge based on a percentage of the total estate. On the other hand, remember that a good lawyer can be worth many times his fee when you add up the time, trouble and dollars he can save for you.

LEGAL REVIEW

1. Call on the Legal Referral Service for low-cost counsel. There is usually no need to eschew essential help from a lawyer because of the fear of a high fee.
2. If no LRS is available where you live, call the nearest bar association for a lawyer who can help you.
3. Get to know a good local lawyer whom you can count on in an emergency. In other words, have a family lawyer.

4. Use a lawyer who is a specialist for a serious legal problem.
5. Determine the fee promptly when you consult a lawyer, any lawyer. Know the approximate fees for special work, obtainable from the local bar association. If necessary, shop for a good lawyer, evaluating the qualifications of each for your work, his suitability for you, as well as his approximate fee. But a low fee should not be the deciding factor in choosing one.
6. Don't hesitate to question a lawyer whose performance for you seems inadequate, ineffective or incompetent. If necessary, report your problem to the grievance committee of the local bar association which, if justified, often can make a lawyer toe the line.
7. Two good books explain, among other things, facts about the law and what lawyers can and cannot do for you. They are *The Legal Encyclopedia for Home & Business* by Samuel G. Kling ($.95 in paperback), and *How to Avoid Lawyers* by Edward Siegel ($6.95 at bookstores).

24

why every man and woman
should have a **will**

*Reasons for a legal will · Common myths · Writing a will
properly · The cost of wills*

A will could be one of the most important documents you will ever sign in your life, yet an estimated 70 percent of all Americans who have reached legal age do not have wills. That's asking for trouble, especially since a will ordinarily can be drawn up quickly and at low cost.

■ Steve Willoughbe had always said, "Why should I bother with a will? If anything happens to me everything goes to Kathy and the kids." Besides, he was in the prime of life, a 32-year-old sales engineer with much going for him. But, returning home one fog-bound night, he was killed in a freak accident. His bank accounts were frozen and Kathy was plunged into a series of agonizing legal procedures. Steve had died intestate—without a will—and state law where he lived directed that two-thirds of his property go to the children, one-third to his wife. That's the law in most states and with no will most of the rest divide the money half to the widow, half to the surviving children. Kathy discovered that she had to apply to the court to be named administratrix of the estate as well as legal guardian for her three children. She had to post expensive bonds and must submit regular accountings to the court for all expenditures for the children until each reaches 21. Thus, no will is costing Kathy substantial fees for bond premiums and other costs, which is money she could well use for herself and the kids, and she must make continual trips

189

to attorneys' offices and the courthouse. Most if not all of this money, time and trouble could have been avoided if Steve had spent at hour or so to have a proper will written.

■ Jack Philpepper put his house in his wife's name and not long afterwards she died unexpectedly. They had no children and his state law decreed that a good portion of her estate, including his house, go to *her* closest blood relative, a ne'er-do-well brother with whom Jack had long feuded.

■ Phil Macdade was killed instantly in a car crash but his wife, Hazel, riding with him, lived three hours longer before she died. They had no children, and because Hazel outlived Phil all of his portion of their joint property and possessions first passed on to Hazel and then from her estate to her nearest relatives. Nothing went to Phil's widowed sister and children whose welfare had concerned him and whom he had been helping to support. They were left out in the cold.

Lawyers' files are filled with examples like those as a result of people dying intestate. A will is the only real assurance that money and property will be distributed as a person wants. It's how to minimize what could be stiff court expenses and estate settlement charges and also to prevent such things as taxes from taking an overlarge bite from one's estate. And it's usually the only way to guarantee that all of a man's money and property will pass on directly to his wife and children, or from a wife to her husband and the children, with no middlemen or court bureaucracy taking an excessive portion of the estate. The cold statistics say that more than eight out of ten wives outlive their husbands, which puts top-priority importance on a married man's having a will.

Many people don't have wills because of three common myths. They mistakenly believe that a surviving husband or wife always will automatically receive everything one owns. Others believe that their assets are so small that a will is unnecessary (another myth when you add up the value of personal possessions, such as house, car, bank balances, pension fund and profit-sharing rights, household furnishings and even life insurance). And third, making out a will is associated with the idea of death, which nobody likes to contemplate. The tendency to ignore it, however, is ignoring the future well-being of one's family. No man is immortal.

What's more, a will is not a will unless it's drawn properly, which requires adherence to the laws of your state. In most states, for example, a husband may not disinherit his wife without her prior consent, and conversely a wife generally may not disinherit her husband. That, by the way, has led to messed-up estates in cases where couples have fought bitterly and separated but never consummated a divorce. In such cases, the death of one could result in much, if not all, of that person's estate passing back to the hated separated spouse, though that is the last thing in the world desired. The will must be properly drawn to prevent this.

In short, you can't beat city hall and the local probate court without a good will. The cost is comparatively little, usually no more than $25 to about $50 for a simple will, plus 50 percent more for a second will done at the same time for a husband or wife. A complex will, setting up trusts, making special provisions and fulfilling special requirements, will generally cost from $250 to $500, more for a really elaborate document.

Many people disdain lawyers and write their own wills, but these have doubtful value. Such wills (called holographic wills), written and properly dated and signed, are valid only in about half the states. Even when valid they're often thrown out by the courts because the wording is unclear, inadequate or subject to other flaws. (Judges and lawyers have fine-tooth combs that can discover flaws in almost anything.) Some states, however, are more likely to accept a holographic will and even an oral will made by a member of the armed services overseas, provided it is properly witnessed.

So, alas, whether we like it or not, paying the fee and having a will drawn up properly by a lawyer is sound advice. Your will also should be reviewed and brought up to date periodically (you can't win) especially when you move to another state, when a witness to the will dies and when there is a change in your family status due to marriage, death of a close relative or children reaching 21.

The names of lawyers who can prepare a will for you should be obtainable from your local bar association, from the nearest Lawyer Referral Service or from friends or relatives. Get two or three names, if necessary, and call each. Determine the cost in advance. Sometimes money can be saved by writing your own will in advance and then having it checked by a lawyer, with changes made, if necessary, to make it valid. Or write down for the lawyer everything you want included in your will. In either case, you're saving time and trouble for the lawyer and may deserve a reduced fee.

REVIEW
1. Get a will and have it drawn up properly.
2. Keep your will up to date. It generally requires revision when you move to another state, when one or both witnesses die, following a change in family status for you, a close relative, or a beneficiary, and also due to changes in state laws which can occur at any time.
3. Don't rely on a do-it-yourself (holographic) will.

eight

a family **life insurance** checkup

The editors of *Consumer Reports* say, "Americans are sold on life insurance—yet they often spend more than they should to buy less than they need."

But unlike most things you may buy, many life-insurance policies can, after purchase, be modified, changed or even exchanged for better coverage and sometimes at lower cost and you could even get the equivalent of a refund on previous premiums paid. There is, in other words, excess fat in many policies now in force which can be trimmed to save you money with little or no loss in insurance.

Life insurance has played a vital role in family life ever since the first policy was sold to a London salt merchant, one William Gybbons, in 1583. But it need not be excessively expensive and it need not be a confusing thicket of incomprehensible legal print (often wrapped up in a fancy-name cover). The key to coping with your life insurance—and mastering it—is to check your insurance against a few fundamental facts about what *you* need, with no loopholes and at the best protection and lowest price.

25

the two best kinds
of **life insurance**

Determining how much insurance you need · Social Security benefits that reduce the insurance you need · "Term" insurance versus "straight life" · "Family," "limited payment" and endowment policies · "Buy term and invest the difference"

There are really only two basic considerations to resolve about a family's life insurance: How much life insurance do you really need? And what kind of policies should you buy to get it?

The answer to the first is simplified by concentrating life insurance on the family breadwinner, usually a husband and father. The second can be simplified greatly by narrowing down your choice to two different kinds of life insurance, term and straight life, and virtually forgetting about all the rest (unless you have a lot of money that you don't know what to do with).

How much insurance do you need?

One rule of thumb says a family man should have insurance equal to four to five times his annual income. Another says that his insurance should provide his wife and children with about 60 percent of his income. But these are starting points. To determine what you need, break down your insurance requirements like this, according to life stages:

■ Minimal monthly income for a family until the children are grown up (though this is less insurance than you may think because of Social Security benefits for a widow and children).

■ Educational fund for the children, which means enough money to get them started in college, but not necessarily a full packet of money for four years of college.

■ Estimated cash sum needed for final medical, burial and other expenses, plus readjustment money so that, among other things, a widow can return to work. (Insurance companies usually pay within a short time after receiving a copy of the death certificate plus the policy.)

■ Monthly income for a woman to live on until she qualifies for a Social Security retirement pension; then, if necessary, the reduced monthly income needed to augment Social Security payments.

■ Mortgage insurance for a widow to pay off a house mortgage.

■ Estate-tax insurance, a sum that might be required to help pay estate taxes at a time when the sale of securities or other property may be difficult or unwise. The greater one's wealth or potential estate, the greater the possible need for this, which can be important for a business or professional man.

Not everyone will require insurance to cover all of the specific points just cited above. Whatever your total insurance comes to, it's also a good idea to jack it up to allow for about 2 percent a year future inflation for the period spanned by your insurance. On the other hand, the amount of insurance required will be reduced according to the Social Security insurance you already have.

Counting in Social Security benefits

That money taken out of your paycheck every month for Social Security is not just for old age but it also offers some money-saving younger-age benefits, too, the equivalent of from about $50,000 to as much as $200,000 of life insurance. That's the effective value of payments a widow and children receive from Social Security on the death of a father—from about $250 up to $600 or so a month, depending on the number of children. It's paid monthly until children reach 18, plus additional payments for each child continuing in school until age 22. The exact monthly income you are entitled to varies from person to person and is determined from a statement of your account obtainable from the government, as described at the end of this chapter. Social Security benefits, of course, are paid only to those whose jobs are covered by it, including self-employed people. Most people are covered by it, receiving, in effect, a bundle of basic insurance at an important stage of life.

Social Security widow checks cease, however, when the last child grows up, leaving no benefits for a widowed woman until she reaches her sixties and qualifies for an old-age pension. That's called the widow's gap, a period in a woman's life when she may have no income, unless she goes to work or remarries. Neither of these possibilities is guaranteed, which ordinarily calls for plugging the widow's gap with life insurance.

Here's how a young couple we'll call Fred and Sally Gibson figured their insurance needs, using the basic requirements we mentioned above, though in a different order, and eliminating the last. They have three young children and Fred earns $12,000 a year. They sat down and worked out their initial figures like this:

1. For burial, medical, other immediate expenses upon death, plus paying off the car and other debts...... $ 3,000
2. To pay off the house mortgage.................. 20,000
3. $100 a month (in addition to Social Security payments) until the youngest child is 18, in this case for 16 years................................. 15,000
4. Minimum fund to get the children started in college. Later this fund will be increased with savings or additional insurance............................. 5,000
5. Widow income of $100 a month for 20 years. This is from the time the youngest child reaches 18 until the widow is 62............................. 18,000
6. $75 a month for 15 years starting at age 62 (which is really thinking ahead) to supplement Social Security retirement checks...................... 11,000

Estimated Total Insurance....................... $72,000

That's a lot of insurance and more than the Gibsons could afford, especially when the first salesman they talked to blithely quoted a cost of over $1,000 a year for $72,000 of insurance. Like most people, therefore, they started to prune.

They had some money in the bank and certain assets, which came to about $3,000. They cut that much from their total. In addition, Sally figured that if her husband died, she could sell their house when the children were grown, invest the money to live on and, if necessary, find a job. That would cut out another $18,000 in insurance (the "widow income"). Fred had a $20,000 policy where he worked. In all, they figured that they could safely aim for $40,000 of insurance now. They might get more later, if and when they could afford more.

That's the usual trial-and-error method by which you estimate the total insurance you will need versus the minimum you can afford now. More-over, $40,000 of insurance is by no means a huge sum for a family with three children and $12,000 a year income. As you can see, and counting in Fred's $20,000 of insurance at work, it's exactly five times his annual salary.

What's more, that much insurance need not cost a small fortune. The Gibsons' agent had recommended a $40,000-insurance plan for $764 a year, which included an endowment policy for the children. But that was more than they could pay. The agent dug into his briefcase and came up with another $40,000 plan for $585, which eliminated the expensive endowment policy.

The Gibsons persisted. They thought they could do even better than that. Very sensibly, they wanted, above all, adequate insurance on Fred. The agent dug deeper into his bag and came up with his large, economy-size insurance plan, also for $40,000, but this time for only $196 a year, or less than $17 a month. It was what is called term insurance and all on Fred, their first concern. If they can afford it later, they may buy other insurance and also start a separate investment savings program. Right now, however, their main concern is getting adequate insurance at the lowest possible cost.

This experience illustrates why the total amount of insurance you need, however great a sum it may seem, does not have to overwhelm you. The price you pay for it hinges greatly on the specific type you buy.

The two best types of insurance

Actually, there's no best insurance for everybody, but for most people two of the best are *term* insurance, the kind the Gibsons loaded up with, and *straight life* insurance. With few exceptions, we think that one or both of these can provide excellent all-around insurance for most people, and you can forget all the rest.

Term insurance is cheapest of all. It is sold for a specified period of time, or "term," usually 5, 10 or 20 years. Generally, it is renewable at the end of each term until you are 65, but the price, or "premium," goes up on each renewal.

Term insurance is cheap, because it is pure, stripped-down insurance.

It provides for payment of a specified sum of money on the death of the policyholder. If the policy is canceled or dropped or runs out before the death of the insured, however, that's it. Unlike straight life insurance, described in a moment, you get no money back from term insurance. It has no cash value; like fire or auto insurance, it simply provides protection for a stated length of time.

There are two kinds of term insurance, *level term* and *decreasing term*. A five-year, level-term $10,000 policy, for instance, provides $10,000 of insurance for five years. To be sure that it can be renewed after the five-year period, you should get "renewable" term. This costs slightly more than nonrenewable term, but you can renew it to the age of 65 with no need for further medical examinations; remember, though, that the premium goes up each time it's renewed.

A decreasing term policy falls off in value each year. It costs even less than level term, since with decreasing term you get a little less insurance each year. It is ideal for meeting decreasing insurance needs, such as providing enough money for a wife to pay off a house mortgage if her husband dies before this has been done.

Take that $20,000 mortgage the Gibsons have, for example, which has 20 years to run. They can get a 20-year decreasing term policy for $20,000. Each year as the mortgage is reduced by $400 to $500, the insurance coverage drops off by about the same amount. Say that Fred happens to be one of the three of every ten men who do not live to 65 and there's $6,000 due on the mortgage when he dies. The insurance, having declined at about the same rate as the mortgage each year, will provide the needed $6,000. A good agent can get a decreasing term policy to match almost any mortgage.

Banks and other financing agencies also sell such insurance, making it part of the mortgage package, although the cost could be a little more than if a family buys its own decreasing term policy. Also a policy built into a mortgage usually stipulates that the insurance money automatically goes to the mortgage lender to pay off the mortgage. But a woman may have more urgent needs for the money. A family considering such a policy should decide whether or not the mortgage lender should receive the money and make sure that the policy reflects its choice. If you already have such a policy, you can check the relevant clause and ask to have it changed if you wish.

Straight life insurance (also called "ordinary" or "whole" life) generally costs about three to four times as much as five-year term insurance. But with straight life the yearly cost, its premium, remains the same for the rest of your life, unlike term insurance whose cost, as we have seen, goes up at each renewal interval. And the earlier you buy a straight life policy, the lower this yearly cost will be, since the cost reflects the statistical fact that the younger a person is, the longer he is likely to live.

The premiums for straight life remain steady over the years because insurance companies base the cost of insuring a person for the "whole" of his life, for statistical reasons usually set at 95 or 100 years. Then the companies strike a yearly average. Compared with term insurance, then, a man pays more for straight life when he is young and less for it when he is older; the same for a woman.

For instance, if a man takes out a straight life policy when he is in his twenties or thirties, he will be paying more for it than for the same amount of term insurance until he gets to be about 50 or 55. At that crossover point, however, term insurance is more expensive—and it continues to go up in price at the regular renewal dates until the age of 65. After that, term insurance is usually unobtainable. This, of course, is a point in favor of straight life. If you believe you will want insurance in your later years, particularly after 65—as many people do—you should buy at least some straight life.

Straight life has another advantage. It is "cash-value" insurance. Part of the premium paid each year goes toward guaranteeing that if, for example, a man who has a $10,000 policy dies, his beneficiary will receive $10,000. But the rest of the premium goes toward building up the cash value of his policy during his lifetime. The exact cash value varies from company to company, but you can always tell what the cash value of a straight life policy is at any time, now or in the future, by consulting a table in the policy.

Insurance companies also pay compound interest on the cash value building up in a policy—usually $2\frac{1}{2}$ percent to $3\frac{1}{2}$ percent—so that the money "saved" inside the policy grows each year by that much. The cash value becomes yours, however, only if the policy is cashed in, in which case, of course, you lose your insurance coverage. But in case of emergency you may cash it in at any time. If you don't want to do that, but still need money, you may borrow on your policy from the insurance company with little difficulty, as explained later.

A straight life policy is also versatile. You can add term insurance to it as a "rider," to fill gaps in your insurance coverage, and the term insurance will be a little cheaper than the same amount bought separately.

One of the most popular term riders often added to straight life is the "family-income" rider. This can assure a woman an income of say, $50,

$100 or $200 monthly after the death of her husband, the policyholder, until a stipulated year in the future, until, for instance, the youngest child is 18, at which time the income would come to an end.

You may be told that the only way to buy such insurance is as a rider to a straight life policy, but this isn't true. A family-income rider is actually decreasing term insurance with a catchy name. You can get the very same insurance with a separately bought decreasing term policy— simply tell the agent how much monthly income you want and the period you want it to span. You may have to pay a little more for it than for a comparable family-income rider, but on the other hand you can buy it at any time without having to buy a straight life policy at the same time.

"Modified life"

This is a special low-cost version of straight life insurance and the cheapest of all cash value insurance. It's a policy whose coverage automatically is reduced, usually in half, at age 65 or 70. A $10,000 modified life policy, for example, gives you that much insurance plus the usual build-up of internal cash value, but at 65 or 70—you decide which—the coverage is automatically reduced in half, or $5,000 in this case. That's all right for many people because at that age one's insurance needs are usually reduced. The big advantage of modified life is that its cost can be decidedly less than that of a comparable straight life policy.

Another form of modified life is tailored for a young married couple on a lean budget. It is basically a straight life policy with a reduced premium cost for the first three to five years, sometimes longer. During that period the cash value of the policy builds up more slowly than in a regular straight life policy, but after the initial "modified" period, the policy automatically becomes a regular straight life policy with regular cash-value build-up and the annual premium cost also goes up to the price of a regular straight life policy. The advantage is that the premium is based on the age of the buyer at the time he initially takes out the policy. That means a lower cost for the insurance compared with waiting a few years and then taking out the same amount of straight life insurance. The exact terms and prices for such policies vary from company to company.

Modified life insurance is now available for veterans of World War II and later who still have GI insurance from those days. Such GI insurance generally can be converted now or anytime later to modified life, and in many cases this can be a good thing. Get details from your nearest Veterans Administration office.

The "family policy"

A *family* policy is the next step up from straight life, costing more because it insures a father, mother and children in one package. It may sound like a good way to get the whole family insured at a bargain rate, but this is not necessarily so.

A family policy is actually straight life insurance on the father, usually combined with a smaller term policy on the mother, plus term insurance on each child. But remember that, unlike a shipboard emergency where the rule is "women and children first," the first rule with life insurance is "men first." Because the man is usually the chief source of a family's income, insurance on other family members is not recommended until he is fully insured.

If a wife and mother also works, the loss of income that her death would occasion should be taken into consideration, of course. But in most families, for practical reasons, adequate life insurance on the father takes priority. For one thing, there's the mortality-table fact that more than eight out of every ten women outlive their husbands (a grim fact for men, perhaps, but as women's lib progresses and more women go to work and undergo the stress and pressure of workaday jobs the mortality figures may change in the future toward more of an actuarial balance in life spans between men and women).

For another, after a husband is adequately insured it is always possible to insure a wife, assuming the money's there to buy additional insurance. At that time, insurance for a nonworking wife also may be advisable. After all, replacing a wife with a paid housekeeper can cost money, which is the main purpose of such insurance.

As for children's insurance, it's a highly questionable expenditure and generally unnecessary. One reason given for it is to cover final medical bills and funeral expenses in case of a child's death. But many families have medical insurance to pay such bills and, coldly speaking, funeral costs can be offset by that part of a family's expense that went into the care of the child.

Some agents also promote insurance for a child to be sure he will have it when he is grown. They stress the possibility that childhood diseases or a hazardous occupation as an adult may disqualify him for insurance but if he has a policy as a child, he can retain it as an adult. This is largely nonsense. Such possibilities are very slim, and the amount of insurance usually recommended for a child would hardly be enough to protect him and his family in later years. Saving for children in bonds, a bank account or a mutual fund seems a wiser course, and certainly children themselves are best protected if their father is adequately insured.

"Limited life"

This is the next step up in cost, a cash-value policy whose premiums are so geared that the policy will be entirely paid for in a certain number of years. For instance, with "30-payment life" a man bunches up his total lifetime insurance premiums, paying steeper premiums than for straight life, so that after 30 years he will no longer have to pay premiums at all; his insurance is paid for life. There is also 20-payment life, with even greater bunching up and thus steeper premiums over a shorter time span. But the higher cost makes these policies impractical for most families. Limited life policies are advantageous mainly for people whose peak earnings come early, like movie stars and ballplayers.

The "endowment" policy

The whole idea of spending a lot of money for insurance reaches the peak of folly in an endowment policy, especially for a married couple hard put to bring up children in these days of high-cost inflation. The endowment policy was at one time a favored way to provide for a child's education, but no longer. It's a policy written for a specific period of time, say 20 or 30 years, or to a specific age, often 65. If the policyholder dies in that period, his beneficiary receives the face amount of the policy; if he lives, the amount is paid to him.

Although endowment policies have been widely sold as a way for parents to save for their children's college education, most insurance experts say that there are better ways to do this. The Public Affairs Committee, a nonprofit consumer-education group, calls them "ill-suited," pointing out that premiums are so high for a really adequate college endowment that paying them is often a hardship. A top New York insurance agent, David Mack, generally recommends that a family buy term or straight life instead of an endowment and put the difference in cost into savings bonds or a portion into a good mutual fund for later use in paying for college.

Which type of insurance for you?

Term or straight life, as we have seen, are the two most practical kinds of life insurance for most families when cost and protection are considered. When should you have one or the other?

Because term provides the most insurance for the least money, it's particularly good for a young family on a tight budget. It is often the only way a family can obtain all the insurance it needs at a price it can afford. Term also excels in providing blocks of insurance for specified periods. When children are growing up, for instance, their father needs more insurance than when they are self-supporting, and at that point he can drop blocks of term insurance.

Of course, the cost of term insurance rises periodically, usually every five years, but the increase is not great for people in their twenties, thirties or even forties. And if a man buys "convertible" term policies, which cost a little more, he can switch them later to straight life without a new physical examination. That would be at a time when his earnings will have increased and he can afford to pay the higher premiums for cash-value insurance.

Straight life, on the other hand, bought at an early age, may be a better bet for the insurance you may desire throughout life, since the annual premium stays the same every year and you can continue such insurance after the age of 65 (when term insurance is unobtainable). Also, straight life builds a growing cash-value cushion on which a family can draw in time of emergency. When insurance needs are reduced—when children are grown and a man retires on a pension plus Social Security income— a straight life policy can be turned in for its cash value. A $10,000 policy bought when you're in your twenties or thirties would generally pay you about $6,000 to $6,500 if cashed in at age 65 (which, by the way, is usually a little more than it will have cost you over the years.) You'll get back less cash from a "modified" straight life policy but this policy will have cost you less.

"Buy term and save the difference"

This brings up what is probably the most controversial question concerning life insurance today: Should you use insurance as a crutch to force you to save?

Many authorities believe that families who use insurance as a way to save money are making a big mistake. They say flatly, "Buy term and save the difference." In other words, buy the cheapest term insurance and put the difference in cost between it and higher-priced cash-value insurance into savings that earn interest at a higher rate than the 2½ or 3 percent that insurance savings usually pay. A study by *Consumer Report* shows that you not only will get just as much insurance, but that you'll be better off financially in later years if you follow through consistently.

How it works

Consider, for example, twin brothers, saver Sam and life-insurance Mike, who disagreed about how to buy life insurance. Sam was a believer in buying term and saving the difference, so at age 25 he bought $50,000 worth of term insurance for $240 a year. That much straight life insurance would have cost him about $680 a year for life. He put the difference in cost ($440) into a savings account. Every five years his insurance cost rises, but as his separate savings grow, they amount to "insurance" too, and he gradually reduces his term insurance by an equal amount. According to a *Consumer Reports'* study, at the age of 65 his total separate savings will amount to about $28,000, based on an average return from his savings of 3½ percent interest a year. (Many banks today pay as much as 6 percent, but the conservative 3½ percent figure is used to reflect the fact that bank interest fluctuates and can fall as well as rise. He will also owe income taxes each year on the interest earned but 3½ percent interest is his assumed net return after income taxes.)

Brother Mike goes the other route and at 25 buys a $50,000 straight life policy for a steady $680 a year. When he is 65, the cash value of his policy will also total $28,000, more or less, depending on the company he bought it from. He could cash in his policy at 65 and would be, it seems, just about as well off as his brother who saved his money separately.

But by buying term and consistently saving the difference in cost between it and straight life, Sam has two other things going for him. First, his separate savings grow faster than the cash value in a straight life policy because they grow at a higher interest rate. If he should die before he reaches 65, his family would get, depending upon his age, anywhere from $400 to nearly $5,000 more money all told—insurance plus separate savings—than it would get if he left only a $50,000 straight life policy.

Second, Sam can always draw on his separate savings account in an emergency. Brother Mike can borrow against the growing cash value in his straight life policy, but he must pay interest on what he borrows.

The really big advantage of saving by yourself shows up if you get more than 3½ percent interest on it, which isn't very hard to do. You can get 5½ percent-a-year interest today from government savings bonds and up to 6 percent or more from other risk-free government bonds as well as from banks. Save the difference in cost between $50,000 of term and straight life and at the age of 65 a man would have a tidy nest egg worth about $35,000 to $45,000, depending on the return on his savings and the age at which he started. That's up to $17,000 more than he and his family would get from a $50,000 straight life policy if he converted it to cash at the age of 65.

If you really want to shoot high, you might invest the separate savings in blue-chip stocks, or in a good common-stock mutual fund that could well bring an average return of over 6 percent a year. That is by no means a farfetched expectation; since 1945 about half of all mutual funds have grown at an average rate of 10 percent a year or better.

If saver Sam starts his program at age 25, and receives an average of 6 percent a year net on his separate savings, he would really be in clover at age 65. Then all his term insurance expires but his separate savings account will amount to $67,000!

Sounds great, doesn't it? It will be, but *only* if you diligently follow through each year and really save the difference in cost between straight life insurance and term insurance. That's the catch, as many an insurance man is eager to point out. Be realistic and hard-headed about it, and the fact is that most of us are jellyfish and really don't have the self-discipline to follow through on a separate savings program. Besides, that separate savings account is so temptingly easy to draw on at any time that it could easily be milked, off and on, for nonemergency use and as a result reduce your total "insurance" backup fund.

Your financial situation in later years could be precarious. You might protect your family with term insurance, but wind up with no savings and no insurance later. Then you might look back sadly and wish that you had bought straight life.

Thus, the choice between term and straight life (or any other cash-value insurance) really comes down to whether or not you can save regularly, in a disciplined manner, or whether you need to be forced to save.

There are, of course, other ways besides insurance in which you can force yourself to save—automatic payroll-deduction plans, monthly investment plans or automatic transfers by your bank from a checking account to a savings account. There are also mutual-fund savings plans that combine the purchase of life insurance with an investment program, an excellent way to combine low-cost term insurance with investments, particularly for children's education.

However, you need not choose all of one or the other. You could hedge and buy some insurance, save or invest some money on your own and buy some straight life insurance. Try one or the other for a few years to determine which combination works out best for you and then you can concentrate on that method.

Life insurance costs: Typical annual premiums for $10,000 of life insurance

"Participating" insurance

Male age	25	30	35
5-Yr. Term (R & C)*	$ 50.10	$ 54.20	$ 62.00
20-Yr. Decreasing Term	38.40	43.40	46.20
Straight Life	156.60	183.70	218.80
Family Plan	219.30	247.10	287.46
20-Payment Life	280.10	309.00	343.70
30-Payment Life	220.70	243.90	278.50
20-Yr. Endowment	471.90	477.60	487.40

"Nonparticipating" insurance

Male age	25	30	35
5-Yr. Term (R & C)*	$ 55.00	$ 56.80	$ 65.40
20-Yr. Decreasing Term	45.60	48.76	56.00
Straight Life	132.70	188.70	218.00
Family Plan	219.30	247.00	283.10
20-Payment Life	280.10	209.06	343.30
30-Payment Life	220.10	243.90	273.50
20-Yr. Endowment	471.90	477.60	487.40

* Renewable and Convertible.
NOTE: The table above lists average annual costs from two typical life insurance companies. Rates for other companies may be higher or lower. Though the price varies greatly according to the kind of policy, in each case the amount of insurance is constant—$10,000. The cost for more or less than $10,000 of insurance will be roughly proportionate. Annual premiums for "participating" policies are higher than for "nonparticipating" policies. But a policyholder generally can expect an annual dividend paid back to him on a participating policy, so its net cost may be as low as or lower than the cost of nonparticipating insurance, which does not pay a dividend.
SOURCE: Institute of Life Insurance.

26

life insurance questions and answers

Buying the lowest-cost insurance · Dividend versus non-dividend insurance · Choosing a beneficiary · How insurance proceeds are paid · How to compare prices and shop for a good policy · Special features to include in policies

First, look for low-cost group insurance, or more of it, at work or from a union or fraternal or other association, or such groups as the Institute of Electrical and Electronics Engineers (one of the best group plans of all) or the Teachers Insurance and Annuity Association (TIAA). Get facts and prices and compare with other insurance available.

If you live or work in New York, Connecticut or Massachusetts, one of the best buys of all is savings-bank life insurance, available only in these three states. It's generally 10 to 15 percent cheaper than standard insurance; some kinds, such as savings-bank term insurance, are 30 to 40 percent cheaper and savings-bank insurance also pays high dividends. You must write or see a savings bank for it, because it is not sold by agents. (There is a ceiling, however, on the top amount of savings-bank insurance you may buy, depending on the state. In New York State, for example, the ceiling is $30,000 per person.)

Some 1,700 different companies sell life insurance in the U.S. and they vary greatly in size, competence and value received per dollar of insurance bought. Like health and other insurance, life insurance should be bought only from a company licensed to sell insurance in your state.

Settling a claim with a company not so licensed could be troublesome and expensive. The states in which a company is licensed to do business are sometimes listed in the company's sales literature. This and other information about an insurance company, including its financial rating, also can be had from the industry guidebook, *Best's Life Insurance Reports*, available at some libraries or through your insurance agent.

Only about 370 of the more than 1,700 life-insurance companies in the United States are recommended in *Best's*. In general, these are the biggest and best-established companies, recommended "for soundness, stability, permanence of operation, and safety from the viewpoint of the policyholder." If an agent says he does not have this book for you to see, the chances are that his company is not recommended and you may do better with another company.

About 55 to 60 percent of all regular life insurance is sold by "mutual" companies, which are supposed to operate for the mutual benefit of their policyholders. The rest are stock companies, owned and operated to make a profit for their stockholders. Experts say, however, that buying from a mutual company is not necessarily better than buying from a stock company.

Insurance that pays dividends

Some insurance policies pay you an annual dividend—a percentage of your premium returned to you at the end of the year—while others do not pay dividends. Dividends are paid by most mutual companies but only by some stock companies.

Life insurance that pays you an annual dividend is called "participating" insurance. You participate in the annual surplus, if any, and your net cost therefore is the annual premium you pay *less* the dividend returned. But dividends are not guaranteed; they may increase or decrease from year to year and could even be abolished if a company falls on hard times.

There is also "nonparticipating" insurance, which is sold chiefly by stock companies. You get back no annual dividend, but the price you pay (its annual premium) for this insurance can be as much as 25 percent lower than the list-price premium for the same amount of insurance from a company that pays dividends. The difference in premiums between typical participating and nonparticipating insurance policies is shown in the accompanying table.

However, since the end of World War II, dividend life insurance (the participating kind) has generally been lower in cost than nondividend (nonparticipating) insurance. Though you pay a somewhat higher annual premium for a dividend-paying policy, the money returned each year in dividends has more than offset its higher premium cost. Dividend insurance from most companies is also cheaper according to an exhaustive 1972 study of insurance costs by Dr. Herbert Denenberg, Commissioner of Insurance for the State of Pennsylvania. Denenberg's study (below) gives the 10 companies selling the lowest-cost life insurance in Pennsylvania and the 10 companies there with the highest-cost life insurance. Nine of the 10 companies with the lowest-cost, best buys in insurance are companies that sell dividend-paying policies. Eight of the highest-cost companies sell nonparticipating insurance that pays no dividends. All other things being reasonably equal, therefore, you'll generally save money by buying insurance that pays dividends.

The "fifth-dividend" option

When you buy dividend-paying insurance, shop for the kind that offers what is called the "fifth-dividend option." This little-publicized option is one of the biggest bargains available in cash-value insurance. It can give you from 50 to over 100 percent more insurance coverage each year at no increase in the premium paid.

With a $10,000 straight life policy, for example, you can get from $5,000 to as much as $12,000 of additional term insurance a year added to the policy, thus a total of from $15,000 to about $22,000 from a basic $10,000 policy. You get it only from dividend-paying companies by letting the company retain the dividend. In return, the chunk of extra insurance received can help you reach the total insurance you need at the lowest possible cost. But you must buy from a company that gives you the benefit of what agents call the "full" fifth-dividend option. Many companies offering the option put a ceiling on the amount of extra insurance that can be bought each year in lieu of dividend, sharply restricting the cheap extra insurance obtainable. (In this case you may be better off using the dividends to reduce premium payments.) The full fifth-dividend option is offered by the banks that sell savings bank insurance and by many mutual companies.

Besides leaving your dividends with the company and obtaining extra insurance for them, dividends can be used to reduce your annual premium or left with the company to earn interest. This last, however, could cost you money because of the low-interest rate paid by some companies. You might do better by taking the dividends and putting them in a bank at a higher interest rate.

The 10 best and worst buys in life insurance

Best buys	Average annual cost
1. The Bankers Life (Iowa)	$61.97
2. Home Life	64.03
3. National Life (Vt.)	66.80
4. Connecticut Mutual Life	67.27
5. Phoenix Mutual Life	67.63
6. Northwestern Mutual Life	67.87
7. Central Life Assurance (Iowa)	68.33
8. State Mutual Life (Mass.)	70.17
9. Modern Woodmen of America	70.40
10. Lutheran Mutual Life	70.60

Worst buys

1. Georgia International Life	$119.30
2. The State Life (Ind.)	114.67
3. Valley Forge Life	113.77
4. Old Republic Life	113.07
5. Pennsylvania Life	112.77
6. Puritan Life	111.13
7. Security Life & Accident (Colo.)	110.80
8. The Travelers	110.73
9. Monumental Life	110.53
10. Government Personnel Mutual Life	110.20

NOTE: Above figures are based on the average annual cost for a $10,000 straight life cash-value insurance policy over a 20-year period. All but one (Modern Woodmen of America) of the 10 best buys are insurance policies that pay dividends. Eight of the 10 worst buys are nondividend-paying insurance companies; the two that pay dividends are The State Life (Ind.) and Security Life & Accident (Colo.). The cost figures are the average annual net cost of policies for people of different ages. They are what insurance men call "interest-adjusted cost figures," which take into account such things as cash value build-up, dividends, if any, as well as premiums. The figures reflect the cost in 1972 of insurance sold only by 165 companies which sell in the state of Pennsylvania.

SOURCE: *A Shopper's Guide to Life Insurance*, available for 25 cents from the Pennsylvania Building Insurance Dept., Harrisburg, Pa. 17120; enclose a stamped, return-addressed envelope.

Are your beneficiaries up-to-date?

One young man neglected to change his insurance beneficiary when he got married. He died prematurely and his insurance proceeds went to his mother; his wife and child were left out in the cold. Another mistake sometimes made is failure to add new children as beneficiaries to policies bought before their birth. (It's usually better, however, not to name children as beneficiaries. That's because money left to underage children can be tied up by the courts, costing a widow and her children considerable time and expense, just as it can when a person dies without a will. The problem can be avoided, however, by leaving insurance to children through an executor named in a policy or named in a will. The law on this can vary from state to state.)

How should your insurance be paid?

There are four usual options:

1. Lump-sum payment to the beneficiary. A beneficiary can then draw part or all of the money, use some for the inevitable expenses following death, invest the rest, or leave part or all of the rest of the proceeds to be disbursed in any of the other three following methods.

2. The proceeds are paid in monthly installments over a period of years, which depends on the amount of the insurance. A typical $10,000 policy will, for example, pay you about $100 a month for a little over nine years, or pay about $95 a month for 10 years. If an emergency requires a lump sum payment and the beneficiary also has the right to exercise option 1, above, he or she could draw out the money needed, but then, of course, less money remains to be paid in future monthly installments.

3. The proceeds are converted to an annuity paying a stipulated income for life, "life income," regardless of how long the beneficiary lives. A $10,000 policy would pay a 65-year-old woman a life income of about $75 a month, more or less, or about $900 a year. But it stops on her death. If she lives long, it would mean a substantial return; if not, it's a small return. Or the proceeds can be paid as "life income with installments certain" for the beneficiary for a stipulated period, such as 10, 15 or 20 years. If the principal beneficiary dies before the end of the period, the payments continue to his or her designated beneficiary.

4. The proceeds are left with the insurance company and earn interest which is paid to the beneficiary. But remember that some insurance companies pay a mere 2½ or 3 percent a year interest while others pay

up to 6 percent and a company could at any time change the interest rate paid, so that this option is a questionable one.

Since no one can foresee future needs, it's generally best not to tie the hands of a beneficiary by limiting the method of paying insurance proceeds. It's generally best, therefore, to give a beneficiary the right to choose any or all payment plans.

On the other hand, stories abound of people who squander large insurance payments and others who unknowingly short-change themselves by choosing to receive insurance proceeds in an uneconomical way. If one has doubts about the money-handling capability of his beneficiary, the method of insurance disbursement will require serious consideration. Discuss it with your insurance man. A husband and wife should also discuss this, even though it bears on the subject of death, which some people cannot accept. Nearly every beneficiary should be allowed to draw out at least a portion of the proceeds of insurance in a lump sum, with the rest, if desired, being directed to a dependable trustee or executor of one's estate to save or invest for the beneficiaries.

How can an existing policy be changed or improved?

Virtually every policy can at any time be scaled down in coverage on written instructions from the policyholder (you). A $10,000 policy, for example, can be changed to any lower sum, such as $5,000, and the premium reduced accordingly. Some cash-value policies can be scaled down in type of policy, thus a reduced annual premium cost, but no reduction in policy coverage. An endowment or 20- or 30-payment life policy, for instance, usually can be scaled down to a basic straight life, and its annual premium is not only reduced, but often you will also receive a refund because of the reduced cash-value schedule for the scaled-down policy. And, depending on the company, many cash-value policies, including the straight-life type, can be changed to modified life insurance at a lower annual cost. Remember, though, that the insurance coverage will be automatically reduced at age 65 or 70, as described in the preceding chapter.

When should existing insurance be cancelled and replaced?

Almost never, except when a policy is no longer desired or needed. A favorite game of some slick insurance salesmen is persuading people to cancel old policies in favor of buying new ones that are purportedly better. This can be an expensive trap because new insurance almost inevitably costs you more than the same sum of insurance bought in the past at a younger age. That is immutable insurance law, the older you are, the more you pay per dollar of insurance.

Before cashing in an old policy, call in someone from the company who sold it to you to check the new proposal and possibly counter with an even better proposition. Often an old policy can be changed, modified or peeled-down, as mentioned above, without losing its low-cost advantage based on your age when you bought it. In some rare instances, new insurance may be better than an old policy, but in most cases, an old policy can't be beat on cost, though sometimes it must be modified to compete with a new policy.

How do you shop for low-cost insurance?

Not everyone can buy group or savings bank insurance, generally the lowest cost of all life insurance, and, besides, people who may buy such policies usually need at least some additional private-company insurance. Obviously, you will want to buy insurance from a company with a low price, compared with another whose price is high. But when shopping for insurance and comparing prices you must draw a line between the purchase of term and cash-value insurance.

Term insurance is easier to compare and price, since its premium cost by and large is a good indication of its true actual cost to you. Merely compare the premium charged for a term policy with that charged for the same term insurance offered by another company and this will generally tell you quickly which is cheaper. Though price is important, remember that other factors (discussed elsewhere) are also important.

Determining the true cost of cash-value insurance is another matter, however. The price for life insurance sold by the more than 1,700 companies in the business not only varies from company to company, but also the price on the package (the policy) is not its true cost. As we have seen, the premium is usually lower for nondividend insurance than for dividend insurance, but a dividend-paying policy is often cheaper because of the dividends paid. Other factors, like cash-value build-up, also affect cost, which makes it difficult for anyone but an expert to determine true insurance cost. You can, however, request from each insurance agent you talk to the "interest-adjusted cost" of his policy. That's now considered the closest indication of true cost to you. Then compare that cost figure with the cost of insurance sold by the 50 lowest-cost companies in Pennsylvania, shown in the table starting on the next page.

Should you buy a lot of insurance at once?

Generally yes, because insurance is cheaper by the dozen. The more you buy at one time from one company, the lower the cost per $1,000; therefore, it can pay to concentrate your insurance. Some companies drop the price per $1,000 at every $5,000 to $10,000 purchased. Others drop the price a little for each additional $1,000 of insurance. It may pay, therefore, to investigate these "discounts" and possibly boost your insurance up to the next step for increased protection at low additional cost.

How do you find a good insurance agent?

The same way you find a good doctor, lawyer or repairman: Get recommendations from friends, relatives or others whose opinions you trust. Insurance expert James Gollin, author of the book *Pay Now, Die Later,* also says deal only with an agent who has been in the business for at least five years. That's an arbitrary rule, to be sure. Many young men selling life insurance may be perfectly dependable, but a seasoned agent with more than a few years of experience under his belt can be invaluable. Moreover, a large percentage of new agents don't last long. One who has stuck it out for at least five years, in addition to knowing what he's talking about, is also more likely to be around in later years when you may need him for guidance.

The cost of life insurance sold by 50 large companies

Here is the average annual cost of a $10,000 straight life policy sold by the 50 lowest-cost life-insurance companies in the state of Pennsylvania. The figures were developed by Pennsylvania's Commissioner of Insurance, Herbert S. Denenberg, and they are costs only for large companies (166 in all) licensed to sell insurance in Pennsylvania. Other companies that are small or sell insurance elsewhere but not in Pennsylvania may offer lower-cost policies—or higher-cost. Notice how the premium charged by different companies can be misleading; the average annual cost to you is the important figure. Also see notes at the bottom of the table.

Company	Male age 20 or female age 23			Male age 35 or female age 38			Male age 50 or female age 53		
	Annual premium	Average yearly cost of insurance	Ranking at age 20/23	Annual premium	Average yearly cost of insurance	Ranking at age 35/38	Annual premium	Average yearly cost of insurance	Ranking at age 50/53
1. Bankers Life Company (Iowa)	$149.70	$24.70	3	$229.10	$42.00	1	$400.30	$119.20	1
2. Home Life Ins. Co. (NY)	150.70	23.10	2	228.40	43.10	2	405.10	125.90	3
3. National Life Ins. Co. (VT)	152.70	28.30	5	230.30	46.30	4	389.80	125.80	2
4. Connecticut Mutual Life Ins. Co.	135.00	22.40	1	218.50	46.70	5	397.70	132.70	9
5. Phoenix Mutual Life Ins. Co.	157.00	26.60	4	233.60	48.60	6	392.50	127.70	4
6. The Northwestern Mutual Life Ins. Co.	157.40	28.70	6	234.80	45.50	3	405.40	129.40	6
7. State Mutual Life Assurance Co. of America (Mass.)	149.50	28.80	7	231.60	49.00	7	408.30	132.70	9
8. Massachusetts Mutual Life Ins. Co.	156.30	29.50	10	236.10	50.00	8	407.90	131.40	8
9. New England Mutual Life Ins. Co.	155.20	31.70	13	232.50	50.50	10	398.80	129.70	7
10. New York Life Ins. Co.	152.40	32.50	17	233.40	52.40	13	400.50	127.70	4
11. Sun Life Assurance Co. of Canada	153.30	29.10	8	234.00	50.10	9	409.00	137.90	11
12. Provident Mutual Life Ins. Co. of Philadelphia	149.50	29.80	11	229.40	54.50	16	401.10	138.90	12

13. Great-West Life Assurance Co. (Canada)	131.30	16	31.90	206.00	52.20	12	366.80	140.70	13
14. Confederation Life Association	143.40	9	29.30	219.30	51.20	11	380.60	148.00	26
15. General American Life Ins. Co.	160.80	14	31.80	242.30	55.50	17	414.20	142.50	16
16. The Equitable Life Assurance Society of the U.S. (NY)	152.70	19	33.60	233.20	56.60	22	404.50	141.10	14
17. North American Life Assurance Co. (Canada)	146.10	12	31.00	223.80	54.30	15	392.70	146.00	21
18. The Manufacturers Life Ins. Co.	127.80	32	37.10	197.00	56.00	19	343.70	142.50	16
19. The Penn Mutual Life Ins. Co.	153.00	24	35.60	235.40	58.30	26	412.70	144.10	19
20. State Farm Life Ins. Co.	146.10	18	32.60	227.40	53.60	14	409.20	152.80	29
21. Nationwide Life Ins. Co.	150.90	27	35.90	235.00	55.70	18	409.80	147.60	22
22. Crown Life Ins. Co.	119.70	24	35.60	189.30	56.10	20	347.90	147.70	24
23. Mutual Benefit Life Ins. Co.	158.00	22	34.90	238.70	58.00	25	412.30	147.60	22
24. Aetna Life Ins. Co.	160.60	39	42.00	239.50	56.40	21	408.50	142.30	15
25. John Hancock Mutual Life Ins. Co.	157.00	26	35.70	242.10	61.60	32	415.70	144.90	20
26. Pacific Mutual Life Ins. Co. (Calif.)	152.40	30	36.60	231.90	57.50	24	406.20	148.80	27
27. Continental Assurance Co.	155.70	28	36.00	241.20	59.10	30	419.90	147.90	25
28. The Prudential Ins. Co. of America	157.10	29	36.40	244.40	63.20	34	438.10	143.90	18
29. The Canada Life Assurance Co.	141.20	23	35.00	214.00	56.80	23	384.60	153.00	30

217

Company	Male age 20 or female age 23			Male age 35 or female age 38			Male age 50 or female age 53		
	Annual premium	Average yearly cost of insurance	Ranking at age 20/23	Annual premium	Average yearly cost of insurance	Ranking at age 35/38	Annual premium	Average yearly cost of insurance	Ranking at age 50/53
30. The Mutual Life Ins. Co of NY	$152.00	$34.20	21	$234.10	$58.50	27	$416.20	$152.60	28
31. The Lincoln National Life Ins. Co. (Ind.)	155.20	36.60	30	235.60	58.90	28	408.60	153.00	30
32. Franklin Life Ins. Co. (Ill.)	146.00	34.10	20	226.30	60.80	31	399.80	154.70	32
33. The Guardian Life Ins. Co. of America	147.90	31.80	14	230.50	58.90	28	400.00	163.10	35
34. Occidental Life Ins. Co. of California	153.30	42.10	40	233.50	65.80	35	401.30	156.30	33
35. The Minnesota Mutual Life Ins. Co.	156.40	39.70	36	238.90	62.50	33	414.80	162.10	34
36. Metropolitan Life Ins. Co.	158.60	37.20	33	248.10	66.80	37	427.10	165.80	36
37. Pilot Life Ins. Co.	138.40	43.20	42	216.80	65.90	36	393.50	170.00	38
38. Connecticut General Life Ins. Co.	139.40	39.50	35	220.40	70.70	38	398.80	175.30	39
39. American National Life Ins. Co.	155.80	38.40	34	239.70	71.30	41	423.50	180.20	40
40. Northwestern National Life Ins. Co.	177.80	51.90	48	262.80	71.10	39	439.50	167.40	37

Company									
*41. The National Life & Accident Ins. Co.	116.50	40.30	37	190.80	73.60	42	343.70	180.60	41
42. The Western and Southern Life Ins. Co.	156.60	43.60	43	246.30	73.80	43	426.30	184.40	42
43. Republic National Life Ins. Co.	138.70	40.60	38	222.00	75.70	44	401.60	188.70	44
*44. Allstate Life Ins. Co.	109.00	42.50	41	176.00	71.10	39	343.00	194.80	49
*45. Provident Life and Accident Ins. Co. (Tenn.)	108.80	48.10	45	177.30	77.80	46	328.70	184.70	43
*46. Life Ins. Co. of Virginia	117.90	45.40	44	192.50	76.90	45	356.40	191.50	45
*47. United Benefit Life Ins. Co.	116.40	51.00	46	189.50	82.00	47	345.90	191.70	47
*48. Business Men's Assurance Co. of America	118.20	51.70	47	188.50	83.60	48	339.70	191.50	45
*49. The Travelers Ins. Co.	118.90	53.10	50	190.90	84.70	49	348.10	194.40	48
*50. Old Republic Life Ins. Co. (Ill.)	122.00	52.30	49	196.30	85.90	50	357.90	201.00	50

* Nonparticipating insurance policies, thus no dividends paid. All other insurance shown pay dividends; i.e., are participating policies.
NOTES: The average yearly cost is based on the "interest-adjusted cost" of each policy over twenty years. The companies are ranked according to the average annual cost over twenty years of all three of the different-age policies given. The usual premium for a woman is the same as that for a man three years younger (because women live longer, thus pay less for life insurance).
SOURCE: The State of Pennsylvania Insurance Department.

What special features should you know about?

Ask for a *waiver of premium* option with every policy you buy. This is a miniature disability policy, widely recommended and costing only a little extra. It will keep a policy in force if you are disabled and can't work. The company waives premium payments for the period of disability and the insurance is kept in full force. When you recover and resume paying the premiums, the premiums missed are not repaid; they're chalked off.

When you buy cash-value insurance, get an *automatic loan* option written into the policy (not available with term insurance). It automatically keeps the insurance going if you forget or cannot pay a premium, and it costs nothing. The company will automatically borrow against the cash value in the policy to pay the premium. You pay interest on the sum borrowed but without this option the policy could lapse.

Don't pay extra for *double indemnity*, and if you have it now in present policies, consider dropping it. Though its price is low, it's of highly questionable value; it's better to spend the money on additional insurance. It pays the beneficiary twice the face value of an insurance policy when death is due to an accident. But this is paying extra for a very long-shot possibility, the odds against accidental death being very high. Besides, the dependents of a person killed in an accident frequently receive a damage settlement.

Life insurance review

▪ Estimate the insurance you need according to life stages, what's needed while children are growing up, usually less afterwards for a widow during the "widow gap" period, plus that needed later to supplement Social Security payments.

▪ Determine your monthly Social Security benefits, as they are, in effect, the equivalent of life insurance and reduce the amount of life insurance to be purchased. To determine your Social Security benefits, you will need a statement of your Social Security account. This is obtainable by sending your name, address and SS number to the Social Security Administration, Baltimore, Md. 21233; also ask for their booklet on Social Security benefits for survivors.

▪ Buy term insurance and save the difference in cost between it and cash-value insurance, but *only* if you can genuinely follow through on a lifetime savings program. Most people will be wise to buy some straight life (cash-value) and some term insurance. Remember that at a young age term insurance is very low in cost but later it gets increasingly expensive.

■ Consider a cash-value (and preferably straight-life or modified-life) policy of at least $10,000, preferably bought early at relatively low cost, as your basic long-term life insurance.

■ Straight life insurance is the lowest-cost of all cash-value insurance with the exception of modified-life.

■ It generally does not pay to spend extra for a "family" policy, a 20- or 30-year 20- or 30-payment life, or an endowment policy, the most expensive and least suitable of all life insurance. Such insurance seldom makes sense.

■ Don't use insurance to save money. The primary reason for life insurance is to insure support for dependents in case their source of support dies. You can almost always get a higher return on money saved in a bank or in savings bonds than is possible with money "saved" in life insurance.

■ Do not cash in an existing policy you already have in favor of new insurance unless you're certain that it is wise. New insurance almost always will cost more than insurance bought at a younger age.

■ Be sure that beneficiaries are chosen and cited properly in your insurance policies. Do you have a secondary beneficiary? Are the beneficiaries up to date?

■ Will the proceeds of your insurance be paid in the most advantageous method? A danger to avoid is rigidly limiting the payment to a method that does not pay the optimum return later. Ordinarily, a beneficiary should be allowed to choose among all possible payment methods.

■ Are you getting the most mileage from dividends received from insurance? Interest being earned on dividends left with an insurance company should earn as much as they would in a bank or elsewhere, or the money can be withdrawn to work elsewhere at a higher return.

■ Try to buy low-cost group insurance. But if you leave the group involved, remember that you generally cannot take it with you, though it usually can be converted to an individual policy.

■ Buy from a reputable company and only one that is licensed to sell insurance in your state.

■ Insurance that pays dividends (participating insurance) usually is cheaper than insurance that does not pay dividends (nonparticipating). When you buy dividend-paying insurance, seek a policy that offers a "fifth-dividend option" with more than a year of term insurance given in lieu of the dividend.

■ Deal with an experienced agent who is well recommended. Talk to two or three different agents and then choose.

■ If you live or work in New York, Connecticut or Massachusetts, savings bank insurance can be one of your best insurance buys. In Wisconsin consider buying insurance from Wisconsin's State Life Fund.

■ Don't buy a lot of little policies, since the greater the amount of insurance in one policy, the lower its cost per $1,000.

■ Special features that are good to include in your policies are the *waiver-of-premium* and *automatic loan* options. Paying extra for double indemnity is not recommended.

Obtain copies of *How much life insurance is enough?* and *Understanding Your Life Insurance*, both free from the Institute of Life Insurance, 277 Park Ave., New York, N.Y. 10017.

investing your money

About 32,000,000 Americans, one out of every seven people, have investments in the stock market, according to the New York Stock Exchange. About 8½ million people and their families (including some of the above 32,000,000) have investments in mutual funds, according to the Investment Company Institute, the mutual fund industry association.

It is virtually incumbent on anyone saving money for use tomorrow to consider investing a portion of it in one of those two ways just to stay even with inflation. That is, unless you don't mind discovering later, to your dismay, that the nest egg you have fathered has, over the years, shrunk in value. That unfortunately has happened to literally hundreds of thousands of Americans who since 1940 have been saving all their money in bank savings accounts, in saving bonds or in life insurance. Each dollar saved in one of these ways has since shrunk in real value to as little as 40 cents today. A grim reward for people who had been led to believe that thrift and husbandry of one's money were right up there pretty close to godliness. Investing money in the stock market or in a mutual fund involves risk, to be sure, compared with putting your money in a guaranteed interest-bearing savings account. What few bankers and other advocates of such fixed-dollar savings blithely avoid mentioning is the loss in the value of dollars attached to their saving methods as a result of inflation.

223

27

how to protect your **savings** from **inflation**

How inflation shrinks your money · Comparison of different methods of savings and investing · "Fixed" vs. "variable" dollars · How to beat inflation

How much of a bite will inflation take from your savings, money being put away today for children's college expenses in the future, for your retirement or for any other future goal? A look at the past can give you an idea.

Back in 1940 one of the great American dreams was to retire on $200 a month. That was a glorious lot of money in those days. Today, however, you would need about $500 a month income to live on the same scale possible in 1940 with $200 a month. That's what inflation can do to your savings. It has reduced the value of the 1940 dollar to about 40 cents at the beginning of the 1970's.

Future inflation could reduce the value of your 1973 dollars by about 25 percent in 10 years and by about 50 percent in 20 years. That's based on an average future inflation of roughly 2 percent a year. It means that you would need a retirement income 20 years from now of about $1,000 a month to live on the same scale as you can today on $500 a month.

No one, of course, can predict the exact rate of future inflation. A small increase (1½ to 2 percent a year) is highly likely, as it has become a way of life in nearly every advanced industrial nation of the world. It's the price we pay for continual growth and prosperity. However, the galloping inflation of recent years, due to the Vietnam war, is higher than that. There are records of inflation 4,000 years ago in Babylonian days (along with fast-and-loose royal attempts to control it); it accompanied the rise and particularly the fall of the Roman Empire; and it has accompanied the rise of Great Britain since the Dark Ages. Inflation, to be sure, was less pronounced in America during the 19th century when the industrial revolution was taking hold (but then the advent of factory mass production would naturally tend to reduce prices). And in the past three decades, three wars caused three upward leaps in inflation.

The problem is that certain common savings methods—bank savings, bonds, and life insurance and regular annuities—are particularly vulnerable to inflation. Other types of savings are less vulnerable as shown by the comparison of different kinds of savings during the 1960's in the accompanying table.

How savings fared in the recent past

The table opposite shows what happened to money saved or invested in nine different ways during the 1960's. Say, for example, you had a $10,000 windfall in 1960 to save or to invest in any way you chose. What would you have done with it? How much would your money have grown or diminished in purchasing value during the inflationary 1960's?

If you had kept the money in cash, under a mattress or in a safe deposit box, it would be worth only $7,949 in purchasing value 10 years later. Invested in government savings bonds or a bank account, the money would have grown to a dollar value of about $15,000, depending on the specific savings method used. The purchasing value of your money, however, would have shrunk to about $12,000 or less, again depending on the savings method.

If you had invested the $10,000 in selected stocks or in an average mutual fund, it would have grown in dollar value from $16,448 to as much as $25,458, depending on the stocks or type of mutual fund you had chosen, as the table shows. The purchasing value of your money in each case would be some 20 percent less, as with savings accounts.

Each of the savings methods shown assumes that the annual dividends and other earnings on your money were automatically reinvested each year (but no allowance is made for income taxes). The 10-year period spanned by the table experienced relatively slow year-to-year inflation during the first half, and a relatively fast annual inflation during the second half. It was a period during which bank interest rates ranged from

3 to about 5 percent a year, and stock prices did not perform especially well because of three sharp stock market declines (1960, 1962 and 1969). The price increase in the stock and mutual fund shares during the 10-year period was less than the growth of the same investments in most other 10-year periods since 1945.

Comparison of various savings methods
January 1, 1960 to January 1, 1970

Original amount 1/1/60		Dividends, interest, accrued capital gains	Total dollar value, 1/1/70	Actual purchasing value, 1/1/70
Cash	$10,000	None	$10,000	$ 7,949
Series E U.S. Government Bonds*	10,000	$ 4,581	14,581	11,590
Savings Account in a Commercial Bank**	10,000	4,310	14,310	11,346
Savings Accounts in Savings & Loan Associations***	10,000	5,234	15,234	12,110
Average Growth Stock Mutual Fund#	10,000	12,044	25,458	20,237
Average Common Stock Mutual Fund Average#	10,000	11,544	23,061	18,331
Average Balanced Mutual Fund#	10,000	10,494	17,745	14,106
Stock Investment, Based on Dow-Jones Industrial Average, Adjusted for Dividends#	10,000	Not Available	16,448	13,075
Stock Investment Based on Standard & Poor's 500 Average, Adjusted for Dividends##	10,000	5,006	20,967	16,646

NOTE: The interest rate on U.S. Series E Savings Bonds was increased in 1969 to 5.5 percent a year compounded, and at this new rate a $10,000 investment in savings bonds for ten years would grow to $17,268.

SOURCES: * U.S. Treasury Dept.; ** American Bankers Association; *** U.S. Savings & Loan League; # Investment Company Institute; ## Standard & Poor Corporation.

"Fixed" vs. "variable" dollars

The table illustrates the difference between the two basic methods of savings. Fixed-dollar, or fixed-income, savings is money put into a savings account, savings bonds, cash-value life insurance, a life insurance annuity, gilt-edged bonds, high-grade preferred stocks or real estate mortgages (bought as an investment; not the mortgage on your own house).

Each of these is a conservative method of saving, with very little risk involved. You know fairly accurately how much your money will earn in interest or dividends over the years and how much the dollar value of your money is likely to grow. Your money earns a fixed return virtually regardless of economic boom or bust, and is hardly, if at all, affected by the ups and downs of the stock market.

The trouble is that a fixed-dollar savings method is exceptionally vulnerable to inflation. As shown in the table, it will give you a guaranteed small growth in the dollar value of your savings, but the purchasing value of your dollars can be subject to large shrinkage.

You can protect your long-term savings against inflation by putting a portion of your money into a good "variable dollar" investment, also called "equity" savings. This includes money invested in good common stocks, a common-stock mutual fund or a variable insurance annuity. The value of such savings tends to increase with inflation, though not always and naturally it cannot be guaranteed. (During the 1969-70 stock market debacle, stock prices and many—though not all—mutual funds declined in value while at the same time inflation roared steadily ahead. Many good stocks and mutual funds bounced back afterwards, more than offsetting their 1969-70 losses.) Nevertheless, and no question about it, a variable-dollar investment entails risk.

For that reason, a variable-dollar investment is recommended only for long-term savings that you will not need for five years at the very least and, preferably, not for 10 years or more. The stock market might decline at any time, and if you needed your money shortly after investing it in stocks, you could suffer a loss. Over the long pull, however, history has shown that a sound variable-dollar investment generally grows in value, despite periodic stock market declines. It's a good hedge against long-term inflation.

A personal savings program

Before anyone puts money in the stock market or in any other variable-dollar investment, it's advisable to build an emergency cash reserve fund and have adequate life insurance for wife and children in case of the father's death. Your emergency fund should be cash in the bank, bonds or any other fixed-dollar medium that can be drawn out immediately in an emergency, such as a loss of a job. It should be large enough to pay your family living expenses for three to six months; some experts recommend an emergency savings fund large enough to cover a year's living expenses. If you have cash-value life insurance, the growing cash reserves being built up in your insurance can be considered part of your emergency fund, since you can borrow against it at any time.

Investing in "equities"

One of the best long-term hedges against inflation is owning a good house. In the past, real estate has tended to increase with inflation. Besides, with a house of your own, your basic housing cost remains fixed according to the price paid when you bought the house, but the value of the house is likely to increase from year to year.

Probably the next best hedge for the average person is an investment in a carefully chosen selection of good common stocks. You can buy a number of individual stocks by yourself; or, better still for most people, buy a share in a large number of different stocks by investing in a good mutual fund. Individual stock buying is recommended only for the person who has the time, acumen and knack of managing his own stock-market investments. That means knowing when to buy and sell stocks, as well as what stocks to buy for long-term growth.

A mutual fund may offer you less opportunity to make a killing in the stock market, but it also means less risk and greater diversification of your investment (spread over a large number of different companies' stock). Remember, however, that not all mutual funds are alike. Look again at the table accompanying this article and you'll notice that the average growth of that $10,000 investment in three different kinds of mutual funds varied greatly during the 1960's. This emphasizes the importance of choosing a good growth-stock mutual fund for inflation protection.

To save for your retirement, you can also consider a "variable-dollar" annuity that is sold by insurance companies. Unlike regular life-insurance annuities, which have suffered greatly from inflation in the past, a variable-dollar annuity involves an investment partly in stocks that are likely, though not guaranteed, to increase in value over the years along with inflation.

Other variable-dollar investments to beat inflation include buying real estate or land for future profit and investing in such specialized things as rare coins, antiques or works of art. Each of these, however, is recommended only if you are willing to devote the time and effort to become an expert on the subject and turn such an investment into a full-time avocation. Otherwise, you could lose your shirt and your savings. For these reasons, more people invest in the stock market, either directly or through a mutual fund, than in any other kind of variable-dollar investment, the subjects of the next two chapters.

28

investing in the stock market: part 1, personal investing

How much money can be made in the stock market · Your investment objective · Diversification · Choosing a stock broker · How to invest · The emotional equipment required for successful investing · Investment counselors, investment clubs and the Monthly Investment Plan

A primary reason for investing in the stock market is, of course, to earn a greater return on your money, your capital, than obtainable from bank savings or savings bonds. A second reason is to make a lot of money fast, which smacks of speculation and gambling (though that's all right if it's fun for you and you can afford to lose).

The trouble is that dreams of glory continually lure unsuspecting souls to the stock market. The dream is to buy $5,000 worth of stock and sell out a little later for $10,000. Hope springs eternal. Many books have been written to exploit this fanciful appeal of the stock market, but in this book and in this chapter we are concerned with the first reason above, sensible investing with a reasonably good return on your money.

To hedge against inflation, a reasonable if not minimal goal is an average annual compounded return of 8 to 10 percent a year, perhaps a little more. (A 10 percent return compounded annually doubles your money every seven years.) That's required just to stay ahead of inflation. Money

231

in the bank or in gilt-edged bonds will earn you a guaranteed compounded return of up to 6 or even 7 percent a year with little or no risk. But that kind of investment does not grow of itself, though it may have illusionary growth as a result of reinvested interest. It's illusionary because the deceptive growth of that capital is due to your own interest's being plowed back. Putting it another way, should the interest from a savings account or from bonds be withdrawn each year (to live on, say), your capital remains a fixed sitting-duck target for inflation. Your capital *also* should grow of itself as well as earn you an acceptable return.

Since 1870, when stock market averages were first kept, the market has increased in value at an average annual compound rate of 9.1 percent a year, according to John Bogle, president of the Wellington group of mutual funds and a keen student of stock market performance. From 1926 to 1965 all the stocks on the New York Stock Exchange, the Big Board, produced an average annual return, compounded, of 9.8 percent a year according to a study by two University of Illinois professors, Lawrence Fisher and James Lorie. And from 1960 to mid-1968, the stocks on the Big Board increased at an average annual rate of 9.2 percent, according to Standard & Poor's 500 stock index.

Doing the same by yourself, however, is not all that easy. Only about one-third of all stocks tend to rise in price. The rest either mark time or decline; it is that one-third minority of stocks that have pulled the stock market continually into higher ground over the years, which puts obvious emphasis on choosing stocks carefully to profit in the stock market. Brokers say that an intelligent layman investor should expect to earn up to about 10 percent a year on his investments, assuming he doesn't trade in and out of the market frequently, and earning a higher return is rare in real life except for professional investors.

True, folklore abounds with stories of people who have hit the jackpot in the stock market. But there's precious little documentation of such stories about people who allegedly have struck it rich on Wall Street, except for a few rare cases and again except for professionals—and a few legendary multi-millionaires like Bernard Baruch, an advisor to presidents; Joe Kennedy, the father of a president; and Jessie Livermore, who ended up broke and killed himself in the men's room of New York's Sherry-Netherland Hotel.

So here the usual cautionary sermon words also should be clearly stated. The stock market is no game for casual play. Risk is attached to every dollar invested in the market, as if glued on with unbreakable cement. There's no guarantee that you will make money in the stock market. There is also no guarantee that the stock market will continue to rise in the future as it has in the past. The likelihood of a continually rising stock market, not without inevitable intermediate declines, is good, most experts say. But that's about as far as any person can say for sure, based on the assumption that the U.S. economy and the world economy in general will continue to expand and grow.

Your investment objective

What is your goal: long-term growth of your capital or present-day income from it? The first is the usual goal for a person who is investing for tomorrow, or at least five to ten years in the future. The second is for the person who requires present-day income from his capital, to live on, for example.

Choosing one or the other objective and sticking to it is important because it determines the kind of stocks, and bonds sometimes, that should be bought. It immediately directs you either to "growth" or "income" stocks. Many people do not clearly resolve this basic decision and end up nowhere as a result, like a person who takes any train that comes along with no idea of its destination.

Diversification

This big word, bandied about often, simply means the opposite of putting all your eggs in one basket. It means spreading an investment among a number of different stocks to spread your risk, the greater the number of stocks chosen, the less the risk. Put all your chips on one or two stocks and you might possibly have a big winner, but you could also have a big loser and no money left. Even the bluest blue-chip stock is not immune to going nowhere, or even to losing money. Blue-chip stocks have attained an unfortunate Gibralterlike aura of safety and almost sure-fire profitability, but that's not true. A blue chip is the stock of a large, well-known company with a long, stable record of good earnings and dividend payments over the years. But in the past 10 to 20 years roughly half of the 30 blue-chip company stocks that make up the well-known Dow-Jones Industrial stock average have increased in value by hardly anything and some have suffered long-term declines. And then there's that former blue chip, the Penn Central Railroad, which went into bankruptcy in 1969, its stock falling sharply in value from over $80 a share in the 1960's down to less than $5 a share in 1972.

Minimal diversification generally requires spreading your money over at least five or six different stock investments. Of course, there can be too much diversification, the result of being a watered-down potential for profit. The thinner the diversification, the greater the risk. And reasonable minimal diversification generally requires an investment kitty to start with of at least $10,000 and preferably $20,000 to $25,000.

Choosing a stock broker

This is clearly important since one's broker is usually instrumental in the choice of investments and other decisions, such as the all-important time to buy and sell. Thus, for most people, investment success—or lack of it—depends more on the broker than on anything else. But, alas, finding a good broker is not easy, especially if you're a small investor or live in a small city or town. Even in a big city like New York, Chicago or Boston, where stock brokers abound, finding a good broker is not so easy. (Read *How to Keep What You Have, or, What Your Broker Never Told You*, by Charles V. Neal, published by Doubleday & Co.)

The choice of a broker also extends to choosing a good brokerage firm. It's generally best to deal with a firm that's a member of the New York Stock Exchange. A member firm of the N.Y.S.E. must conform to stiffer standards than other broker firms who are not members. At last count, there were some 3,000 licensed stock broker firms in the U.S., but less than 600 were members of the N.Y.S.E. In addition, fewer than 400 of these member firms are retail brokers who deal with the public. A directory of N.Y.S.E. members, including those with branch offices in various parts of the country, can be had by writing for *Member Firm Directory*, the New York Stock Exchange, P.O. Box 1971, Radio City Station, New York, N.Y. 10019.

A broker firm that is not a member of the New York Stock Exchange can still be good, but you should be sure about this. Request a copy of its last annual financial report to check that it's on sound footing. (Anyone who doesn't know how to read an annual report or doesn't learn need not bother; he shouldn't be dabbling in the stock market.) About 75 stock broker firms went broke as a result of the 1969-70 stock market decline, according to the Securities & Exchange Commission, the SEC (the government's watchdog over Wall Street), and another 75 or so on the verge of failure were saved by being bailed out by other brokerage firms.

Check on the investment research that a brokerage house provides for its clients. Review some of its recent reports to determine if they provide the hard facts and financial information that you'll want for your investing.

Then comes choosing a particular individual within the firm, the "registered representative," for your personal broker. Try for one who has been in the business for at least five to ten years. It's a big plus if he has a solid background in economics or finance. Ask him for a business autobiography. Also, he should follow the kind of stocks you like. Most brokers concentrate on the stocks of no more than a few dozen different companies—it's not humanly possible to keep close track of more. And keep in mind that there are more than 5,000 different securities listed on our various stock exchanges.

Try to find out how well the broker has performed for his clients in the past. This is a vital question, of course, but it may be tough to answer because brokers' batting averages are unobtainable. You can get some idea by talking to a few of his clients. Get their names from him just as you would ask for references from any other businessman you deal with. Also, ask him for the names of specific companies he has been bullish about in the past. In the 1960's, for example, which stocks did he recommend? If he mentions such companies as Avon Products, Eli Lilly, IBM, National Can, Snap-on Tools and Xerox, he had some big winners.

A stockbroker earns his money through the fee or "commission" you pay each time you buy or sell stock. This fee generally ranges from about 1 to 2 percent of the total cost of the stock being bought or sold, but it can range as high as 6 percent for small transactions. The larger your transaction, the smaller the percentage you pay as commission to the broker. The fees charged are set by the New York Stock Exchange and are the same for all brokers, except for large transactions for which the fees vary and can be negotiated.

Find a really good broker and you're three-quarters of the way to successful investing. You could skip the rest of this chapter. But a really good broker is a rare bird, and besides, most good ones confine their business to well-heeled clients with stock portfolios of at least $50,000 to $100,000. It doesn't pay a top-notch broker to buy and sell stocks for smaller clients. (He'll often advise you to invest in a mutual fund or politely refer you elsewhere.) For the same reason a number of broker firms shy away from small investors. The New York Stock Exchange says that anyone who perseveres will find a suitable broker, though that may be painting a rosier picture than reality.

Intelligent investing

You've probably heard the old advice, put forth by the SEC and many others, "Investigate before you invest." Yet Wall Street observers are continually amazed at the seemingly inexhaustible stream of naive people, eyes swimming with fantasy, who put money into stocks they know virtually nothing about. (And there are plenty of sharp-fanged wolves who are delighted to take money from such sheep.)

At the country club on Sunday, Joe Swizzlehut hears about a new stock, Amalgamated Zenith Ltd., that's "absolutely guaranteed to go up 15 points." First thing Monday morning Joe calls his broker and orders a hundred shares. The stock goes down a couple of points to take a long rest and a year later Joe sells out in disgust, taking a loss. Nancy Hipplemeyer comes into a windfall and her friends insist that she put her money into a new cable television company that's due to get a license to set up business in their area. "You can't lose," everybody tells her, so she buys a bundle of the stock. At the last minute, the Federal Communications Commission declares a moratorium on new cable television franchises and Nancy's stock declines sharply. There is an endless flow of such stock tips, though many people do not realize that they often are deliberately generated to boost a particular stock and make money for insiders who want to sell out at a tidy price. You'll even read rosy stories about a company in the newspapers or in a big magazine. But it could well be a story generated by an energetic press agent who is paid to publicize the company and build up the demand for its stock. Lesson: Be skeptical of any company puff that you read about.

Mickie Siebert, the first woman member of the New York Stock Exchange and a top-notch investment analyst, as well as broker, gives this down-to-earth advice: "Collect as much information, facts and figures— what brokers call 'the numbers'—that you can on the corporation you're interested in. Find out how the stock has performed recently, what products or services the corporation produces, which ones are new, what the competition is, and try to get information on the caliber of the executives running the corporation. This information is readily available and it's free."

That kind of homework may be beyond the scope of a typical investor, but it's exactly what professional stock analysts do every day, their full-time job. Not long ago this author could not reach Mickie Siebert by phone because, we were told, "Miss Siebert just flew to the West Coast on a research trip." She had flown out to visit a certain company, and then on the way back was stopping at Denver to check on still another company. That's common practice among stock market analysts. Though you cannot investigate that thoroughly, you can obtain the resulting information in the follow-up research reports written by such analysts on their return. You get them by dealing with a good broker whose firm provides first-hand research. One warning here, however: Often, you must read between the lines, and also remember that negative information about a company is seldom ever presented in its raw truth.

If your objective is long-term growth, rather than current income from capital, you will probably seek the stock of "growth" companies. They are companies whose sales and earnings are expected to grow, and then so should the value of their stock. Such companies may earn good profits but as a rule they pay out small or no annual divdends. Dividends are largely withheld so that the profits can be plowed back for greater future growth. In short, the dividend-paying record of a company is no longer as important as it formerly was for judging the worth of a stock. A company's potential for growth has become more important.

One of the classic growth companies of recent years is Xerox, the maker of the Xerox copying machine, which pays out very little in cash dividends, yet the value of Xerox stock has climbed continually as a result of sharply mounting sales of its photocopy machines. Just from 1960 through mid-1972 it increased more than 60 times. If you had invested $1,000 in Xerox in early 1960, in 1972 your stock would have grown to a value of more than $60,000!

That does not mean, however, that Xerox or any other recently popular growth stock (such as International Business Machines, Avon or Polaroid) will continue to grow in the future as in the past. Its growth, in fact, could be slowing down. Also remember that $1,000 put in another so-called growth stock in 1960 might be worth less today. Thus, choosing a good growth stock—or any other stock—is not easy, which is what makes the business of Wall Street fascinating as well as risky.

On the other hand, the dividend-paying record of a company is indeed important if your objective is current income. That's where a good blue-chip stock comes in. Such companies generally forgo the possibility of substantial future growth in favor of paying out attractive annual dividends. The blue chips include companies like Detroit auto maker General Motors, some of the big utilities, some of the railroads and, among others, some of the large international oil companies most of which are chiefly income stocks (though some of these last could become future growth companies as a result of the energy crisis).

The right emotional equipment

Some people, to be blunt, are simply not emotionally constituted to invest in the stock market. It's not for the faint of heart and not for a person who soars with jubilation when his stocks go up and sinks into despair when they go down. The ideal temperament is one that does neither, remaining cool and skeptical in both cases. You must believe in your investments (presumably they were bought on a sound premise), be capable of holding on and not selling in panic when the stock market goes through its inevitable downswings and then not suffer sleepless nights and nervous days. Conversely, there comes a time when nearly every stock should be sold, often at a loss, and this, too, requires no-nonsense decisiveness, coolly selling without the typical emotional restraint that prevents many amateur investors from selling until too late.

Investment clubs

A good way to test your aptitude for the stock market and also to gain experience at a small price is to join an investment club, which can also be an agreeable social activity. There are some 60,000 investment clubs in the country, many with as few as five to ten members. About one-third are all-male clubs, another third all-women and the rest sexually mixed. Most clubs meet monthly to discuss their investments, give research assignments to members and discuss investments made, with "dues" as little as $10 to $20 a month invested per member. Each member owns a proportionate share of the investments made and shares in the profits and losses. Many people who belong to investment clubs also invest on their own, and graduates say that it is excellent experience, like playing in the minor leagues before going on to the major leagues on your own. Write for information to the National Association of Investment Clubs, 1515 E. Eleven Mile Road, Royal Oak, Mich. 48067.

Hiring your own investment counselor

With as little as $10,000 to invest, sometimes less, you can forgo reliance on a stock broker or on yourself and put your investments in the hands of a paid professional investment counselor. Investment counselors were formerly all big-time money managers who concerned themselves only with the accounts of people with at least $100,000 to invest and often at least a million dollars. They are full-time professionals concerned entirely

with managing the investment portfolios of others, which include corporation and labor-union pensions and other funds, as well as individual accounts. Two well-known ones for large investors are the T. Rowe Price
people in Baltimore and Scudder, Stevens & Clarke of Boston and New
York. But, as often occurs in this business, both firms plus quite a few
others also manage mutual funds which any person may invest in.

There are also now a growing number of private investment counseling
firms for individual investors with as little as $10,000 to invest. They
charge you a counseling fee of from ½ to 1 percent a year of the total
money invested, sometimes a little more or less, depending on the sum
involved. Counselors who do this include banks and they advertise in
the financial pages of newspapers and in financal magazines. Not all,
however, are necessarily as good as they might be. Again, you must check
on a counselor before hiring one. Ask for, among other things, the firm's
investment record (batting average) for other accounts managed, and
of course find out all you can about the firm.

If you wish to invest a small sum of money regularly, as little as $40
every three months, you may do this with the New York Stock Exchange's
Monthly Investment Plan, or MIP. You choose the stock or stocks you
want and mail in a check periodically. An MIP account can be opened
through a New York Stock Exchange member broker, such as Merrill
Lynch, Pierce, Fenner & Smith, the giant brokerage firm that, among
other things, specializes in MIP accounts. In addition, the broker handling your MIP account can give you advice on choosing stocks to invest
in. MIP, incidentally, is also a good way to make large investments by
mail. For information, send a self addressed stamped envelope to Merrill
Lynch, Pierce, Fenner & Smith, 70 Pine St., New York, N.Y. 10005; ask
for the pamphlet, *Monthly Investment Plan.*

Basic information about stock investing especially for beginners can
be had in the *Investors Information Kit,* available for $1.07 from The
New York Stock Exchange, Dept. AW, Box 252, New York, N.Y. 10005.
It includes booklets on how the New York Stock Exchange works and
on understanding financial reports, bonds, preferred stocks, plus financial
facts about various stocks. Also look into books about the stock market
at the library or at a book store (many are available in low-cost paperback editions).

The following stocks are those with the greatest total value of all the
nearly 1,500 stocks listed on the New York Stock Exchange, as of
July 1, 1972. They accounted for just over 29 percent of the total value
of all stocks on the Exchange on that date.

The 25 stock market giants

	Listed shares (millions)	Market value
International Business Machines	116.0	$45,462
American Tel. & Tel.	549.3	22,865
General Motors	287.6	21,535
Eastman Kodak	161.6	21,428
Sears, Roebuck	156.3	17,273
Standard Oil (N. J.)	226.6	16,797
General Electric	185.1	12,171
Xerox Corp.	78.4	11,818
Texaco Inc.	274.3	8,914
Minnesota Mining & Mfg.	112.8	8,598
Coca-Cola Co.	59.7	7,971
E.I. duPont de Nemours	47.6	7,801
Procter & Gamble	81.9	7,640
Johnson & Johnson	56.5	6,931
Avon Products	57.8	6,599
American Home Products	54.6	5,813
Mobil Oil	103.1	5,800
Merck & Co.	73.3	5,700
Gulf Oil	211.9	5,165
Standard Oil (Indiana)	73.9	5,143
Standard Oil of Calif.	84.8	5,111
Ford Motor	76.5	4,889
Kresge (S. S.)	36.7	4,658
Eli Lilly	68.8	4,576
Westinghouse Electric	87.6	4,445

SOURCE: The New York Stock Exchange.

The 50 most widely held stocks

Company	Stock-holders	Company	Stock-holders
American Tel. & Tel.	3,010,000	Niagara Mohawk Power	167,000
General Motors	1,291,000	Phillips Petroleum	166,000
Standard Oil (New Jersey)	783,000	Greyhound Corp.	160,000
Int'l Business Machines	581,000	Transamerica Corp.	160,000
General Electric	514,000	Philadelphia Electric	157,000
General Tel. & Electronics	447,000	Public Service Elec. & Gas	157,000
U.S. Steel	342,000	Westinghouse Electric	156,000
Ford Motor	340,000	Detroit Edison	156,000
RCA Corp.	308,000	International Tel. & Tel.	154,000
Texaco Inc.	300,000	Pan Amer. World Airways	147,000
Standard Oil of California	280,000	Atlantic Richfield	145,000
Consolidated Edison	272,000	Xerox Corp.	144,000
Sears, Roebuck	254,000	Northeast Utilities	142,000
Gulf Oil	249,000	International Harvester	140,000
Tenneco Corp.	242,000	Penn Central	139,000
E. I. duPont de Nemours	229,000	American Brands	132,000
Eastman Kodak	223,000	American Motors	129,000
Mobil Oil	223,000	Sperry Rand	129,000
Bethlehem Steel	218,000	General Public Utilities	129,000
Union Carbide	207,000	Cities Service	128,000
Chrysler Corp.	202,000	Litton Industries	127,000
Columbia Gas System	175,000	El Paso Natural Gas	126,000
Standard Oil (Indiana)	173,000	Anaconda Company	123,000
Commonwealth Edison	170,000	American Can	122,000
Pacific Gas & Electric	169,000	R.J. Reynolds Industries	121,000

SOURCE: The New York Stock Exchange.

REVIEW

If you can honestly answer yes to each of the following review questions, you could well achieve financial success in the stock market:

1. Can you risk losing money in the stock market?
2. Have you a basic financial cushion in bank savings, insurance or other liquid assets to tide you over a financial storm?
3. Have you decided on your clear-cut investment objective— usually long-term growth or current income? Can you stick to it?
4. Do you have the willingness plus enough money to diversify your total investment among at least half a dozen or so different stocks?
5. Have you found a good broker? Is he really good?
6. Will you do the research and homework usually necessary for successful investing? (Less emphasis on this if you have a good broker.)
7. Do you have the proper emotional temperament for the ups and downs of personal investing?

29

investing in the stock market: part 2, mutual funds

The record of mutual funds · Mutual funds versus the stock market · What a mutual fund is · Advantages and disadvantages of mutual funds · Choosing a mutual fund for your investment objective · The five basic types of mutual funds · Three key tests for evaluating a mutual fund · Cost of investing in a mutual fund · Finding out about specific mutual funds

If you had invested $10,000 in an average mutual fund in 1950, at the end of 1971, 22 years later, your investment would have grown in value to $94,008. That's an average return of 10.7 percent a year compounded, which isn't bad. It's the average annual performance of all regular mutual funds each year since 1950, as shown in the accompanying table. By contrast, $10,000 put in a 5-percent-a-year-compound interest savings account in 1950 would have grown in value over the same 22 years to $29,256.

That's the story of mutual funds since World War II when roughly half of all mutual funds have increased in share value by more than 10 percent a year. Some have increased by an average of up to 14 percent a year while others have grown as little as 6 to 7 percent (though some of these don't promise to do much better than this). In other words, there are mutual funds and there are mutual funds, and the trick is knowing how to choose one among the better half of all funds. How to do that is less difficult than you may think and is the subject of this chapter.

What happened to an investment of $10,000 in the average fund on January 2, 1950 is shown in the following table.

The record of mutual funds since 1950

Year	$10,000	% Change	Gain	Loss	5% interest compounded annually $10,000
1950	$11,089	+10.89	$ 1,089		$10,509
1951	12,734	+14.84	1,645		11,025
1952	14,166	+11.24	1,432		11,576
1953	14,150	− .11		−$ 16	12,155
1954	20,233	+42.99	6,083		12,763
1955	23,805	+17.65	3,572		13,401
1956	25,604	+ 7.56	1,799		14,071
1957	23,023	−10.08		− 2,581	14,775
1958	32,088	+39.37	9,065		15,514
1959	36,198	+12.81	4,110		16,290
1960	37,403	+ 3.33	1,205		17,105
1961	46,911	+25.42	9,508		17,960
1962	41,484	−11.57		− 5,427	18,858
1963	48,519	+16.96	7,035		19,801
1964	54,866	+13.08	6,347		20,791
1965	66,256	+20.76	11,390		21,831
1966	62,785	− 5.24		− 3,471	22,923
1967	84,294	+34.26	21,509		24,069
1968	99,138	+17.61	14,844		25,272
1969	85,100	−14.16		−14,038	26,536
1970	78,616	− 7.62		− 6,484	27,863
1971	94,008	+19.58	15,392		29,256

NOTE: Figures in this table are based on annual performance averages of funds listed in the Management Results section of Wiesenberger's *Investment Companies*, excluding the categories of bond and preferred stock funds, tax-free funds and international funds. Annual average performance was derived by adding each fund's performance and dividing by the number of funds. New funds were added as they appeared in the annual Wiesenberger volumes that were used. In 1950, 1961 and 1970, for example, the number of funds was 45, 145 and 307 respectively. Investment results assume an initial investment of $9,150 following deduction of an 8.5 percent sales charge and subsequent reinvestment each year of dividends and capital gains.

The table illustrates how an investment of $10,000 in 1950 in a mutual fund would

But first, a few basic facts and assumptions about mutual funds should be clearly understood. An investment in a mutual fund is by no means risk-free. It is, in effect, a broad-based investment in the stock market, and the likelihood of future profits—or losses—in mutual funds are tied directly to the future course of the stock market, and also, therefore, to the future course of the U.S. economy. Mutual funds have performed well since World War II simply because the U.S. economy and the stock market have prospered since then. Thus anyone who invests in a mutual fund today must realize that such an investment is likely to do well tomorrow *only if the stock market as a whole continues to thrive in the future as in the past.* That's fundamental.

A good mutual fund can be a sensible investment because it could increase in share value in the future at an average annual rate a little higher than the average increase in the stock market as a whole (assuming again that the market continues to rise). Mutual funds have outperformed the market in the past as shown by their average 10.6 percent annual increase since 1950 versus the average stock market increase in past years of 9.1 to 9.6 percent reported in the last chapter.

Mutual funds, to be sure, have been criticized and scorned by some people, including some who supposedly know all about the stock market. Part of this criticism has to do with the sales and management fees levied by mutual funds and the way mutual funds are sold. These charges were taken up by 1971 changes in the U.S. investment laws governing the operation of mutual funds. Other criticism has been directed at a certain group of speculative funds which declined sharply in value during the

---

have fared, year by year, measured by the average performance of mutual funds; it would have grown by the end of 1971 to $94,008, or a net gain of $84,008. The table also indicates the extent to which a mutual fund investment can fluctuate each year as conditions in the stock market change. Note how such an investment went down during the bear market years of 1962, and 1969–70, during which time a short-term investor's shares would have lost value. But over the long term the number of years with gains exceeded the years with losses by nearly three to one and long-term gains far outpaced losses. It should also be remembered that the record of any individual fund will, of course, vary according to its investment objective and its particular performance. Most of all, perhaps, the table demonstrates the advantage of long-term investing in a mutual fund. While past performance is no guarantee of future performance, the mutual fund record, as shown above, is not bad at all. The same $10,000 invested in a 5 percent compound interest savings account would have produced a guaranteed net gain of $19,256 over the same 22-year period, and a total of $29,256 in the account, as shown in the table. But that can be misleading because bank interest rates are not necessarily guaranteed. Interest rates paid by banks ranged from about 1 to 3 percent a year in the 1950's, up to 5 percent at the end of the 1960's.

SOURCE OF TABLE FIGURES: Investment Company Institute, copyright © 1972, The Investment Company Institute.

1969-70 stock market crash. (Many of the same volatile funds have since bounced back and more about them in a moment. On the other hand, one of every five stocks listed on the New York Stock Exchange, the Big Board, and on the American Stock Exchange, its kid brother, closed out 1971 at a price 70 percent or more lower than its high in 1967-68. In 1971, a good year, all the stocks on the New York Stock Exchange showed an average over-all increase of 14.1 percent, according to the Standard & Poor 500 index adjusted for dividends; all mutual funds increased by an average of 18.2 percent.) And, finally, some critics have charged simply that funds are lousy, yet the record clearly shows that many of them can indeed be a good investment. We are clearly in favor of mutual funds, though not blindly and not without recognizing their warts and limitations, which brings up another underlying assumption that should be clearly stated.

In this book and in this chapter our discussion of mutual funds is chiefly for readers who are concerned with *investing* for future years and as a hedge against inflation, as opposed to speculating (or gambling). The rest of this chapter is therefore not for anyone bent on making a lot of money fast. The nature of mutual funds precludes that.

What mutual funds are

A mutual fund is an investment vehicle in which a number of people can pool their money with the expectation of receiving a higher return on their capital than ordinarily possible by people investing on their own. The first mutual fund was started by William I of Belgium. The idea was taken up in England in 1868 (where they are called Unit Trusts) and a number of mutual investment companies were subsequently formed and prospered. The first regular mutual fund in America was the Massachusetts Investment Trust, which was launched in 1924 and is now a giant fund. It is an "open-end" mutual fund, the most common type of mutual fund with, at last count, over 800 such funds in the U.S. and over 1,600 operating in some 60 different countries of the world.

An open-end mutual fund invests in the stock market where the value of its shares fluctuates as the total value of all its securities fluctuates. The total assets of the Friendship Fund on a given day may add up to $100 million dollars, according to the prices of all its securities. It owns, say, 5,000 shares of General Motors, 8,500 shares of General Electric, 10,000 shares of IBM, and, in all, shares of different companies which add up in value to $100 million on that day. At the same time assume that Friendship has issued 20 million shares of its own stock. These shares are therefore worth $5 apiece, their net asset value. That's $100 million divided by 20 million. As the value of the fund's total investments goes up—or down—on the market, so does the prorated net value of each share you own, based on the total sum of all shares owned by people who have bought into the fund.

To buy shares in an open-end fund on the above day, you would pay a price based on that day's share value. Depending on the fund's sales policy, you would pay a flat $5 per share, or $5 plus a sales commission of up to about 9 percent of the money invested. To sell shares that day, you would receive $5 for each share sold, with a few exceptions where a redemption fee of 1 to 2 percent is charged. That's oversimplifying things a bit but generally is how mutual funds work.

There are also mutual funds that are closed-end investment companies with only a few dozen or so with wide appeal in the U.S. Most are listed on the New York or American Stock Exchange like regular corporate stocks. A closed-end fund has a fixed number of shares for sale and cannot create new shares on demand as an open-end fund may do. To buy and sell its shares, you go to a stock broker who handles the transaction just as he buys and sells corporate stocks. The price you pay to buy or sell the shares of a closed-end fund, however, is not necessarily proportionate to the total value of the fund's stock market holdings at the time of purchase or sale. Instead, it may fluctuate as much as 20 to 30 percent higher or lower than the actual value of all its securities. This complicates things with closed-end funds and introduces the need for special knowledge for successful investing in them. Chiefly for this reason, the open-end mutual funds, the most popular and by far most numerous kind, are the subject of this chapter and from here on the term mutual fund refers to open-end funds.

Why invest in a mutual fund?

The main reasons are the same as those for investing directly in the stock market: To protect your capital from inflation and to earn a greater return on your money than obtainable in a bank savings account or in other fixed-dollar return investments, like bonds. Compared with investing directly in the stock market, an investment in a mutual fund offers special advantages that can take the terror out of investing. The primary advantage of a mutual fund is, as we've mentioned, the professional management of your money. Stock market professionals take charge of investing your money.

Other advantages of a mutual fund are:

Diversification. A typical fund spreads your risk—diversifies it—over a number of different company stocks and securities. A disaster in any one or two of them will have small effect on the fund and on your investment.

Reduced emotional entanglements. Investing in a mutual fund minimizes the inevitable emotional knots that can tie up and hurt people who invest by themselves in individual stocks and bonds. Nearly everybody—ego-motivated, hungry for profit, fearful of loss, and stirred with a bagful of crosscurrents—is buffeted by emotion in the stock market. You've got to be cool-headed and cold-blooded to invest successfully in the stock market and few amateurs come this way.

Investment flexibility. A mutual fund account can be started with as little as $50 to $100 and additional investments often can be made at any time with an even sum equally small, and sometimes with as little as $10 a month.

Automatic reinvestment of dividends and capital gains. The annual dividends and other annual earnings from a mutual fund can be automatically converted to additional shares in the fund, thus creating an automatically growing and compounding investment. That eliminates the human loss that can occur when the owner of a stock receives an odd-sum dividend check which is not so easily convertible to additional shares, and instead is usually spent. As a result, a comparable investment in stocks often does not increase so fast as in a mutual fund where the compounding principle works with greater fluidity.

Reduced study and homework. Compared with buying individual securities, which demands continual study and homework, a mutual fund investment is easy. Less time and effort are needed to choose a good fund and keep abreast of its fortunes.

Known performance records. How a mutual fund has performed, its batting average, is a known quantity and a matter of record. This is not so, of course, for stock brokers, bank trust departments and virtually all other kinds of money managers handling stock investments for others.

Simplified record-keeping. This can be a boon at income-tax time. At the end of each year, a mutual fund sends out a paper listing the total dividends and other distributions made during the year and your tax liability for each. And at any time the status and value of a mutual fund account can be determined in a moment.

Another nice thing about mutual funds is the convenience of a single security representing your share ownership in a fund. That does away with the fuss and bother of safekeeping individual stock and bond certificates, not to mention the paperwork involved with exercising warrants, rights, splits, and so on. In most cases, you never need see your security of ownership; it's kept by a separate company which also handles a fund's money and keeps in its vaults a fund's stock certificates.

Mutual funds are a heavily regulated and controlled segment of the investment industry. They are policed by the federal government's Securities & Exchange Commission, the SEC, and by the nongovernment National Association of Security Dealers (NASD), one of the toughest industry watchdogs in all U.S. industry. Hank-panky is not unknown among mutual funds, but serious instances have been markedly less frequent in it than in almost any other corner of Wall Street.

Mutual fund pitfalls

Probably the greatest pitfall with mutual funds is the expectation of making a lot of money fast and then not doing so and possibly losing money. This happened particularly after 1967 and 1968 when the so-called "go-go" funds rose in value as much as 50 to 100 percent in a year's time. That garnered them much publicity, followed by a great rush of people to invest in these top funds of the year. Such people anticipated that similar record performance would follow and they could almost taste it. But the stock market went into a tailspin in 1969 and 1970 causing many of the very same volatile funds to decline as much as 50 to 60 percent.

But that's typical, since the funds that climb the most in good years tend to be the very same funds that decline the most in bad years. Such mutual funds can be very risky. Over a period of years they could turn in the highest performance of all mutual funds, assuming that the stock market goes up more than it goes down. But, if the opposite occurs, an investment in a speculative go-go fund carries the risk of losing the most money, too.

The other possible pitfall of a mutual fund is for the person who forgets that, like the stock market, the safety of an investment in a mutual fund is by no means guaranteed and that there is no assurance that money put in a mutual fund will grow in value.

Choosing a mutual fund

Also like the stock market, investing in a mutual fund requires, first, a clearcut choice of your investment objective. Do you seek long-term growth of your capital, or a fairly consistent and respectable annual income from it?

An objective of "growth" or "growth of capital," the same thing, is achieved by investing in a mutual fund (or stock) whose basic dollar value, or share price, will tend to increase, while at the same time the dividends paid by the fund (or stock) are likely to be small, if not nonexistent. The term "income" is the reverse, being an investment for which one expects to achieve a reasonably good dividend income while at the same time the dollar value of your capital invested should not be expected to grow much from year to year.

There are five basic categories of mutual funds according to investment objective. They range from those that strive hardest for maximum long-term growth on the one hand, across the spectrum to those that strive for maximum annual income and little or no growth, as follows:

Maximum growth funds. These are also called maximum capital gains funds and sometimes are referred to as the "performance funds." They go all out for growth, often investing in small, little-known companies which they think will be future Xeroxes and IBMs. Dividends are of virtually no concern to them. As a result, they hold within themselves the greatest risk of potential loss of all mutual funds, the greater the striving for growth, the greater the possibility of loss. They also tend to be volatile, often declining sharply in value when the stock market declines.

Maximum growth funds account for roughly 30 percent of all mutual funds, and they include the so-called go-go funds, that special breed of volatile performance funds mentioned above, which brought notoriety to the mutual fund business in 1969 and 1970.

Not all maximum growth funds, however, are alike, some being more or less speculative than others. The degree of volatility and risk in a particular maximum growth fund can be determined by a look at the fund's specific stock holdings listed in its prospectus or in its latest financial report. Because of its volatility and built-in risk, a maximum growth fund is not for the faint-of-heart investor; this is stated, in effect, in the prospectus of each. Choosing a good one requires a little care and knowledge plus the willingness to accept greater-than-average risk.

Growth funds. These also strive for long-term growth but with less risk and less volatility than the maximum growth funds. Regular growth funds invest in more established growth companies that may have less potential for future growth (compared with those chosen by maximum growth funds) but that's in return for greater stability. Dividends are of secondary importance.

A good straightforward growth fund is recommended for most people investing for the future with emphasis on beating inflation. Since World War II most growth funds have increased in share value by an average of 10 to 12 percent a year; though, again, that is no guarantee that they will continue to do the same in the future.

Growth-income funds. This is a grayish group of funds which straddle the fence, choosing a middle course between growth and income. They are more conservative than growth funds, sacrificing some growth possibility for greater stability and some dividend income. But, like the other categories of mutual funds, there are different shadings within the growth-income group. One may emphasize growth more than income, while another does the opposite, putting more of its chips on stocks with good dividend-paying records. A growth-income fund is for a person who would like some possibility of growth, thus some hedge against future inflation, but with not too much risk, plus some income each year.

Income funds. These strive for a liberal annual income and sometimes you may even get a little growth on the side, too. They are conservative funds that invest chiefly in solid, blue-chip company stocks and sometimes in corporate and government bonds. As a result, they cannot be expected to return 10 percent a year or so on your money. Most income funds in the past have performed at an average rate of about 6 to 8 percent a year return on capital invested in them.

Balanced funds. This fifth category of mutual funds is one of the smallest in number of funds—about 30 in all—but it contains two of the very largest mutual funds (the $3 billion Investors Mutual and the $1.2 billion Wellington Fund), though large size is not necessarily a good thing in mutual funds. According to Wiesenberger's *Investment Companies,* the basic mutual fund reference guide, "The objective of a Balanced Fund is to minimize investment risk as far as this is possible, without unduly sacrificing possibilities for long term growth and current income." To do that, a balanced fund generally holds at all times in its portfolio a certain proportion of bonds and preferred corporate stocks, as well as common stocks. But that's like trying to be all things to all people. There are a few good balanced funds, but on the whole, balanced funds have the dreariest performance records of all funds and they have moved up comparatively little in past decades.

There are also funds that strive for "relative price stability" (which is not a good cup of tea for protection against inflation), plus specialty funds, dual-purpose funds, hedge funds, real estate, oil and cattle funds. Some of these are gimmick funds designed to exploit a particular field of investment, while others are relatively new with no real track record for gauging their stamina and performance potential, so we do not favor them. Many hedge funds, in particular, have turned in poor records since their introduction in the mid-1960's, and dual-purpose funds were heralded as the greatest invention since sliced rye bread, but so far they have performed in unexciting fashion.

Three key tests for evaluating a mutual fund

Which fund should you invest in? You choose the category of funds that meets your investment objective and then narrow down your choice to a good fund within the category according to three key tests: the caliber of management, the past performance record, and the size of the fund.

Obviously, the people who run a mutual fund are the key to how well it will perform, just as the caliber of players determines whether a base-ball team will win more games than it loses. Who runs the fund? What are their qualifications? How long have they been in the investment business? Some of this information can be obtained from a fund's prospectus, and often a fund salesman can fill in details. Literally dozens of new funds are being started up each year and thus a special trap to avoid here is the new fund sponsored by people with no clearcut qualifications for managing a mutual fund.

The best test of management caliber is a fund's past performance record, its batting average for at least the past ten years. The performance of every fund, its annual increase or decrease in share value and annual dividends paid, are a matter of open record. Check the performance of a fund you're interested in not only for the past ten years but also for the most recent three years. A good fund should display a consistently good, if not superior, past performance compared with all other funds of the same breed. A growth fund, for example, should have performed better than the average of all other growth funds in the past three years, as well as in the past ten years. Any growth fund, in fact, that has not performed at an average annual growth rate of about 10 percent a year or better in the past decade should be viewed skeptically. Similarly, the performance of a growth-income fund should be compared with the average performance of all growth-income funds; and so on. Also check the performance of a fund against the stock market as a whole. How well has a fund performed each year in comparison with all stocks? Compare the fund's performance, for instance, with the annual change in Standard & Poor's 500 index, which is more representative of stock market performance than the much-publicized Dow-Jones Industrial Index.

Suppose you like a new fund that has been in existence for only a short period and therefore has little or no past record. Be wary here, since you're dealing with a rookie fund. Be wary even if the fund has just racked up an excellent record for the past year. A sterling one-year record can be highly deceptive, just as a horse may win the Kentucky Derby but never again place in the money. Best test for a new fund is its management's performance compared with sister funds that are older. A new fund started by people with no track record with other funds should be avoided until it has proven itself, unless you live dangerously. Mutual fund performance records can be obtained from sources given at the end of this chapter.

Fund size

The larger a fund, the more difficult it is to manage successfully, particularly if it's a growth fund. Mutual funds generally range in size from a few million dollars in total assets (total money invested in them) up to several billion dollars for a handful of giant funds. As a rule, it's best to invest in a fund no larger than about $500 million to $1 billion in size. For long-term growth, it's generally best to invest in a fund with no more than $50 to $250 million or so in size. Funds larger than that tend to have reduced potential for future growth, though there are exceptions, to be sure. Size is less important if your objective is income; then a larger fund, with up to $500 million or even $1 billion in assets, could do well for you. A fund larger than $1 billion, however, will tend to be handicapped, like an elephant, by its large size.

What it costs to invest in a mutual fund

Naturally you pay a price for a mutual fund to invest your money, with the price varying a bit from fund to fund. All funds charge a management fee which averages about $\frac{1}{2}$ of 1 percent a year of the money you have invested. With some funds it's as little as 0.2 percent, up to about .75 percent for others. In addition, there are operating expenses (for overhead, legal and accounting costs, printing, mailing, and so on). In all, the total cost for management fees and expenses generally runs between .5 and 1 percent a year. Thus, for example, $1,000 invested in a mutual fund will cost you a total of from $5 to $10 a year; $5,000 will cost $25 to $50 a year; and so on. Some funds cost more, though the total charge is generally less than 1 percent because that's the maximum permitted by law in most states.

Sales charges

Roughly 80 percent of all mutual funds also charge a sales fee, or "load" charge, on money invested in them; they are called "load" funds. This charge is generally about 8½ percent of the money invested, less as the total money invested hits certain levels. The sales charge on a $1,000 investment in a mutual fund would therefore cost you $85, more or less, depending on the fund, and you would receive $915 worth of shares in the fund. Actually, that $85 sales charge works out to be 9.3 percent of the net sum ($915) invested in the fund.

The sales charge generally decreases to about 6 percent on investments of $25,000 or more, and then down in steps to as little as 1 percent with sums of several hundred thousand dollars invested. The exact step-down charge schedule also varies according to the fund. The sales charge is based, not just on the amount of each investment in a fund, but on your investment plus the sum you have already invested in a fund. You may have, for example, $22,000 invested in a mutual fund and decide to invest $3,000 more. The sales charge on that $3,000 would be the reduced rate based on the total of $25,000 you will have invested in the fund.

The other 20 percent of all U.S. mutual funds make no sales charge on money invested in them; they're the no-load funds. A handful of no-load funds, however, do charge a redemption fee of up to 2 percent when you sell shares (redeem them) back to the fund. Like load funds, all no-load funds also charge a management fee and have annual expenses which will cost you up to 1 percent a year on the money invested, sometimes more.

Load versus no-load funds

Why pay a sales charge to invest in one mutual fund when you may invest in another, a no-load, at no sales charge? The answer is that despite the sales charge a load fund could be a better investment for you, giving you a better return on your money. Over a period of, say, ten years, a load fund has to outperform a no-load fund by a mere 1 percent or so a year to offset the sales charge, but there's more to it than that.

Probably the main advantage of a load fund is that the salesman selling it can be quite helpful, particularly if you are unfamiliar with mutual funds. He can answer your questions, help steer you into a good fund. Of course, not all salesmen are as good as you may desire, but you need not buy from the first one you talk to. Incidentally, the salesman himself generally earns no more than about half the sales charge, or 4 to 4½ percent; the rest is usually split between the mutual fund dealer (the firm the salesman works for) and the sponsor of the mutual fund.

A second advantage of load funds is that, by and large, they tend to possess broader management and research capabilities than no-load funds. That's not because they are load funds but simply because there are many more older and more-seasoned load funds than no-load funds. Load funds also offer special investment plans which, for example, combine the purchase of life insurance with a mutual fund investment program (not available with no-load funds).

No-load funds

There are some excellent no-load funds, but you, the investor, must seek them out and find a good one on your own, since they're not sold by salesmen. The typical no-load fund sells its shares by mail, though a few can be bought on the phone. A serious pitfall of the no-load fund is psychological, the blind purchase of one simply because it can be bought without a sales charge.

The way to invest in mutual funds is to divorce your emotions from the existence of a sales charge and evaluate funds according to the key criteria we've mentioned (objective, management capability, performance record, size, and so on). Narrow your choice down to a few funds that seem best for you, again irrespective of the sales charge factor. Then, if you have a choice between a good load and a good no-load fund and all other things are equal, choose the no-load fund, since you save the sales charge. Everything isn't always equal, however, and seasoned investors in mutual funds often spread their money among two or three different funds, a load fund or two, and a no-load fund.

How to invest in a mutual fund

There are basically two ways to invest in a mutual fund, with a "voluntary" plan or with a "contractual" plan. The first generally lets you start with an initial investment ranging from about $100 to $500, sometimes more, and then you may invest an even sum as small as $50 to $100, depending on the fund, at any time. Some people invest a lump sum all at once and that's it. Others open an account and invest additional sums off and on, continually building up their investment in the fund. A voluntary account generally puts no obligation on you to invest regularly, and the sum you invest is usually up to you.

A contractual plan does obligate you to invest regularly, usually every month, for a period of usually ten years or longer. An initial investment of several hundred dollars up to about $500, more or less, is generally required but after that your monthly investments may be as little as $10 to $20 a month. At the same time you may buy supplementary life insurance tied into the mutual fund program.

The chief advantage of a contractual plan is that it is a method of forced savings. Because you are obligated to invest regularly, you are likely to continue to do so over a period of years. The chief disadvantage is that the sales fee is "front-loaded," a large portion of the money you put into the fund in the beginning being taken out for the sales fee, based on the total sales fee to be paid over the full term of your investment program.

Joe Dukes, for example, signs up for a ten-year contractual plan calling for investments of $50 a month, or $6,000, in all, over the next decade. His total sales charge over those ten years will be in the neighborhood of $540 (9 percent of $6,000). However, as much as half of that $540 fee could be taken out of his first year's payments of $600 for the front-load sales charge. Moreover, if Joe decides to drop out of the plan early, very little, if any, of his sales charge may be returned. That's even though he has paid a sales charge for a greater amount of money than he had invested at the time he decided to drop out. The exact sales charge schedules for contractual plans not only can vary from fund to fund, but they also depend on the type of contractual plan you may choose. Thus anyone investing in a contractual plan should determine them before signing up and also determine the different options available.

Because a contractual plan will tie you down to a particular mutual fund for a number of years, taking a little time to choose a good one is particularly important. You will not necessarily be tied down to one mutual fund, however, if you start a contractual plan with a fund that is a member of a family of different mutual funds operated by the same management company. Many such multifund management companies permit investors in any of its funds to switch to other funds it operates, with no penalty and no second sales charge. The same free-switching privilege is also available, by the way, with most load funds when you have made investments on a voluntary plan and the fund is one of a family of funds run by the same management company.

How to find out about specific mutual funds

Much basic information about mutual funds along with performance records for most funds is given in the annual edition of *Investment Companies*, the thick, basic guide to mutual funds published by Wiesenberger Services, Inc., available in many libraries. It can be bought for $55 a year, for which price you also receive a subscription to Wiesenberger's quarterly performance records of mutual funds. Wiesenberger also publishes *Mutual Funds PANARAMA*, a handy semiannual directory of all active mutual funds and their addresses. At $5 a copy it is an excellent buy and can be obtained from Wiesenberger Services, Dept. AW, 1 New York Plaza, New York, N.Y. 10004.

The names and addresses of many mutual funds also can be obtained free from the Investment Company Institute, 1775 K Street N.W., Washington, D.C. 20006, a fund association whose members account for about 90 percent of all U.S. mutual fund investments, including both load and no-load funds. A list of no-load funds can be obtained from the No-Load Mutual Fund Association, 375 Park Ave., New York, N.Y. 10017.

Detailed performance records of mutual funds are published by the monthly magazine, *Fundscope*, available at libraries or for $50 a year, individual issues available separately, the price varying according to the issue. For example, the March issue each year provides a summary of the performance records for all funds for each of the preceding eight years, the July issue usually publishes "Results for all 10-, 15- and 20-year periods" for all funds. *Fundscope*, Suite 700, 1900 Avenue of the Stars, Los Angeles, Calif. 90067. Reports on mutual funds are also made in financial magazines and papers like *Forbes* (especially its annual mutual fund issue in August) and in *Barron's*.

Books about mutual funds also can provide helpful information. A new book on the subject, with emphasis on the performance of mutual funds and annual performance data for many funds is *Making Money in Mutual Funds*, by the author of this book, published in July 1973, available at book stores, or for $9.95 from AAH Co., 855 River Road, Piermont, N.Y. 10968.

SUMMARY

1. A mutual fund is chiefly an investment vehicle for five to ten years or more; it is not a way to make a quick buck in a short time.

2. Choose a mutual fund, first, according to your objective. Remember that funds range in objective from the most speculative, risky and volatile maximum-growth type to the most conservative income funds.

3. A typical investor interested in long-term protection from inflation and reasonably good growth potential generally will do well to invest in either a straight growth or, to play it safe, growth-income fund. Maximum growth funds are only for those who can afford to accept a higher-than-usual degree of risk.

4. The caliber of management is particularly important with a mutual fund. This should be obvious, since the skill of the people who manage a fund's investments largely determines the fund's performance. Look for good management.

5. The best test of management ability is a fund's past performance record. How well has it performed in the past ten years? Has it performed consistently better than average for all funds of the same type? How well has it performed in the most recent three years?

6. Be wary of a new or young fund with little or no performance record. Some could be great in the future, others not so great. Invest in a new or young fund only if its management has a good record compared with other funds. If the fund's management, however, has no real record with other funds, beware, regardless of how well the fund has been doing in the past year or so.

7. How large is a fund? Remember that funds with no more than $50 million to $100 million in asset size tend to have the greatest potential for future growth. Funds ranging in size from $100 million to about $500 million in size may have less growth potential, but often they are more seasoned funds with great built-in stability and less volatility. And in general, giant funds of greater size, particularly those with $1 billion or more in assets, are handicapped by such large size.

8. Should you buy a load or a no-load fund? The sales fee (load charge) should not necessarily be a prime consideration in choosing a fund. It's more important to choose a good fund with a top management and a good record, irrespective of whether or not you must pay a sales fee to invest in it.

9. Read the terms of agreement when you invest in a mutual

fund. You may choose a voluntary plan, which enables you to invest virtually any even sum of money at any time. Or you may choose a contractual plan, which obligates you to invest a sum of money periodically, usually with at least 120 consecutive payments. But if you drop out of a contractual plan within the first few years, you could lose money.

10. On the other hand, a contractual plan could increase the likelihood of following through on a long-term investment program, since it forces you to invest regularly. Without such compulsion, you (along with most of the rest of us) would not save or invest regularly; at the end of a given period of time you might have a smaller, if not zero nest egg, compared with the investment built up in a forced-saving, contractual plan that you have stuck with. Contractual plans also offer supplementary life insurance that can be attractive, especially if you want to guarantee a total investment to be realized in the future, for a child's college expenses, for example.

section ten

how to save on **income taxes**

According to tax experts, as many as ten million Americans unknowingly make mistakes on their income tax returns and as a result pay more tax than necessary. Often it's because legitimate deductions are overlooked or not deducted to the full extent allowable. On the other hand, there are also people, of course, who underpay, which can mean a penalty plus interest added to the bill for the additional tax due.

Master computers now scan all of the estimated 80 million or so personal federal tax returns received annually by the Internal Revenue Service (IRS). Thus, errors are more likely than ever to be caught. Many overpayment errors, however, cannot be caught simply because the smartest computer will find it difficult, if not impossible, to sniff out an allowable deductible item omitted from your return; only you could know about that.

Obviously, the way to save money on your income tax and not overpay—or underpay and ask for trouble—is to compute your tax accurately, and pay no more and no less than due. (True, that's not always easily done, considering the many complicated and confusing income-tax rules, but don't blame this on the IRS; blame it on the U.S. Congress whose members write our income tax laws.)

To save money and take full advantage of every deductible

261

item that you're entitled to, the final section of this book includes a review of the most common mistakes made on income tax returns and how to avoid them. But, first, you should also know about the key changes in our income tax laws made in 1969 and 1971 which offer savings to everybody.

Much of this section is based on material prepared for us by Dennis R. Cunynghame, CPA, a partner in the New York firm of Henry Warner & Co., Certified Public Accountants. It is also based in part on interviews by the author with Internal Revenue Service staff members in Washington, D.C.

30

what the new **tax laws**
mean to you

*Increased exemption limit · Higher deductions · Better break
on dependent care expenses · More generous income
averaging · Increased capital gains tax · Reduced tax on
high-bracket incomes*

In 1969 Congress passed the first major tax reform law in 15 years and
two years later the Revenue Act of 1971 made additional changes in the
income-tax laws. Neither the first nor the second law was all "reform,"
though some loopholes were closed and some glaring inequities were
made less glaring. On the whole, the two new laws were attempts to
distribute income taxes more evenly. Here are the key changes for most
typical taxpayers.

Personal exemption increase. The exemption allowed for each
of your dependents goes up in 1972 to $750 (from $675 in 1971). It
applies to all exemptions you have, including an old-age dependent, for
example, as well as a wife and children. The larger your family, of course,
the more you will benefit (but also, of course, the greater your family
expenses).

Higher standard deduction. This is a break for people who
formerly lacked enough deductible expenses to make itemizing them
worthwhile, such as a single person, a young married couple and a
family that rents rather than owns its own home. Beginning in 1972 you
may deduct 15 percent of your taxable income up to a maximum of

$2,000 when you file the short-form return and do not itemize your deductions. The standard deduction was formerly less. Remember, however, that a married couple filing separate returns is limited to a $1,000 top deduction on each return.

Increased dependent-care deductions. Beginning in 1972 you can deduct up to a whopping $400 a month of the expenses paid out to care for any dependent at home while you're at work. That includes any child up to 14 years plus any other dependent, any age, who is incapable of self-care, such as an invalid wife or an incapacitated grandparent. The deduction is allowed only if such care is required to enable you to go to work, and there are certain qualifications and technical requirements. For example, the allowable deduction is reduced by one dollar for every two dollars that your taxable income exceeds $18,000, and regardless of income the top allowable deduction for outside-the-home care is $200 a month for one child, $300 for two, and $400 for three or more children. All inside-the-home expenses paid out for dependent care, such as hiring a maid, cook or baby-sitter, are deductible up to the maximum $400-a-month limit; the total inside- and outside-the-home expenses, however, may not exceed $400.

New political deduction. Political contributions are tax deductible on your income taxes starting in 1972, though the maximum savings are modest. You get a break on your tax in either of two ways. The first is a 50 percent tax credit allowed on total political contributions up to $50. That means that $50 or more of political contributions lets you reduce your income tax by $25 on a joint return, and $12.50 on other returns. The limit on a joint return applies no matter who makes the contributions, husband or wife. Or, secondly, you may deduct from your taxable income up to $100 of political contributions on a joint return, $50 on other returns. just as you deduct any other allowable deduction.

An allowable contribution is money you give to any candidate for federal, state or local office in a general, primary or special election. It also applies to a contribution made to a committee sponsoring a candidate or to any federal, state or local committee of a national political party.

More liberal income averaging. The rules on this were eased considerably by the 1969 Tax Act, and they offer possible tax savings when, during the year, you get a big raise, for example, or receive a windfall, or earn a large capital gains profit. Your income tax on that sharp increase in your total income ordinarily can be reduced when your average annual taxable income for the four preceding years was appreciably less. It's determined in this way: Add up your taxable income for the four preceding years (the base period) and divide it by four. Compare 120 percent of the answer to your taxable income this year. If this year's taxable income is the greater of the two by more than $3,000, income averaging could reduce your tax for the year.

For example, Chuck Riser's taxable income went up sharply to $20,000, compared with an income in each of the past four years of $10,000, $11,000, $13,000 and $14,000. Can he benefit from income averaging? That's an average of $12,000 a year in those four years, and 120 percent of that is $14,400 (or 6/5ths of $12,000). This year's income ($20,000) is more than $3,000 greater than $14,400, so he could indeed benefit by income averaging. The difference is $5,600 ($20,000 minus $14,400) and this difference is subject to a lower-than-usual tax rate. The income tax on $20,000 of income for Chuck who's a bachelor (or anyone else filing an individual return) comes to $5,230, but, with income averaging, Chuck's tax was reduced to $5,070, a saving of $160.

Increased employer tax withholding. New tables determining how much tax is withheld from your pay went into effect on January 15, 1972, but they increase the tendency for more money than necessary to be withheld. The tables reflect the increase in exemptions and in the standard deduction, and were also introduced to offset the former tendency toward underwithholding, especially for working couples and moonlighters. Too much money withheld from your pay for income taxes will be returned later if you file for a refund, but why let somebody else keep your surplus money for you? To avoid overwithholding, check the figures being used for your pay, as described in the following chapter.

Increased capital gains taxes. What the government gives away with one hand it takes back with the other, though this change applies chiefly to high-bracket taxpayers. For years, the capital gains tax on a profit from the sale of a capital asset (such as stocks or a house) owned more than six months was 50 percent of the usual income tax for the same amount of money earned, up to a maximum capital gains tax of 25 percent of the profit. Now the top capital gains tax on such profits of $50,000 or more in any one year has been increased to 35 percent. Certain qualifications and special rules apply here, too, but anyone involved with that kind of money should have his tax accountant clear up the technicalities.

Reduced maximum tax on earned income. This applies only to high-bracket taxpayers and it means that no one can be taxed more than 50 percent of his earned income in 1972 and thereafter. It was 60 percent in 1971, the first year that the maximum tax on earned income became effective.

31

the 25 best ways to **save** on your annual **income tax**

Planning ahead to save money on income-tax day · End-of-the-year tax strategies · The most common costly errors to avoid

Like a three-act play, saving the most money on your income tax comes down to dealing with your tax in three stages: monthly control over tax-affected expenditures (which is not as large a chore as it may sound), end-of-the-year tax action and, in the final act, pulling together the figures efficiently without missing deductions you're entitled to.

Action during the year to save money later

Keep track of tax deductions as they occur. Don't wait till the weekend before next April 15th to begin assembling your figures. That kind of last-minute accounting makes you a sitting duck for errors that could cost you money. An easy way to avoid losing tax deductions is to place paid bills and cancelled checks promptly in separate folders or envelopes, according to tax subject. At the end of the year you merely add them up. (You might even avoid separate files for cancelled checks by using a page-by-page check register record, rather than the usual checkbook with old-fashioned stubs. A check register will vastly simplify a review later of all checks written during the year.)

Keep a record especially of the bills paid for such major purchases as a car, home furniture and furnishings and jewelry, because the sales tax paid often can be deducted in addition to the usual average sales tax

266

allowed in the Internal Revenue Service tables. Other key expenses to keep records of include money spent for the support of dependents not living with you (which might entitle you to a deduction for reasons given below), and personal expenditures that are in part business—for example, the business use of your house or car. The best time to segregate bills is when you pay them; the best time to segregate checks is just after going over your monthly bank statement.

Keep a business-expense diary. Do this especially for travel and entertainment expenses not reimbursed by your employer. A diary for such expenses is indispensible, especially if you are called in later by the IRS to substantiate such items. Then, no diary usually means no deduction. What is and isn't deductible plus the kind of records to be kept are given in the IRS booklet *Travel, Entertainment and Gift Expenses,* usually available at local IRS offices or the U.S. Government Printing Office, Division of Public Documents, Washington, D.C. 20402.

Because the tax laws and the rules applying to various deductions are often changed from time to time and because space limitations prevent listing the numerous qualifications and rules concerning every tax item, here and elsewhere in this chapter we refer you to basic guidelines for different income-tax subjects; they're usually given in one of the many pamphlets published by the Internal Revenue Service and available from them or from the Government Printing Office, address above.

Get your tax withholding statement when you change jobs. This is important when you work for more than one employer during the year. Each employer is required by law to issue this statement to you within 30 days after you leave. A company that neglects this, preferring to wait till the end of the year, could complicate things for you, since two or more jobs during the year often result in excessive tax and Social Security money withheld by all employers, at your new job as well as at your last one.

Be sure that the proper tax is withheld from your pay. This, of course, is when your salary is subject to income-tax withholding by an employer (as opposed to a self-employed person). Then find out from the payroll department when you last filled out an employee's withholding exemption certificate, Form W-4. This form was revised in December 1971 and now allows greater flexibility in determining the tax your employer withholds from your paycheck. To prevent overwithholding, the rules now permit a new withholding allowance (not applicable, though, if a man and wife both work or if one or the other holds more than one job concurrently). You may also qualify for an additional withholding allowance if you have substantial itemized deductions.

On the other hand, you may desire to have a greater tax withheld than

the law requires, and the new Form W-4 lets you authorize extra withholding. (There's usually no real reason for this, however, especially
since the money could be in the bank earning interest for you. The usual
reason for extra withholding is that it's forced savings, money you would
otherwise spend but prefer to save. Then you might have it automatically
put into a payroll savings plan.) The proper withholding amount is determined from the new tables introduced in 1972. Compute the total
amount that will be withheld from your pay for the whole year, based on
the new tables. Estimate your total income tax for the year, based on
last year as a yardstick; be sure, of course, to allow for a major change
in income or in deductions. And then compare the two figures. If the tax
withheld is much larger, fill out a new Form W-4.

Keep permanent records of all expenditures related to every
house you own. This means things like bills, receipts and other documents
from the purchase and sale of a house you own, including a cooperative
apartment, condominium or vacation house. Practically everyone knows
by now that the property taxes and mortgage interest paid on a house
are tax deductible (on itemized returns, of course). But, in addition,
other records could come in mighty handy some day, and these include
records of capital improvements on a house and bills relating to the
purchase and sale of each house you buy or sell, possibly going back to
the very first house you ever bought. That means closing costs, real-estate
broker fees, and even moving and telephone bills (which are evidence
that may be required some day to prove that a house meets the "principal
residence" test).

That's because when you buy a house and later sell it at a profit, the
profit is subject to a tax. But many expenses, including those just mentioned, could serve to reduce that tax. Some people think that when you
sell a house at a profit and promptly build or buy another house you
escape that tax, but this is untrue. Then the tax is deferred, *not* cancelled.
It is deferred if you use the proceeds from the sale of one house to buy
another house within a year, or build a new house within 18 months.
Someday later you will be subject to a tax on that profit and also on the
profit of any other house you sold before or afterwards. You get a tax
break, however, on the profit made from the sale of a house that occurs
when you are 65 years or older, provided you owned the place and it
was your principal residence for 60 months during the eight years prior
to the sale. (Sorry—it is virtually impossible to report this in plain
English because of the jungle of tax-law ins and outs.)

So, to play safe, the relevant records relating to any house you buy
should be put into a permanent file. And don't throw them out when you

move, as they could be important to you someday, however long you
must keep them.

Be alert to tax consequences before it's too late. Like an alba-
tross, the ubiquitous income tax can hang over your head when you
participate in a variety of personal or business transactions. But find out
the ramifications promptly and often things can be worked out so that
you benefit from a lower tax, rather than suffer a higher tax. This includes being involved in such things as stock options, deferred compensa-
tion plans, in the stock market with short sales "against the box" or puts,
calls, and straddles, divorce and separate maintenance agreements (alimony, for example, being tax deductible for the giver, but not child-
support payments), plus the tax on the profit from the sale of a house even
though it may not be payable till long after the sale.

Knowing how to work out such things to minimize your tax is obviously
important, compared with ignoring the tax consequences till later when
you might owe money that otherwise could have been saved. To be sure,
the tax ramifications of such transactions can be involved and complicated, and then it's wise to consult a tax expert.

Don't accept a stock broker's periodic statements as correct.
The paper explosion in Wall Street brokerage firms in recent years has
led to an unbelievably high incidence of errors. Read your broker's statement promptly to catch errors and have them corrected early. If you own
mutual fund shares or belong to an investment club, keep a running
record of (1) your cash payments to the fund or club, and (2) the
periodic distributions received from one or the other, including those
reinvested in additional shares. You will need this information to determine the tax "cost" of the shares you own when you later sell all or
part of your investment. Distributions to you that are reinvested in additional shares increase the tax "cost" of your investment; partial sales
and redemptions reduce it. If you buy bonds between interest dates, note
the amount of the interest you "prepay." This amount is not part of the
cost of the bond; it should be deducted from any interest income you
receive from the bond. If you do not receive interest income until the
year following the year of purchase, the deduction of the "prepaid"
interest is also deferred to the next year.

Those end-of-the-year tax-saving strategies

Actually, most end-of-the-year tax-saving devices are the stuff of life for
corporation lawyers and businessmen. Some good ones, however, do
apply to individual taxpayers. As December 31st approaches, certain

family money activities can be shaped to reduce the income tax you will owe on April 15th.

Bunch itemized deductions of two years into one. This is chiefly for the person who from year to year may file the "short-form" income tax because his—or her—itemized deductions do not exceed the standard deduction allowed each year. Then you might get more mileage from your deductions by bunching them into one year, both at the start and at the end of the year; and then repeating this every other year. You can take advantage, in effect, of itemized deductions from two years piled up in one year. The next year you file an income tax return with the standard deduction accepted, the third year reverse the process, and so on.

For example, start with a year in which your itemized deductions will be close to or exceed the amount of your standard deduction; then pay all possible tax-deductible bills you owe—large medical bills, next January's installments on estimated state or local income taxes or on property taxes—on or before December 31st. The next year defer payment of tax-deductible items as much as possible until the following (third) year and take the standard deduction. In the third year, start the cycle over again. If you start in a year in which your itemized deductions are less than the amount of your standard deduction, defer your deductions this year and bunch them in the following year.

Shift deductions into the year in which you expect higher income. If your annual income fluctuates, you should pay as many of your itemized deductions as you can in the year your income is higher. If, for instance, you are getting a bonus this year, bunch your deductions into this year; if a raise or bonus is expected next year, defer payment of your deductible bills until next year. But be careful here if medical expenses are involved, as a medical deduction will decline by 3% of the increase in income.

Shift income into the year in which you expect lower income or higher deductions. This often can arise, for example, with investments, or when one has a small business on the side or, among other times, when there's a family windfall. Then things often can be arranged for a financial shift to the better year for you. Knowing how to handle profits and losses in the stock market can be particularly important.

Whenever possible, for example, shift security profits into a year in which you expect lower income or higher deductions or where they can offset losses. If, however, you are compelled to sell a stock this year for any reason and you want to defer the gain or loss to next year, you could make a short sale this year and close it out after January 1st. But check the rules on this each year, not only because they are tricky but also because they may change.

Be sure that a long-term loss sustained is wholly tax deductible. You pay a tax on a profit made in the stock market but a loss in the same year could offset part or all of the tax on that profit. However, you get a deduction of only 50 cents for each dollar of long-term loss that is not absorbed by a short-term gain up to a limit of $2,000 of loss in one year. (And bear with us, since a few more long- and short-term mentions are unavoidably coming up.)

Try to avoid a net short-term loss in a year in which you have a long-term gain. The short-term loss would be offset by the long-term gain, in effect converting the long-term gain into a short-term gain. You then would lose your 50 percent long-term capital gains deduction. A long-term gain or loss is, of course, the profit or loss sustained by owning something for at least six months and a day before selling (and woe to the person who forgets that one day). "Short-term" means, in tax language, a gain or loss sustained on a buy-and-sell transaction that was completed within six months or less.

Be alert for future tax-rule changes. You might profit by a coming tax change that will be favorable for you by accelerating your deductions. If it is unfavorable, defer your deductions. Some recent examples are the lower tax rates for single people which became law in 1971; extending the tax surcharge through June 30, 1970; and dropping the alternate tax on long-term capital gains in excess of $50,000, as mentioned earlier. In each case obvious tax savings were possible by taking the appropriate action at the right time.

The most common causes of income-tax mistakes that cost people money

Medical deductions. Many people mistakenly think that medical expenses are tax-deductible only above 3% of their income, but that's only partly true. Half of your medical-insurance premiums up to $150 are deductible, even if your medical expenses do not exceed the 3% figure. That's for Blue Cross, Blue Shield, major medical and other such medical insurance (but not insurance against loss of income because of accident or illness). The other half of your medical-insurance premiums is also deductible when all medical expenses exceed the 3% limit; you lump the medical-insurance balance in with these.

Other medical expenses commonly overlooked include the cost of travel to and from a doctor's office or a hospital, including a parent's travel expenses taking a child for treatment; medical bills paid for dependents including a child in college, even though he also works; and the cost of maintaining a relative in a nursing home when medical care is the principal reason for his being there; if it isn't, only payments for medical or nursing care are deductible medical expenses.

Medical deductions for dependents. You may deduct the medical expenses paid for a dependent even though he is not a tax exemption for you. For example, Jack Hofflewhit's daughter got married in December and on the following April 15th she filed a joint income-tax return with her happy new husband. That meant, Jack thought ruefully, that he could not take a dependency exemption for her on his tax return even though he had supported her for eleven of the twelve months of her last year under his roof. Jack was pleased to learn, however, that he could deduct on his return medical bills he paid when Mary broke her leg in a skiing mishap the previous winter. Mary qualified as a dependent of Jack's through the test of "support and relationship."

If, by the way, one of your dependents has medical expenses, they should be paid by you rather than by the dependent. Do this even if it must reduce other support payments to him. You'll get a medical expense deduction as well as a dependency exemption.

Overlooked dependents. A legitimate dependent will, of course, reduce your tax but many people overlook dependents they could take credit for. A dependent may be an adult son or daughter who works, as well as a married child, an elderly relative in a rest home, in addition to young children at home. A key test for dependency is that you contributed more than half of a person's annual support.

Did you do this for, say, a daughter who recently married and left home, or for a married daughter who is living with you while her husband is in the armed forces? If you did, you may well rate an additional dependent. Certain other requirements, having to do with such things as the person's own income, student status, relationship to you, and citizenship-residency status, also must be met in order to qualify for an additional dependent. See the special stipulations for dependency in the Federal Income Tax guide sent to you with your income-tax form.

Some people overlook the multiple support rules. If they apply to you, another family member or you may claim an exemption for a dependent. An example is an aged grandmother whom you and a brother and sister support. If all three of you together contribute a total of more than half the support, any one of you who contributes more than 10 percent of the support is entitled to a dependency exemption. That's provided, of course, that you would be entitled to the exemption had you alone furnished more than half the support. However, only one of you may take it each year. Decide among you who that will be this year and the other two declare on Form 2120 that they will not claim an exemption this year for grandmother. Next year, another one of you can claim the exemption and the others will furnish him with Form 2120.

Be sure that you and everybody else providing support, as above, keep records to prove support. You may have to prove that the dependent did not use all of his own income for his or her own support. This involves the gross-income test. Your children under 19 and those over 19 who are full-time students—5 months or more in the year—don't have to meet this test. You include only the dependent's taxable income; thus, most scholarship and fellowship grants are exempt from tax. Another example is a dependent parent over 65 who sells his house at a profit and is exempt from a tax on the profit because he's over 65. The untaxed profit is not considered part of his gross income for the year.

Charitable contributions. Some people go hog-wild (followed by a call to visit IRS); others overlook certain deductible items. For example, expenses you incur doing volunteer work, such as driving your car for the local blood bank or the Girl Scouts, are deductible. A gift of furniture, clothing, or anything else to a recognizable charity is also deductible—but get a receipt for its value. You must be able to substantiate all such contributions. If you can't, part or all of your contributions may be disallowed. If you deduct a really sizeable contribution, check the recipient's eligibility to qualify as a charity as well as the allowable value that you put on your gift.

Buried interest charges. What you pay for interest is tax deductible but it's easily missed because of being buried in other payments, such as within your total monthly mortgage payment, or inside a monthly charge-account bill. The total annual interest paid on a mortgage should be reported to you each year by your mortgage lender. Other interest charges may require ferreting out by you, such as interest you may have paid for late payment of property taxes. If you own a condominium or a co-op apartment, the manager or his agent should give you your interest deduction at the end of the year. Did you buy or sell real property during the year? If it involved a mortgage and there was an interest adjustment between buyer and seller, be sure to adjust your deductible interest. (See below under "Taxes.")

A bank or installment loan may require a little juggling on your part to get the proper deduction. If you take out a loan and repay it in the same year, the full interest is deductible in that year. Often, however, the bank deducts such interest in advance and you repay the loan in a later year and then you may deduct only a prorated share each year. If you renew the loan, the renewal date is the date of payment of the old loan. If you increase the loan before it is due, the bank will adjust—or discount—the interest deducted in advance on the old loan. Interest on auto loans and other installment purchases, like major home appliances, must also be prorated over the number of months you are making the payments. Some installment loans, however, include charges for insurance and service charges, which are not deductible.

Other interest sometimes missed is that paid for a bank loan, which is usually charged directly against your bank account balance; interest on charge-account and credit-card purchases, which generally requires (alas) going through a whole year of statements to pull out the monthly interest charges; interest paid on a margin account with a stock broker; and interest on life insurance loans.

Deductible taxes. Many day-to-day taxes you pay can be deducted, such as state and local retail sales and gasoline taxes, all non-federal income taxes, state and local transfer taxes on the sale of securities, as well as real-estate and personal propery taxes. If you bought a house during the year, remember to add the portion of the property tax the seller prepaid and allocated to you on the closing statement. On the other hand, if you sold a house or other property and charged the seller the taxes you prepaid, this charge should be removed from your deductible tax.

A large state transfer tax on the sale of securities owned more than six months should be deducted as a tax, not as part of the selling price on your capital gains schedule, as is often done. Otherwise, you will lose half of your deduction because only 50 percent of a long-term gain is taken into taxable income. If the sale gives you a net long-term loss, you would also lose part of your deduction.

An auto registration or license fee is deductible if it is based in full or in part on the value of the auto. The portion of the fee based on value is deductible as a personal property tax.

What can be deducted for sales and gasoline taxes can be found in the guideline tables with your income-tax instructions. But if your sales taxes are unusually high or if, for example, you spend a lot of money eating in restaurants where the sales tax is added to your check, you can add the extra sales taxes to the figure from the guideline table.

Dividends and bond interest. Remember that the first $100 of dividends received from most U.S. corporations can be excluded from your income. A wife may not want to get involved in the stock market but that's no reason to lose her right to this exclusion. Just put enough dividend-paying stocks in your joint names and the saving could pay for more than one new Easter bonnet.

Exclude interest from state and local bonds—the so-called municipal bonds—from your federal tax return. Interest from "municipals" outside of your state are generally taxable on state and local income-tax returns, but interest from federal bonds and other federal obligations is exempt from state and local income taxes. An end-of-the-year statement of the dividends and interest you received should be sent to you (Form 1099) by the source of the payments. A stock broker sends you this information on Form 1087, or he will show it on your last monthly statement for the year. Because broker statements are not dependable, be sure to check the figures against what you actually received when a broker carries your stock in his name. Pay special attention to capital gains distributions from mutual funds, since they mean a lower tax, and for nontaxable, or return-of-capital, dividends (which mean no tax).

"Head-of-Household" tax benefit. This may save money for a single or divorced person, a widow or widower, a man or woman married to a nonresident alien and a married person who is legally separated. It's for people who are not entitled to use a joint return but do maintain a household for at least one other person, young or old. You may qualify even if you maintain a household for a grown child who works, or if you support a relative under another roof. You must pay more than half of all regular household expenses (rent, mortgage, taxes, food, and the like) for one or more others. But you don't count personal expenses (clothing, medical bills, car, and so forth) that a grown child, say, paid out of his own earnings. You get a break on your tax by using the Head-of-Household table. It cannot be used, however, if a husband or wife died within the past three years. If the survivor stays unmarried and has one or more dependents, a joint return can be used for that three-year period; the Head-of-Household table is used after that period.

Overpaid Social Security tax. As mentioned earlier, this can occur when a person works at two or more jobs during the year. Each employer by law must withhold your total Social Security tax starting from scratch (even though you've paid part or all of it for the year at your first job). That can mean an overpayment, especially if in 1972 you earned $9,000 or more. (It was $7,800 in 1971.) Then you must ask the government for a refund, with one exception: If only one employer withheld too much Social Security tax, go to him for the refund, not to the government.

A tax refund due from a past year. You suddenly learn about a deduction omitted from last year's return, but, alas, now it's too late. Actually, it's not. Every taxpayer has up to three tax years to claim a refund for overpaid taxes. You have, for example, up to April 15, 1974 to claim a refund on your 1970 return, unless your 1970 return was filed later than that date and then the three-year grace period begins on the date the return was filed. There's a possible exception here if you've been in business for yourself and you have had a loss; then the special rules for business losses apply.

To get a refund for overpaid taxes, you'll have to spell out your case, of course, but this is comparatively easy to do with the special Form 1040-X available for the purpose. Applying for a few refund dollars may not seem worth the trouble, but getting an appreciable sum back can be—including refunds you may learn about in these pages. The same three-year grace period is also given by most of the 42 states with state income tax, so you should check if you're entitled to a state income-tax refund, too. If so, however, you will probably have to defer filing for the state refund until after your federal refund claim is approved.

Taking the wrong deduction route. Should you itemize your deductions or save time and take the standard deduction? Experts estimate that several million individual taxpayers shortchange themselves as a result of the wrong answer to this question. It therefore can profit you to figure your tax both ways, then use the one that ends up with the smaller tax, especially if at first glance your itemized deductions seem to be about the same as the standard deduction (the percentage standard or minimum, whichever is greater for you). As a rule, if you own a house, itemizing your deductions will pay, but not always, especially as a result of the 1969 and 1971 income-tax changes.

Incidentally, don't use that optional tax table you see on the form just because, like Mt. Everest, it's there and you're entitled to use it. This table is based on the standard deduction or the low-income allowance. Test first whether itemizing your deductions will serve you better. Using the optional table will mean the loss of certain tax breaks you would otherwise be entitled to, such as a wife's right to itemize on a separate return.

Separate versus joint returns. Here again it can pay for a husband and wife to figure their total income tax both ways, a separate return for each versus the tax due with a joint return. Separate returns could save a couple money, for example, if a wife earns more than a nominal income and a husband has had substantial medical bills for the year. (A key item here, however, is that 3-percent-of-income requirement for deductible medical expenses.) A joint return is generally favorable when only one of a married couple earns the lion's share of the family's income and the other's earnings are comparatively small.

Use of the wrong table. Many a man and wife filing a joint return do everything correctly till the end—and then, of all things, pick their tax from the table for a married couple filing separate returns. This means, of course, a higher-than-necessary tax. Conversely, other people use the lower-tax joint-return table when they don't have that option, then wonder why they are later called in for an explanation (and more money) by the IRS. And as many a newly married person has recently found to his dismay, the new tax-law changes effective in 1971 can mean a higher tax compared with the tax on the same income before his wedding, especially when he and his wife file separate returns.

Last-minute errors. These can give fits to the IRS and its computers, and among other things delay a refund that you're waiting for, or call special attention to your entire return. The most common last-minute errors and oversights: missing or wrong Social Security number, including it being left off on tax checks with returns as well as on the returns themselves (this mistake alone being committed by more than 1.5 million people a year); missing documents (Form W-2 or a special schedule that should be attached to your return); wrong addresses; and, of all things, missing signatures (by nearly half-a-million people last year). Quite a few arithmetic errors are, of course, also made on returns. Haste makes waste, especially at the end.

Allow time to put your finished return aside for a few days before going back to it fresh for a final check. An IRS official says that this probably can save you (and them) more time, trouble and expense than any other single suggestion anyone can make.

And if you have questions about a thorny problem—can you deduct such-and-such an item?—you could call or see an IRS person near you, though you'll probably have to wait in line as income-tax day approaches when the IRS is swamped with calls for advice. You might also hire a reputable tax-help man who may charge as little as $10, more or less, to compute a whole return, though that's for the usual routine return. If more than a few dollars are involved, go wild and hire a good tax man for $50 to $100, perhaps more, since he might save you that fee plus more. But to save money on his fee, sort out all your figures beforehand, categorizing your expenses and so on. Be your own bookkeeper, in other words, which will save him time and you money in more than one way. You should save on your tax, since it's easier for him to figure, as well as on his fee.

Some day the preparation of our annual income-tax returns may be simplified, but until then, unfortunately, it can take a bit of time and effort to do accurately and take full advantage of all the allowable deductions one is entitled to. If it's any consolation, that's one of the prices we must pay to live in a reasonably free society.

index